AARIN

Literal Meaning: LIGHT BRINGER
Suggested Character Quality: BRINGER OF LIGHT
Suggested Lifetime Scripture Verse: Psalm 27:1 *"The Lord is my light and my salvation; whom shall I fear? The Lord is the strength of my life; of whom shall I be afraid?"* *

ARRON

Literal Meaning: LIGHT BRINGER
Suggested Character Quality: BRINGER OF LIGHT
Suggested Lifetime Scripture Verse: Psalm 27:1 *"The Lord is my light and my salvation; whom shall I fear? The Lord is the strength of my life; of whom shall I be afraid?"* *

AARYN

Literal Meaning: LIGHT BRINGER
Suggested Character Quality: BRINGER OF LIGHT
Suggested Lifetime Scripture Verse: Psalm 27:1 *"The Lord is my light and my salvation; whom shall I fear? The Lord is the strength of my life; of whom shall I be afraid?"* *

ABBE LEIGH

Literal Meaning: FATHER OF THE MEADOW
Suggested Character Quality: SOURCE OF PEACE
Suggested Lifetime Scripture Verse: Isaiah 26:3 *"Thou wilt keep him in perfect peace, whose mind is stayed on thee, because he trusteth in thee."* *

ABBIE

Literal Meaning: MY FATHER IS JOY
Suggested Character Quality: SOURCE OF JOY
Suggested Lifetime Scripture Verse: John 15:11 *"These things have I spoken unto you, that my joy might remain in you, and that your joy might be full."* *

ABBOT

Literal Meaning: FATHER
Suggested Character Quality: BENEVOLENT HEART
Suggested Lifetime Scripture Verse: I Corinthians 13:13 *"There remain then, faith, hope, love, these three; but the greatest of these is love."*

ABBOTT

Literal Meaning: FATHER
Suggested Character Quality: BENEVOLENT HEART
Suggested Lifetime Scripture Verse: I Corinthians 13:13 *"There remain then, faith, hope, love, these three; but the greatest of these is love."*

ABBY

Literal Meaning: MY FATHER IS JOY
Suggested Character Quality: SOURCE OF JOY
Suggested Lifetime Scripture Verse: John 15:11 *"These things have I spoken unto you, that my joy might remain in you, and that your joy might be full."* *

ABEL

Literal Meaning: BREATH
Suggested Character Quality: FULL OF LIFE
Suggested Lifetime Scripture Verse: Psalm 52:8 *"But I am like a green olive tree in the house of God; I trust in the mercy of God forever and ever."* *

ABIANE

Literal Meaning: GRACE OF GOD
Suggested Character Quality: GOD'S GRACIOUS ONE
Suggested Lifetime Scripture Verse: Psalm 84:11 *"For the Lord God is a sun and shield; the Lord will give grace and glory: no good thing will He withhold from them that walk uprightly."* *

ABIGAIL

Literal Meaning: MY FATHER IS JOY
Suggested Character Quality: SOURCE OF JOY
Suggested Lifetime Scripture Verse: John 15:11 *"These things have I spoken unto you, that my joy might remain in you, and that your joy might be full."* *

ABNER

Literal Meaning: OF LIGHT
Suggested Character Quality: TRUSTWORTHY
Suggested Lifetime Scripture Verse: Psalm 119:44, 45 *"Then I shall keep Thy law continually forever and ever I shall walk with freedom, for I have sought Thy precepts."*
Explanation: One who is of the light is transparently honest.

ABRAHAM

Literal Meaning: FATHER OF MULTITUDE
Suggested Character Quality: RIGHTEOUS PROTECTOR
Suggested Lifetime Scripture Verse: Ecclesiastes 7:12 *"For wisdom is a defense, and money is a defense; but the excellency of knowledge is, that wisdom giveth life to them that have it."* *

What's In A Name?

Over 1500 Names and Their Meanings

Compiled by:
Gayle Palmquist
John Hartzell

Our cover features

Ark Products' Character Name Plaques

made available through your local Christian Bookstore.

Note: Scripture verses selected for Character Name Plaques may differ from the verses found in this book.

SECOND EDITION 1983

Ark Products, Publishers
Bloomington, Minnesota 55420

SECOND EDITION NOTES

*An asterisk following a verse indicates a direct quotation from the King James Version of the Bible.

*Some character qualities are slightly different in this edition than in the first. Periodically, the need for clarity has caused us to make minor revisions.

ISBN 0-934400-06-7

Printed in the United States of America

Editorial/production supervision by Tammy Feigal
Editing and typing services by Jan Davies

INTRODUCTION

When God plans a project, many lives are touched in the process of its development. This book is no exception. It all started when the Mayor of Minneapolis made an unusual request of an unusual cop. He asked Al Palmquist to set up a rehabilitation program for drug addicts.

Most drug users don't ask policemen to rehabilitate them. They ask Al. Most cops aren't preachers. Al Palmquist is. He knew God loved drug users and wanted to set them free. So he trusted God for the wisdom, the staff, the money; and Midwest Challenge became a reality. (The story of this Christ-centered rehabilitation program is told in Al's book, *Miracle at City Hall.*)

Early in 1974, Midwest Challenge began to investigate new areas of production and vocational training for the young people in its program. John Hartzell, an assistant director for Midwest, proposed making something different in the way of decorative name plaques. They were to be unique, personalized, scriptural. John gave the idea to artist Terry Dugan who designed several prototypes. The plaques were made; the response to them was so enthusiastic, Midwest Challenge organized a new company called ARK Products in order to manufacture and distribute them. Chuck Hetland, Ark's manager, soon realized more people needed to be told the story of the plaques and the philosophy behind them. Chuck talked to Linda Francis, who had been doing research for the project, and it was she who compiled the material for this book.

Most name books give mainly literal or cultural meaning. Some will list beside each entry, famous people having had that name. Some will add quotations from well-known literary works. These books are, in a sense, impersonal name dictionaries and are not intended to be otherwise. This book is different!

Throughout the Bible are countless instances revealing God's interest in individuals and in their names. So deep was this interest, He sometimes changed names in order to better work out His plan in their lives. He's also interested in you. We believe God has made you a special creation. He has a unique life for you. He wants you to live up to the potential He has placed within you. He wants you to live up to your name.

Every name has a meaning drawn from the language of its origin. Sometimes that meaning is obscured because of changes in the culture or in the customs. There is more to a name than its literal meaning, however. Each name can and does suggest a character quality—a goal for which to strive. That's why this book is different. It features your name, the literal meaning, the character quality and an applicable scripture verse. This compilation will help you to understand the significance of your name and inspire you to live up to the character quality it suggests.

Sometimes an explanation has been included to help you realize the relationship between character quality and literal meaning. The name *Beverly,* for example, means, "by the beaver dam." Since beavers are known for their industry, Beverly's character quality is *industrious.*

Douglas means "up from the black lagoon." To leave such a place, a person would have to look for the light; therefore, *Seeker of Light* is the character quality assigned.

Included are certain names for which no literal meanings could be found. In such cases we assigned those character qualities we felt were implied in resource materials available to us.

A young boy overheard an uncle speaking to his father. "I don't know why you named that boy Clayton," the uncle said. "Clay is dirt and that's what his name means—dirt. He'll never amount to anything."

"You could be right," the father replied.

Clayton never forgot that conversation. He hated his name and he hated himself. Subconsciously he began to live up to his conception of the name's meaning. Whenever he experienced failure, he chalked it up to his name. After all, he was just dirt, wasn't he? Clayton grew into manhood feeling worthless.

One day on business he contacted Midwest Challenge. After hearing about the name plaques, he told his story to John Hartzell. John looked through our names to see if Clayton had been researched. It had. He discovered Clayton did refer to clay, but there was a special way to look at it. Clay isn't just dirt. It's an important substance, a raw material; when placed in the potter's hand, it becomes a thing of usefulness and beauty. God compared clay to his own special people. That's why the character quality for Clayton is *In God's Mold* and the verse says, "*. . . take notice, just as the clay is in the potter's hand, so you are in My hand . . .*"

That man learned he was unique in God's eyes— that God had special plans for him. As he let God unfold those plans, Clayton became a new person—the person God intended him to be.

Your name is unique and is as important as you are. Let God show you how to live up to it.

THE EDITORS
First Edition

ABRAM
Literal Meaning: FATHER OF A MULTITUDE
Suggested Character Quality: RIGHTEOUS PROTECTOR
Suggested Lifetime Scripture Verse: Ecclesiastes 7:12 *"For wisdom is a defense, and money is a defense; but the excellency of knowledge is, that giveth life to them that have it."* *

ACE
Literal Meaning: UNITY
Suggested Character Quality: PEACEMAKER
Suggested Lifetime Scripture Verse: Matthew 5:9 *"Blessed are the peacemakers; for they shall be called the children of God."* *

ADA
Literal Meaning: HAPPY
Suggested Character Quality: HAPPY SPIRIT
Suggested Lifetime Scripture Verse: Psalm 5:11 *"But let all who take refuge in Thee rejoice. Let them ever shout for joy since Thou dost make a covering over them. Let all who love Thy name be glad in Thee."*

ADAM
Literal Meaning: A MAN OF THE EARTH
Suggested Character Quality: GOD'S CREATION
Suggested Lifetime Scripture Verse: Ephesians 2:10 *"For we are His Handiwork, created in Christ Jesus for good works, which God previously prepared for us so that we should live in them."*

ADAMS
Literal Meaning: MAN OF THE EARTH
Suggested Character Quality: GOD'S CREATION
Suggested Lifetime Scripture Verse: Ephesians 2:10
"For we are His handiwork, created in Christ Jesus for good works, which God previously prepared for us so that we should live in them.

ADDIE
Literal Meaning: NOBLENESS
Suggested Character Quality: WOMAN OF ESTEEM
Suggested Lifetime Scripture Verse: Hosea 12:6 *"So, you return to your God, hold on to love and justice and wait continually on your God."*

ADDISON
Literal Meaning: SON OF ADAM
Suggested Character Quality: MAN OF DISTINCTION
Suggested Lifetime Scripture Verse: Psalm 4:3 *"But know that the Lord hath set apart him that is godly for Himself; . . . "* *

ADDY

Literal Meaning: NOBLENESS
Suggested Character Quality: WOMAN OF ESTEEM
Suggested Lifetime Scripture Verse: Hosea 12:6 *"So, you return to your God, hold on to love and justice and wait continually on your God."*

ADE

Literal Meaning: JOYOUS
Suggested Character Quality: JOYFUL HEART
Suggested Lifetime Scripture Verse: Psalm 5:11 *"But let all who take refuge in Thee rejoice. Let them ever shout for joy since Thou dost make a covering over them. Let all who love Thy name be glad in Thee."*

ADEL

Literal Meaning: NOBLE
Suggested Character Quality: WOMAN OF ESTEEM
Suggested Lifetime Scripture Verse: Hosea 12:6 *"So, you return to your God, hold on to love and justice and wait continually on your God."*

ADELAIDE

Literal Meaning: NOBLENESS
Suggested Character Quality: WOMAN OF ESTEEM
Suggested Lifetime Scripture Verse: Hosea 12:6 *"Go, you return to your God, hold on to love and justice and wait continually on your God."*

ADELE

Literal Meaning: NOBLE
Suggested Character Quality: WOMAN OF ESTEEM
Suggested Lifetime Scripture Verse: Hosea 12:6 *"So, you return to your God, hold on to love and justice and wait continually on your God."*

ADELINE

Literal Meaning: NOBLENESS
Suggested Character Quality: WOMAN OF ESTEEM
Suggested Lifetime Scripture Verse: Hosea 12:6 *"So, you return to your God, hold on to love and justice and wait continually on your God."*

ADELL

Literal Meaning: NOBLE
Suggested Character Quality: WOMAN OF ESTEEM
Suggested Lifetime Scripture Verse: Hosea 12:6 *"So, you return to your God, hold on to love and justice and wait continually on your God."*

ADELLA

Literal Meaning: NOBLE
Suggested Character Quality: WOMAN OF ESTEEM
Suggested Lifetime Scripture Verse: Hosea 12:6 *"So, you return to your God, hold on to love and justice and wait continually on your God."*

ADELLE

Literal Meaning: NOBLE
Suggested Character Quality: WOMAN OF ESTEEM
Suggested Lifetime Scripture Verse: Hosea 12:6 *"So, you return to your God, hold on to love and justice and wait continually on your God."*

ADELYNN

Literal Meaning: NOBLE
Suggested Character Quality: NOBLE HEART
Suggested Lifetime Scripture Verse: I Chronicles 28:9 *" . . . know thou the God of thy father, and serve Him with a perfect heart and with a willing mind; . . ."**

ADOLF

Literal Meaning: "NOBLE WOLF" — Germanic
Suggested Character Quality: COURAGEOUS SPIRIT
Suggested Lifetime Scripture Verse: Psalm 34:4 *"I sought the Lord and He answered me, and freed me from all my fears."*
Explanation: Noble wolf or hero suggests the ability to meet difficulties bravely.

ADORA

Literal Meaning: THE BELOVED, THE ADORED
Suggested Character Quality: BELOVED ONE
Suggested Lifetime Scripture Verse: John 15:9 *"As the father hath loved me, so have I loved you: continue ye in my love."* *

ADRIAN

Literal Meaning: "BLACK EARTH" — Latin
Suggested Character Quality: CREATIVE HEART
Suggested Lifetime Scripture Verse: Psalm 51:10 *"Create in me a clean heart, O God; and renew a steadfast spirit within me."*

ADRIANA

Literal Meaning: BLACK EARTH
Suggested Character Quality: CREATIVE HEART
Suggested Liftetime Scripture Verse: Psalm 51:10 *"Create in me a clean heart, O God; and renew a steadfast spirit within me."*
Explanation: See Adrian.

AGATHA

Literal Meaning: GOOD
Suggested Character Quality: A GOOD HEART
Suggested Lifetime Scripture Verse: Ephesians 4:32 *"Be kind toward one another, tenderhearted, forgiving one another, even as God has in Christ forgiven you."*

AGNES

Literal Meaning: PURE ONE
Suggested Character Quality: PURE ONE
Suggested Lifetime Scripture Verse: Psalm 51:6 *"Surely, Thou desirest truth in the inner self, and Thou makest me to understand hidden wisdom."*

AIDA

Literal Meaning: JOYOUS
Suggested Character Quality: HAPPY SPIRIT
Suggested Lifetime Scripture Verse: Psalm 5:11 *"But let all who take refuge in Thee rejoice. Let them ever shout for joy since Thou dost make a covering over them. Let all who love Thy name be glad in Thee."*

AILEEN

Literal Meaning: BEARER OF LIGHT
Suggested Character Quality: BRINGER OF LIGHT
Suggested Lifetime Scripture Verse: Psalm 37:6 *"And He shall bring forth thy righteousness as the light, and thy judgement as the noonday."* *

AIMEE

Literal Meaning: BELOVED ONE
Suggested Character Quality: BELOVED
Suggested Lifetime Scripture Verse: Song of Solomon 2:4 *"He brought me to the banqueting house, and His banner over me was love."* *

AIMES

Literal Meaning: BELOVED
Suggested Character Quality: BELOVED
Suggested Lifetime Scripture Verse: Song of Solomon 2:4 *"He brought me to the banqueting house, and His banner over me was love."* *

AL

Literal Meaning: CHEERFUL
Suggested Character Quality: CHEERFUL ONE
Suggested Lifetime Scripture Verse: Jeremiah 15:16 *"Thy words were found, and I ate them, and Thy words were to me a joy and a rejoicing of my heart; for I bear Thy name, O Lord, God of hosts."*

ALAINA
Literal Meaning: HARMONIOUS, CHEERFUL
Suggested Character Quality: CHEERFUL
Suggested Lifetime Scripture Verse: Psalm 35:9 *"And my soul shall be joyful in the Lord: it shall rejoice in His salvation."* *

ALAINE
Literal Meaning: HARMONIOUS, CHEERFUL
Suggested Character Quality: CHEERFUL
Suggested Lifetime Scripture Verse: Psalm 35:9 *"And my soul shall be joyful in the Lord; it shall rejoice in His salvation."* *

ALAN
Literal Meaning: HANDSOME, CHEERFUL, HARMONIOUS ONE
Suggested Character Quality: CHEERFUL ONE
Suggested Lifetime Scripture Verse: Jeremiah 15:16 *"Thy words were found, and I ate them, and Thy words were to me a joy and a rejoicing of my heart; for I bear Thy name, O Lord, God of hosts."*

ALASTAIR
Literal Meaning: PROTECTING MEN
Suggested Character Quality: DEFENDER OF MAN
Suggested Lifetime Scripture Verse: Micah 3:8a *"But truly I am full of power by the Spirit of the Lord, and of judgment, and of might . . ."* *

ALAYNA
Literal Meaning: HARMONIOUS, CHEERFUL
Suggested Character Quality: CHEERFUL
Suggested Lifetime Scripture Verse: Psalm 35:9 *"And my soul shall be joyful in the Lord: it shall rejoice in His salvation."* *

ALAYNE
Literal Meaning: HARMONIOUS, CHEERFUL
Suggested Character Quality: CHEERFUL
Suggested Lifetime Scripture Verse: Psalm 35:9 *"And my soul shall be joyful in the Lord: it shall rejoice in His salvation."* *

ALBERT
Literal Meaning: NOBLE, BRILLIANT OR INDUSTRIOUS
Suggested Character Quality: MAN OF HONOR
Suggested Lifetime Scripture Verse: Isaiah 30:18 *"Nevertheless the Lord longs to be gracious to you! Therefore He shall rise up to bestow mercy on you; for the Lord is a God of justice. Blessed are they who wait for Him."*

ALBERTA

Literal Meaning: BRILLIANT AND NOBLE
Suggested Character Quality: WOMAN OF HONOR
Suggested Lifetime Scripture Verse: Isaiah 30:18 *"Nevertheless the Lord longs to be gracious to you! Therefore, He shall rise up to bestow mercy on you; for the Lord is a God of justice. Blessed are they who wait for Him."*

ALDEN

Literal Meaning: OLD WISE PROTECTOR OR FRIEND
Suggested Character Quality: FRIENDLY ONE
Suggested Lifetime Scripture Verse: Proverbs 11:30 *"The fruit of the righteous is a tree of life, and a wise man wins friends."*

ALDORA

Literal Meaning: GIFT OF NOBLE RANK
Suggested Character Quality: NOBLE GIFT
Suggested Lifetime Scripture Verse: Ephesians 2:8 *"For by grace are ye saved through faith; and that not of yourselves: it is the gift of God:"* *

ALDRICH

Literal Meaning: WISE RULER
Suggested Character Quality: FULL OF WISDOM
Suggested Lifetime Scripture Verse: Psalm 111:10 *"For reverence of the Lord is the beginning of wisdom. There is insight in all who observe it. His praise is everlasing."*

ALEC

Literal Meaning: "PROTECTING MEN" — Greek
Suggested Character Quality: BRAVE PROTECTOR
Suggested Lifetime Scripture Verse: Psalm 31:24 *"Be strong and let your heart take courage, all ye who wait for the Lord."*

ALESHA

Literal Meaning: TRUTH
Suggested Character Quality: TRUTHFUL
Suggested Lifetime Scripture Verse: Psalm 51:6 *"Surely, Thou desirest truth in the inner self, and Thou makest me to understand hidden wisdom."*

ALESIA

Literal Meaning: TRUTH
Suggested Character Quality: TRUTHFUL
Suggested Lifetime Scripture Verse: Psalm 51:6 *"Surely, Thou desirest truth in the inner self, and Thou makest me to understand hidden wisdom."*

ALESSANDRA
Literal Meaning: HELPER OF DEFENDER OF MANKIND
Suggested Character Quality: COMPASSIONATE HEART
Suggested Lifetime Scripture Verse: Proverbs 31:20 *"She stretcheth out her hand to the poor; yea, she reacheth forth her hands to the needy."**

ALETA
Literal Meaning: TRUTH
Suggested Character Quality: TRUTHFUL ONE
Suggested Lifetime Scripture Verse: Psalm 51:6 *"Surely Thou desirest truth in the inner self, and Thou makest me to understand hidden wisdom."*

ALETHA
Literal Meaning: TRUTH
Suggested Character Quality: TRUTHFUL
Suggested Lifetime Scripture Verse: Psalm 51:6 *"Surely, Thou desirest truth in the inner self, and Thou makest me to understand hidden wisdom."*

ALEX
Literal Meaning: PROTECTING MAN
Suggested Character Quality: BRAVE PROTECTOR
Suggested Lifetime Scripture Verse: Psalm 31:24 *"Be strong and let your heart take courage, all ye who wait for the Lord."*

ALEXANDER
Literal Meaning: "PROTECTING MEN" — Greek
Suggested Character Quality: BRAVE PROTECTOR
Suggested Lifetime Scripture Verse: Psalm 31:24 *"Be strong and let your heart take courage, all ye who wait for the Lord."*

ALEXANDRIA
Literal Meaning: HELPER AND DEFENDER OF MANKIND
Suggested Character Quality: COMPASSIONATE HEART
Suggested Lifetime Scripture Verse: Proverbs 31:20 *"She stretcheth out her hand to the poor; yea, she reacheth forth her hands to the needy."**

ALEXIA
Literal Meaning: HELPER AND DEFENDER OF MANKIND
Suggested Character Quality: COMPASSIONATE HEART
Suggested Lifetime Scripture Verse: Proverbs 31:20 *"She stretcheth out her hand to the poor; yea, she reacheth forth her hands to the needy."* *

ALEXIS
Literal Meaning: PROTECTING MAN
Suggested Character Quality: SECURE SPIRIT
Suggested Lifetime Scripture Verse: Psalm 32:7 *"Thou art my hiding place; Thou wilt preserve me from trouble. Thou wilt surround me with songs of deliverance."*

ALFIE
Literal Meaning: WISE COUNSEL
Suggested Character Quality: A GOOD COUNSELOR
Suggested Lifetime Scripture Verse: Proverbs 20:5 *"Counsel in the heart of man is like deep water, but a man of understanding will draw it out."* *

ALFONSO
Literal Meaning: OF NOBLE FAMILY
Suggested Character Quality: NOBLE ONE
Suggested Lifetime Scripture Verse: Psalm 74:12 *"For God is my King of old, working salvation in the midst of the earth."* *

ALFRED
Literal Meaning: GOOD COUNSELOR
Suggested Character Quality: A GOOD COUNSELOR
Suggested Lifetime Scripture Verse: Proverbs 20:5 *"Counsel in the heart of man is like deep water, but a man of understanding will draw it out."* *

ALFREDA
Literal Meaning: WISE COUNSEL
Suggested Character Quality: A GOOD COUNSELOR
Suggested Lifetime Scripture Verse: Proverbs 31:26 *"She openeth her mouth with wisdom, and in her tongue is the law of kindness."* *

ALICE
Literal Meaning: TRUTHFUL ONE
Suggested Character Quality: TRUTHFUL
Suggested Lifetime Scripture Verse: Psalm 51:6 *"Surely, Thou desireth truth in the inner self, and Thou makest me to understand hidden wisdom."*

ALICIA
Literal Meaning: TRUTHFUL ONE
Suggested Character Quality: TRUTHFUL ONE
Suggested Lifetime Scripture Verse: Psalm 51:6 *"Surely, Thou desirest truth in the inner self, and Thou makest me to understand hidden wisdom."*

ALIDA
Literal Meaning: LITTLE WINGED ONE
Suggested Character Quality: LIVING IN FREEDOM
Suggested Lifetime Scripture Verse: John 8:36 *"If the Son therefore shall make you free, ye shall be free indeed."* *

ALISA
Literal Meaning: TRUTH
Suggested Character Quality: TRUTHFUL
Suggested Lifetime Scripture Verse: Psalm 51:6 *"Surely, Thou desirest truth in the inner self, and Thou makest me to understand hidden wisdom."*

ALISHA

Literal Meaning: TRUTH
Suggested Character Quality: TRUTHFUL
Suggested Lifetime Scripture Verse: Psalm 51:6 *"Surely, Thou desirest truth in the inner self, and Thou makest me to understand hidden wisdom."*

ALISSA

Literal Meaning: TRUTH
Suggested Character Quality: TRUTHFUL
Suggested Lifetime Scripture Verse: Psalm 51:6 *"Surely, Thou desirest truth in the inner self, and Thou makest me to understand hidden wisdom."*

ALLAN

Literal Meaning: HANDSOME, CHEERFUL, HARMONIOUS ONE
Suggested Character Quality: CHEERFUL ONE
Suggested Lifetime Scripture Verse: Jeremiah 15:16 *"Thy words were found, and I ate them, and Thy words were to me a joy and a rejoicing of my heart; for I bear Thy name, O Lord, God of hosts."*

ALLEN

Literal Meaning: HARMONY
Suggested Character Quality: CHEERFUL ONE
Suggested Lifetime Scripture Verse: Jeremiah 15:16 *"Thy words were found, and I ate them, and Thy words were to me a joy and a rejoicing of my heart; for I bear Thy name, O Lord, God of hosts."*

ALLISON

Literal Meaning: LITTLE TRUTHFUL ONE
Suggested Character Quality: TRUTHFUL ONE
Suggested Lifetime Scripture Verse: Psalm 51:6 *"Surely, Thou desirest truth in the inner self, and Thou makest me to understand hidden wisdom."*

ALMA

Literal Meaning: LOVING, KIND
Suggested Character Quality: LOVING AND KIND
Suggested Lifetime Scripture Verse: Psalm 5:7 *"But as for me, by the greatness of Thy unfailing love I will enter Thy house; at Thy holy temple I will worship in reverence of Thee."*

ALMEDA

Literal Meaning: PRESSING TOWARD THE GOAL
Suggested Character Quality: STEADFAST SPIRIT
Suggested Lifetime Scripture Verse: I Corinthians 15:58 *"Therefore, my beloved brethren, be ye steadfast, unmovable, always abounding in the work of the Lord, forasmuch as ye know that your labour is not in vain in the Lord."* *

ALONZO

Literal Meaning: OF NOBLE FAMILY
Suggested Character Quality: NOBLE ONE
Suggested Lifetime Scripture Verse: Psalm 74:12 *"For God is my King of old, working salvation in the midst of the earth."* *

ALPHA

Literal Meaning: THE FIRST
Suggested Character Quality: FULL OF HONOR
Suggested Lifetime Scripture Verse: Proverbs 22:4 *"By humility and the fear of the Lord are riches, and honour, and life."* *

ALTA

Literal Meaning: HIGH OR LOFTY
Suggested Character Quality: NOBLE SPIRIT
Suggested Lifetime Scripture Verse: Proverbs 2:6 *"For the Lord gives wisdom; from His mouth come knowledge and discernment."*

ALTHEA

Literal Meaning: A HEALER
Suggested Character Quality: HEALER
Suggested Lifetime Scripture Verse: III John 2 *"Beloved, I wish above all things that thou mayest prosper and be in health, even as thy soul prospereth."* *

ALTON

Literal Meaning: DWELLER AT THE OLD TOWN OR ESTATE
Suggested Character Quality: RESOURCEFUL
Suggested Lifetime Scripture Verse: Psalm 1:2 *"But his delight is in the law of the Lord and His law he ponders day and night."* *

ALVA

Literal Meaning: FAIR AND BEAUTIFUL
Suggested Character Quality: FAIR ONE
Suggested Lifetime Scripture Verse: I Chronicles 16:29 *"Give unto the Lord the glory due unto His name: bring an offering, and come before Him: worship the Lord in the beauty of holiness."*

ALVERA

Literal Meaning: EXCELLING
Suggested Character Quality: EXCELLENT SPIRIT
Suggested Lifetime Scripture Verse: Psalm 86:12 *"I will praise Thee, O lord my God, with all my heart, and I will glorify Thy name forever!"* *

ALVIN

Literal Meaning: FRIEND OF ALL
Suggested Character Quality: NOBLE FRIEND
Suggested Lifetime Scripture Verse: Psalm 112:4 *"Light rises for the upright in times of darkness; gracious and merciful is the good man."*

ALVINA

Literal Meaning: BELOVED: FRIEND OF ALL
Suggested Character Quality: NOBLE FRIEND
Suggested Lifetime Scripture Verse: Proverbs 17:17a *"A friend loveth at all times . . ."* *

ALVIS

Literal Meaning: ALL WISE
Suggested Character Quality: WISE ONE
Suggested Lifetime Scripture Verse: Job 28:28 *". . . Behold, the fear of the Lord, that is wisdom; and to depart from evil is understanding."* *

ALYCE

Literal Meaning: TRUTHFUL
Suggested Character Quality: TRUTHFUL ONE
Suggested Lifetime Scripture Verse: Psalm 51:6 *"Surely, Thou desirest truth in the inner self, and Thou makest me to understand hidden wisdom."*

ALYSE

Literal Meaning: TRUTHFUL ONE
Suggested Character Quality: TRUTH
Suggested Lifetime Scripture Verse: Psalm 51:6 *"Surely, Thou desirest truth in the inner self, and Thou makest me to understand hidden wisdom."*

ALYSHA

Literal Meaning: TRUTHFUL ONE
Suggested Character Quality: TRUTH
Suggested Lifetime Scripture Verse: Psalm 51:6 *"Surely, Thou desirest truth in the inner self, and Thou makest me to understand hidden wisdom."*

ALYSSA

Literal Meaning: TRUTH
Suggested Character Quality: TRUTHFUL ONE
Suggested Lifetime Scripture Verse: Psalm 51:6 *"Surely, Thou desirest truth in the inner self, and Thou makest me to understand hidden wisdom."*

AMANDA

Literal Meaning: WORTHY OF LOVE
Suggested Character Quality: BELOVED
Suggested Lifetime Scripture Verse: I John 4:7 *"Beloved, let us love one another, because love springs from God and whoever loves has been born of God and knows God."*

AMBER

Literal Meaning: AMBER JEWEL USED IN HEALING RITUALS
Suggested Character Quality: PRECIOUS ONE
Suggested Lifetime Scripture Verse: Psalm 84:11 *"For the Lord God is a sun and shield: the Lord will give grace and glory: no good thing will He withhold from them that walk uprightly."* *

AMBROSE

Literal Meaning: DIVINE, IMMORTAL ONE
Suggested Character Quality: ENDURING
Suggested Lifetime Scripture Verse: James I:12 *"Blessed is the man who stands up under trial; for when he has stood the test, he will receive the crown of life that God has promised to those who love Him."*

AMELIA

Literal Meaning: INDUSTRIOUS
Suggested Character Quality: INDUSTRIOUS ONE
Suggested Lifetime Scripture Verse: Titus 2:7a *"In all things showing thyself a pattern of good works . . . "* *

AMERIS

Literal Meaning: GOD HAS PROMISED
Suggested Character Quality: BLESSING OF GOD
Suggested Lifetime Scripture Verse: Proverbs 8:32 *"Now therefore harken unto me, O ye children: for blessed are they that keep my ways."* *

AMHERST

Literal Meaning: UNKNOWN
Suggested Character Quality: MAN OF HONOR
Suggested Lifetime Scripture Verse: Isaiah 33:15, 16 *"He that walketh righteously, and speaketh uprightly; he that despiseth the gain of oppressions, that shaketh his hands from holding of bribes, that stoppeth his ears from hearing of blood, and shutteth his eyes from seeing eveil; He shall dwell on high: his place of defense shall be the munitions of rocks: bread shall be given him; his waters shall be sure."* *

AMOS

Literal Meaning: BEARER OF A BURDEN
Suggested Character Quality: COMPASSIONATE SPIRIT
Suggested Lifetime Scripture Verse: Romans 12:9,10 *"Let your love be sincere, clinging to the right with abhorrence of evil. Be joined together in a brotherhood of mutual love . . ."*

AMY

Literal Meaning: BELOVED ONE
Suggested Character Quality: BELOVED
Suggested Lifetime Scripture Verse: I John 4:7 *"Beloved, let us love one another, because love springs from God and whoever loves has been born of God and knows God."*

ANABEL

Literal Meaning: GRACE
Suggested Character Quality: GRACIOUS ONE
Suggested Lifetime Scripture Verse: Psalm 119:112 *"I have set my heart on practicing Thy statutes forever, even to the end."*
Explanation: See Ann

ANDI

Literal Meaning: WOMANLY, STRONG
Suggested Character Quality: STRONG AND WOMANLY
Suggested Lifetime Scripture Verse: Proverbs 31:10, 25 *"Who can find a virtuous woman? For her price is far above rubies. Strength and honor are her clothing; and she shall rejoice in time to come."* *

ANDRA

Literal Meaning: WOMANLY, STRONG
Suggested Character Quality: STRONG AND WOMANLY
Suggested Lifetime Scripture Verse: Proverbs 31:10, 25 *"Who can find a virtuous woman? for her price is far above rubies. Strength and honor are her clothing; and she shall rejoice in time to come."* *

ANDREA

Literal Meaning: WOMANLY
Suggested Character Quality: GODLY WOMAN
Suggested Lifetime Scripture Verse: Psalm 97:12 *"You who are righteous, rejoice in the Lord; be thankful for the consciousness of His holiness."*

ANDRENE

Literal Meaning: WOMANLY, STRONG
Suggested Character Quality: STRONG AND WOMANLY
Suggested Lifetime Scripture Verse: Proverbs 31:10, 25 *"Who can find a virtuous woman? for her price is far above rubies. Strength and honor are her clothing; and she shall rejoice in time to come."* *

ANDREW

Literal Meaning: STRONG, MANLY
Suggested Character Quality: STRONG, MANLY
Suggested Lifetime Scripture Verse: Daniel 2:23 *"I thank Thee and praise Thee, O God of my fathers; for Thou has given me wisdom and strength."*

ANGEL

Literal Meaning: AN ANGEL; MESSENGER
Suggested Character Quality: BRINGER OF TRUTH
Suggested Lifetime Scripture Verse: Psalm 89:1 *"I will sing of the mercies of the Lord forever; I will make known Thy faithfulness with my mouth from generation to generation."*

ANGELA

Literal Meaning: ANGEL OR MESSENGER
Suggested Character Quality: BRINGER OF TRUTH
Suggested Lifetime Scripture Verse: Psalm 89:1 *"I will sing of the mercies of the Lord forever; I will make known Thy faithfulness with my mouth from generation to generation."*

ANGELENE

Literal Meaning: AN ANGEL; MESSENGER
Suggested Character Quality: BRINGER OF TRUTH
Suggested Lifetime Scripture Verse: Psalm 89:1 *"I will sing of the mercies of the Lord forever; I will make known Thy faithfulness with my mouth from generation to generation."*

ANGELICA

Literal Meaning: AN ANGEL; MESSENGER
Suggested Character Quality: BRINGER OF TRUTH
Suggested Lifetime Scripture Verse: Psalm 89:1 *"I will sing of the mercies of the Lord forever; I will make known Thy faithfulness with my mouth from generation to generation."*

ANGIE

Literal Meaning: AN ANGEL; MESSENGER
Suggested Character Quality: BRINGER OF TRUTH
Suggested Lifetime Scripture Verse: Psalm 89:1 *"I will sing of the mercies of the Lord forever; I will make known Thy faithfulness with my mouth from generation to generation."*

ANGINETTE

Literal Meaning: GRACE
Suggested Character Quality: GRACIOUS ONE
Suggested Lifetime Scripture Verse: Psalm 119:112 *"I have set my heart on practicing Thy statutes forever, even to the end."*

ANGUS

Literal Meaning: UNIQUE CHOICE
Suggested Character Quality: CREATIVE SPIRIT
Suggested Lifetime Scripture Verse: Ephesians 2:10 *"For we are His handiwork, created in Christ Jesus for good works, which God previously prepared for us so that we should live in them."*

ANITA

Literal Meaning: GRACEFUL ONE
Suggested Character Quality: GRACIOUS ONE
Suggested Lifetime Scripture Verse: Psalm 119:112 *"I have set my heart on practicing Thy statutes forever, even to the end."*
Explanation: See Ann

ANN

Literal Meaning: GRACEFUL ONE
Suggested Character Quality: GRACIOUS ONE
Suggested Lifetime Scripture Verse: Psalm 119: 112 *"I have set my heart on practicing Thy statutes forever, even to the end."*
Explanation: Graceful does not refer merely to physical ability, but to a quality of graciousness and mercy in the inner person.

ANNA

Literal Meaning: GRACEFUL ONE
Suggested Character Quality: GRACIOUS ONE
Suggested Lifetime Scripture Verse: Psalm 119:112 *"I have set my heart on practicing Thy statutes forever, even to the end."*
Explanation: See Ann

ANNABEL

Literal Meaning: FULL OF GRACE
Suggested Character Quality: GRACIOUS SPIRIT
Suggested Lifetime Scripture Verse: Psalm 119:112 *"I have set my heart on practicing Thy statutes forever, even to the end."*
Explanation: See Ann

ANNE

Literal Meaning: GRACIOUS ONE
Suggested Character Quality: GRACIOUS ONE
Suggested Lifetime Scripture Verse: Psalm 119:112 *"I have set my heart on practicing Thy statutes forever, even to the end."*
Explanation: See Ann

ANNELLE

Litereal Meaning: FULL OF GRACE
Suggested Character Quality: GRACIOUS ONE
Suggested Lifetime Scripture Verse: Psalm 119:112 *"I have set my heart on practicing Thy statutes forever, even to the end."*
Explanation: See Ann

ANNETTE

Literal Meaning: GRACEFUL ONE
Suggested Character Quality: GRACIOUS ONE
Suggested Lifetime Verse: Psalm 119:112 *"I have set my heart on practicing Thy statutes forever, even to the end."*
Explanation: See Ann

ANNIE

Literal Meaning: FULL OF GRACE
Suggested Character Quality: GRACIOUS ONE
Suggested Lifetime Scripture Verse: Psalm 119:112 *"I have set my heart on practicing Thy statutes forever, even to the end."*
Explanation: See Ann

ANTHONY

Literal Meaning: INESTIMABLE
Suggested Character Quality: PRICELESS ONE
Suggested Lifetime Scripture Verse: Psalm 21:6 *"Yes, forever Thou dost make him most blessed; Thou dost delight him with joy by Thy presence."*

ANTOINETTE

Literal Meaning: INESTIMABLE
Suggested Character Quality: PRICELESS ONE
Suggested Lifetime Scripture Verse: Proverbs 31:35 *"Who can find a virtuous woman? for her price is far above rubies."* *

ANTON

Literal Meaning: INESTIMABLE
Suggested Character Quality: PRICELESS ONE
Suggested Lifetime Scripture Verse: Psalm 21:6 *"Yes, forever Thou dost make him most blessed; Thou dost delight him with joy by Thy presence."*

APRIL

Literal Meaning: OPENING; BORN IN APRIL
Suggested Character Quality: NEW IN FAITH
Suggested Lifetime Scripture Verse: Psalm 143:8 *"In the morning proclaim to me Thy covenant love, for I have put my trust in Thee. Make me understand the way I should go, for I lift up my soul to Thee."*
Explanation: April suggests a time of freshness and beginnings, a time for new faith in God.

APRYL

Literal Meaning: OPENING; BORN IN APRIL
Suggested Character Quality: NEW IN FAITH
Suggested Lifetime Scripture Verse: Psalm 143:8 *"In the morning proclaim to me Thy covenant love, for I have put my trust in Thee. Make me understand the way I should go, for I lift up my soul to Thee."*
Explanation: See April

ARCHIE
Literal Meaning: NOBILITY
Suggested Character Quality: MIGHTY AND POWERFUL
Suggested Lifetime Scripture Verse: Proverbs 24:5 *"A wise man is straong; yea, a man of knowledge increaseth strength."* *

ARDELLE
Literal Meaning: WARMTH, ENTHUSIASM
Suggested Character Quality: DEVOTED HEART
Suggested Lifetime Scripture Verse: Psalm 42:1 *"As a deer pants for water brooks so my soul longs for Thee, O God."*

ARDYCE
Literal Meaning: WARMTH, ENTHUSIASM
Suggested Character Quality: ZEALOUS FOR GOD
Suggested Lifetime Scripture Verse: Colossians 3:23 *"Whatever you do, work heartily as for the Lord and not for men."*

ARDYTHE
Literal Meaning: ZEALOUS AND ARDENT
Suggested Character Quality: ZEALOUS FOR GOD
Suggested Lifetime Scripture Verse: Colassians 3:23 *"Whatever you do, work heartily as for the Lord and not for men."*

ARGUS
Literal Meaning: WATCHFUL, VIGILANT
Suggested Character Quality: ALERTLY WATCHFUL
Suggested Lifetime Scripture Verse: I Corinthians 16:13 *"Watch ye, stand fast in the faith, quit you like men, be strong."* *

ARLAND
Literal Meaning: PLEDGE
Suggested Character Quality: DEPENDABLE ONE
Suggested Lifetime Scripture Verse: Psalm 5:8 *"O Lord, lead me in Thy righteousness because of those who watch me; make Thy way straight before me."*

ARLEN
Literal Meaning: PLEDGE
Suggested Character Quality: FAITHFUL ONE
Suggested Lifetime Scripture Verse: Psalm 34:1 *"I will bless the Lord at all times; His praise shall continually be in my mouth."* *

ARLENE

Literal Meaning: A PLEDGE
Suggested Character Quality: FAITHFUL ONE
Suggested Lifetime Scripture Verse: Psalm 34:1 *"I will bless the Lord at all times; his praise shall continually be in my mouth."* *

ARLIS

Literal Meaning: UNKNOWN
Suggested Character Quality: FAITHFUL ONE
Suggested Lifetime Scripture Verse: Psalm 89:1 *"I will sing of the mercies of the Lord forever; with my mouth will I make known Thy faithfulness to all generations."* *

ARLOW

Literal Meaning: FORTIFIED HILL
Suggested Character Quality: STRONG PROTECTOR
Suggested Lifetime Scripture Verse: Psalm 18:32 *"It is God that girdeth me with strength, and maketh my way perfect."* *

ARMAND

Literal Meaning: SOLDIER
Suggested Character Quality: SOLDIER OF CHRIST
Suggested Lifetime Scripture Verse: II Timothy 2:3,4 *"Thou therefore endure hardness, as a good soldier of Jesus Christ. No man that warreth entangleth himself with the affairs of this life; that he may please Him who hath chosen him to be a soldier."* *

ARNE

Literal Meaning: STRONG AS AN EAGLE
Suggested Character Quality: STRONG ONE
Suggested Lifetime Scripture Verse: Isaiah 12:2 *"Behold, God is my salvation; I will trust, and not be afraid, for Jehovah, the Lord, is my strength and my song; yes, He has become my salvation."*

ARNO

Literal Meaning: STRONG
Suggested Character Quality: STRONG ONE
Suggested Lifetime Scripture Verse: Isaiah 12:2 *"Behold, God is my salvation; I will trust and not be afraid, for Jehovah, the Lord, is my strength and my song; yes, He has become my salvation."*

ARNOLD

Literal Meaning: EAGLE RULER OR STRONG AS AN EAGLE
Suggested Character Quality: BRAVE AND STRONG
Suggested Lifetime Scripture Verse: Isaiah 12:2 *"Behold, God is my salvation; I will trust and not be afraid, for Jehovah, the Lord, is my strength and my song; yes, He has become my salvation."*

ARON

Literal Meaning: LOFTY OR EXALTED
Suggested Character Quality: EXALTED
Suggested Lifetime Scripture Verse: Psalm 3:3 *"But thou, O Lord, art a shield about me; my glory and the One who lifts my head."*

ARTHUR

Literal Meaning: NOBLE ONE OR BEAR MAN
Suggested Character Quality: MAN OF INTEGRITY
Suggested Lifetime Scripture Verse: Psalm 37:23 *"A person's steps are confirmed by the Lord; He establishes him and delights in his way."*

ARVID

Literal Meaning: MAN OF THE PEOPLE
Suggested Character Quality: FRIENDLY SPIRIT
Suggested Lifetime Scripture Verse: Ephesians 4:32 *"And be ye kind one to another, tenderhearted, forgiving one another, even as God for Christ's sake hath forgiven you."* *

ASHLEY

Literal Meaning: A DWELLER AT THE ASH-TREE MEADOW
Suggested Character Quality: RESTFUL SPIRIT
Suggested Lifetime Scripture Verse: Psalm 23:1,2 *"The Lord is my shepherd; I shall not want. He maketh me to lie down in green pastures: He leadeth me beside the still waters."* *

AUBREY

Literal Meaning: ELF RULER
Suggested Character Quality: NOBLE ONE
Suggested Lifetime Scripture Verse: Matthew 25:21 *". . . Well done, thou good and faithful servant: thou hast been faithful over a few things, I will make thee ruler over many things . . ."* *

AUDRA

Literal Meaning: NOBLE STRENGTH
Suggested Character Quality: NOBLE SPIRIT
Suggested Lifetime Scripture Verse: Proverbs 31:29 *"Many daughters have done virtuously, but thou excellest them all."* *

AUDREY

Literal Meaning: NOBLE STRENGTH
Suggested Character Quality: NOBLE AND STRONG
Suggested Lifetime Scripture Verse: Psalm 138:3 *"In the day when I called Thou didst answer me, and didst encourage me with strength in my soul."*

AUGUST

Literal Meaning: MAJESTIC; WORTHY OF REVERENCE
Suggested Character Quality: CONSECRATED TO GOD
Suggested Lifetime Scripture Verse: I Thessalonians 5:23, 24 *"And the very God of peace sanctify you wholly; and I pray God your whole spirit and soul and body be preserved blameless unto the coming of our Lord Jesus Christ. Faithful is He that calleth you, who also will do it."* ∗

AUGUSTINE

Literal Meaning: MAJESTIC; WORTHY OF REVERENCE
Suggested Character Quality: CONSECRATED TO GOD
Suggested Lifetime Scripture Verse: I Thessalonians 5:23, 24 *"And the very God of peace sanctify you wholly; and I pray God your whole spirit and soul and body be preserved blameless unto teh coming of our Lord Jesus Christ. Faithful is He that calleth you, who also will do it."* ∗

AUGUSTUS

Literal Meaning: MAJESTIC; WORTHY OF REVERENCE
Suggested Character Quality: CONSECRATED TO GOD
Suggested Lifetime Scripture Verse: I Thessalonians 5:23, 24 *"And the very God of peace sanctify you wholly; and I pray God your whole spirit and soul and body be preserved blameless unto the coming of our Lord Jesus Christ. Faithful is He that calleth you, who also will do it."* ∗

AUSTIN

Literal Meaning: WORTHY OF REVERENCE
Suggested Character Quality: NOBLE HEART
Suggested Lifetime Scripture Verse: Psalm 119:58 *"Wholeheartedly I sought Thy favor; be merciful to me according to Thy word."*

AUTUMN

Literal Meaning: TIME OF YEAR AFTER SUMMER
Suggested Character Quality: IN GOD'S GLORY
Suggested Lifetime Scripture Verse: Psalm 84:11 *"For the Lord God is a sun and shield: the Lord will give grace and glory: no good thing will He withhold from them that walk uprightly."* ∗

AVERY

Literal Meaning: SELF-COUNSEL
Suggested Character Quality: A GOOD COUNSELOR
Suggested Lifetime Scripture Verse: Proverbs 20:5 *"Planning in a man's mind is deep water, but a man of understanding will draw it out."*

AVIS

Literal Meaning: A BIRD
Suggested Character Quality: MIGHTY IN SPIRIT
Suggested Lifetime Scripture Verse: Proverbs 31:30 *"Favor is deceitful, and beauty is vain: but a woman that feareth the Lord, she shall be praised."**

AVON

Literal Meaning: None Could Be Found
Suggested Character Quality: GENEROUS ONE
Suggested Lifetime Scripture Verse: Psalm 54:6 *"With a freewill offering I will sacrifice to Thee; I will praise Thy name, O Lord, for it is good."*

Explanation: No literal meaning could be found for this name. The character quality selected suggests service both to God and man.

AXEL

Literal Meaning: FATHER OF PEACE
Suggested Character Quality: PEACEFUL ONE
Suggested Lifetime Scripture Verse: Psalm 37:37 *"Mark the perfect man, and behold the upright: for the end of that man is peace."**

BAMBI

Literal Meaning: LITTLE BABY
Suggested Character Quality: CHILD OF GOD
Suggested Lifetime Scripture Verse: Matthew 5:44, 45a *"But I say unto you, Love your enemies, bless them that curse you, do good to them that hate you, and pray for them which despitefully use you, and persecute you; That ye may be the children of your Father which is in heaven . . ."* *

BARBARA

Literal Meaning: STRANGER
Suggested Character Quality: COMING WITH JOY
Suggested Lifetime Scripture Verse: I Thessalonians 3:12 *"May the Lord make your love for one another and for everyone abundant and running over, just as ours is for you."*
Explanation: A stranger comes into new surroundings with a certain attitude; one who is in Lord comes with joy and love.

BARBIE

Literal Meaning: STRANGER
Suggested Character Quality: COMING WITH JOY
Suggested Lifetime Scripture Verse: I Thessalonians 3:12 *"May the Lord make your love for one another and for everyone abundant and running over, just as ours is for you."* *
Explanation: See Barbara

BARLETT

Literal Meaning: UNKNOWN
Suggested Character Quality: DILIGENT ONE
Suggested Lifetime Scripture Verse: Deuteronomy 6:17 *"Ye shall diligently keep the commandments of the Lord your God, and His testimonies, and His statutes, which He hath commanded thee . . ."*

BARLOW

Literal Meaning: DWELLER AT THE BARE HILL
Suggested Character Quality: HUMBLE HEART
Suggested Lifetime Scripture Verse: I Peter 5:5, 6 *". . . Yea, all of you be subject one to another, and be clothed with humility: for God resisteth the proud, and giveth grace to the humble. Humble yourselves therefore under the mighty hand of God, that He may exalt you in due time."* *

BARNABY

Literal Meaning: SON OF PROPHECY
Suggested Character Quality: REVERENT SPIRIT
Suggested Lifetime Scripture Verse: Hebrews 12:28 *"Let us, therefore, be grateful that the kingdom we have received cannot be shaken, and so let us serve God acceptably with reverence and awe."*

BARNEY

Literal Meaning: BOLD AS A BEAR
Suggested Character Quality: BRAVE AND STRONG
Suggested Lifetime Scripture Verse: Proverbs 14:26 *"In the fear of the Lord is strong confidence: and His children shall have a place of refuge."* *

BARON

Literal Meaning: NOBLEMAN
Suggested Character Quality: ZEALOUS FOR GOD
Suggested Lifetime Scripture Verse: Titus 2:13, 14 *"Looking for that blessed hope, and the glorious appearing of the great God and our Saviour Jesus Christ; who gave Himself for us, that He might redeem us from all iniquity, and purify unto Himself a peculiar people, zealous of good works."* *

BARRETT

Literal Meaning: BEAR — MIGHT
Suggested Character Quality: STRONG AND MIGHTY
Suggested Lifetime Scripture Verse: Ephesians 6:10 *"Finally, my brethen, be strong in the Lord, and in the power of His might."* *

BARRY

Literal Meaning: SPEARLIKE OR POINTED
Suggested Character Quality: COURAGEOUS
Suggested Lifetime Scripture Verse: Psalm 18:30 *"God! Perfect is His way! The word of the Lord is proven; a shield is He to all who trust in Him."*
Explanation: Where warlike or soldierly meanings occur, qualities necessary for those in combat are selected.

BART

Literal Meaning: SON OF THE FURROWS; FARMER
Suggested Character Quality: DILIGENT ONE
Suggested Lifetime Scripture Verse: Psalm 37:3 *"Trust in the Lord and do good; inhabit the land and practice faithfulness."*

BARTHOLOMEW

Literal Meaning: FARMER'S SON
Suggested Character Quality: INDUSTRIOUS
Suggested Lifetime Scripture Verse: Psalm 37:3 *"Trust in the Lord and do good; inhabit the land and practice faithfulness."*

BARTLEY

Literal Meaning: FARMER'S SON
Suggested Character Quality: INDUSTRIOUS
Suggested Lifetime Scripture Verse: Psalm 37:3 *"Trust in the Lord and do good; inhabit the land and practice faithfulness."*

BASIL

Literal Meaning: KINGLY
Suggested Character Quality: GRACIOUS AND MANLY
Suggested Lifetime Scripture Verse: Psalm 112:6, 7 *"Such a man will never be laid low, for the just shall be held in remembrance forever. He need never fear any evil report; his heart will remain firm, fully trusting in the Lord."*

BEATA

Literal Meaning: BLESSED, HAPPY ONE
Suggested Character Quality: BRINGER OF JOY
Suggested Lifetime Scripture Verse: John 15:11 *"I have talked these matters over with you so that my joy may be in you and your joy be made complete."*

BEATRICE

Literal Meaning: SHE WHO MAKES OTHERS HAPPY
Suggested Character Quality: BRINGER OF JOY
Suggested Lifetime Scripture Verse: Isaiah 30:29 *"But you shall have a song as in the night consecrated for a feasting; and you shall have the gladness of heart as when men march with flutes to come to the mountain of the Lord, the Rock of Israel."*

BEAU

Literal Meaning: OF A BEAUTIFUL NATURE
Suggested Character Quality: BEAUTIFUL SPIRIT
Suggested Lifetime Scripture Verse: Psalm 29:2 *"Give unto the Lord the glory due unto His name; worship the Lord in the beauty of holiness."* *

BELVA

Literal Meaning: BEAUTIFUL ONE
Suggested Character Quality: INNER BEAUTY
Suggested Lifetime Scripture Verse: Hebrews 12:28 *"Let us, therefore, be grateful that the kingdom we have received cannot be shaken, and so let us serve God acceptably with reverence and awe."*

BEN

Literal Meaning: SON OF THE RIGHT HAND
Suggested Character Quality: FAVORED SON
Suggested Lifetime Scripture Verse: Psalm 40:11 *"Thou, O Lord, wilt not withhold Thy mercies from me; Thy lovingkindness and Thy truth shall continually preserve me."*

BENEDICT
Literal Meaning: SPOKEN WELL OF, BLESSED
Suggested Character Quality: BLESSED BY GOD
Suggested Lifetime Scripture Verse: Psalm 119:2 *"Blessed are those who keep His testimonies, who seek Him wholeheartedly."*

BENJAMIN
Literal Meaning: SON OF THE RIGHT HAND
Suggested Character Quality: FAVORED SON
Suggested Lifetime Scripture Verse: Psalm 40:11 *"Thou, O Lord, wilt not withhold Thy mercies from me; Thy lovingkindness and Thy truth shall continually preserve me."*

BENNETT
Literal Meaning: BLESSED ONE
Suggested Character Quality: BLESSED BY GOD
Suggested Lifetime Scripture Verse: Psalm 119:2 *"Blessed are those who keep His testimonies, who seek Him wholeheartedly."*

BENTLEY
Literal Meaning: FROM THE WINDING MEADOW
Suggested Character Quality: PEACEFUL ONE
Suggested Lifetime Scripture Verse: John 14:27 *"Peace I leave with you, my peace I give unto you: not as the world giveth, give I unto you. Let not your heart be troubled, neither let it be afraid."* *

BENTON
Literal Meaning: FROM THE WINDING TOWN
Suggested Character Quality: FOLLOWER OF GOD
Suggested Lifetime Scripture Verse: Romans 14:19 *"Let us therefore follow after the things which make for peace, and things wherewith one may edify another."* *

BERNADETTE
Literal Meaning: BRAVE AS A BEAR
Suggested Character Quality: STRONG; WOMANLY
Suggested Lifetime Scripture Verse: Psalm 18:32 *"It is God that girdeth me with strength, and maketh my way perfect."* *

BERNARD
Literal Meaning: BRAVE AS A BEAR
Suggested Character Quality: MIGHTY, POWERFUL
Suggested Lifetime Scripture Verse: Colossians 4:2 *"Keep persevering in prayer; attend to it diligently with the offering of thanks."*

BERNHARDT

Literal Meaning: BOLD AS A BEAR
Suggested Character Quality: MIGHTY; POWERFUL
Suggested Lifetime Scripture Verse: Ephesians 6:10 *"Finally, my brethren, be strong in the Lord, and in the power of His might."* *

BERNICE

Literal Meaning: HARBINGER OF VICTORY
Suggested Character Quality: VICTORIOUS
Suggested Lifetime Scripture Verse: Isaiah 48:17 *"Thus says the Lord, your Redeemer, the Holy One of Israel: I am the Lord your God, who teaches you to profit, who leads you in the way you should go."*

BERNITA

Literal Meaning: HARBINGER OF VICTORY
Suggested Character Quality: VICTORIOUS
Suggested Lifetime Scripture Verse: Isaiah 48:17 *"Thus says the Lord, your Redeemer, the Holy One of Israel: I am the Lord your God, who teaches you to profit, who leads you in the way you should go."*

BERT

Literal Meaning: SHINING, GLORIOUS ONE
Suggested Character Quality: MAN OF HONOR
Suggested Lifetime Scripture Verse: Isaiah 30:18 *"Nevertheless the Lord longs to be gracious to you! Therefore He shall rise up to bestow mercy on you; for the Lord is a God of justice. Blessed are they who wait for Him."*

BERTHA

Literal Meaning: "BRIGHT" — Germanic
Suggested Character Quality: BRIGHT ONE
Suggested Lifetime Scripture Verse: Psalm 97:11 *"Light is sown for the righteous and joy for those whose hearts are right."*

BERTON

Literal Meaning: OF BRIGHT FAME
Suggested Character Quality: BRIGHT ONE
Suggested Lifetime Scripture Verse: Matthew 5:16 *"Let your light so shine before men, that they may see your good works, and glorify your Father which is in heaven."* *

BERTRAM

Literal Meaning: ILLUSTRIOUS
Suggested Character Quality: MAN OF HONOR
Suggested Lifetime Scripture Verse: Isaiah 30:18 *"Nevertheless the Lord longs to be gracious to you! Therefore He shall rise up to bestow mercy on you; for the Lord is a God of justice. Blessed are they who wait for Him."*

BESS

Literal Meaning: CONSECRATED TO GOD
Suggested Character Quality: CONSECRATED TO GOD
Suggested Lifetime Scripture Verse: Psalm 119:34 *"Give me understanding, and I shall observe Thy law, and keep it wholeheartedly."*

BESSIE

Literal Meaning: CONSECRATED TO GOD
Suggested Character Quality: CONSECRATED TO GOD
Suggested Lifetime Scripture Verse: Psalm 119:34 *"Give me understanding, and I shall observe Thy law, and keep it wholeheartedly."*

BETH

Literal Meaning: HOUSE OF GOD
Suggested Character Quality: ABIDING PLACE OF GOD
Suggested Lifetime Scripture Verse: Psalm 23:6 *"Surely, goodness and unfailing love shall follow me all the days of my life and I shall dwell in the house of the Lord forever."*

BETHANY

Literal Meaning: HOUSE OF POVERTY
Suggested Character Quality: GRATEFUL SPIRIT
Suggested Lifetime Scripture Verse: I Chronicles 29:12, 13 *"Both riches and honor come of Thee, and Thou reignest over all; and in Thine hand is power and might; and in Thine hand it is to make great, and to give strength unto all. Now therefore, our God, we thank Thee, and praise Thy glorious name."**

BETSY

Literal Meaning: CONSECRATED TO GOD
Suggested Character Quality: CONSECRATED TO GOD
Suggested Lifetime Scripture Verse: Psalm 119:34 *"Give me understanding, and I shall observe Thy law, and keep it wholeheartedly."*

BETTY

Literal Meaning: CONSECRATED TO GOD
Suggested Character Quality: CONSECRATED TO GOD
Suggested Lifetime Scripture Verse: Psalm 116:13 *"I will take the cup of salvation and call on the name of the Lord."*

BEULAH

Literal Meaning: THE MARRIED
Suggested Character Quality: FAITHFUL ONE
Suggested Lifetime Scripture Verse: Colossians 2:6 *"As ye have therefore received Christ Jesus the Lord, so walk ye in Him."**

BEVERLY

Literal Meaning: DWELLER AT THE BEAVER MEADOW
Suggested Character Quality: DILIGENT SPIRIT
Suggested Lifetime Scripture Verse: Colossians 3:23 *"Whatever you do, work heartily as for the Lord and not for men."*

BILL

Literal Meaning: RESOLUTE PROTECTOR
Suggested Character Quality: GREAT PROTECTOR
Suggested Lifetime Scripture Verse: Micah 6:8 *"And what does the Lord require of you but to do justice, to love mercy and to walk humbly with your God."*

BIRDIE

Literal Meaning: BRIGHT
Suggested Character Quality: BRIGHT ONE
Suggested Lifetime Scripture Verse: Psalm 97:11 *"Light is sown for the righteous and joy for those whose hearts are right."*

BJORN

Literal Meaning: BEAR
Suggested Character Quality: BRAVE AND STRONG
Suggested Lifetime Scripture Verse: Proverbs 24:5 *"A wise man is strong; yea, a man of knowledge increaseth strength."* *

BLAINE

Literal Meaning: THIN OR LEAN
Suggested Character Quality: IN GOD'S STRENGTH
Suggested Lifetime Scripture Verse: Isaiah 40:31 *"But they that wait upon the Lord shall renew their strength; they shall mount up with wings as eagles; they shall run, and not be weary; and they shall walk, and not faint."* *

BLAIR

Literal Meaning: A MARSHY PLAIN OR BATTLEFIELD
Suggested Character Quality: STRENGTH OF CHARACTER
Suggested Lifetime Scripture Verse: Ephesians 3:16 *"That He would grant you, according to the riches of His glory, to be strengthened with might by His Spirit in the inner man;"* *

BLAKE

Literal Meaning: LIGHT AND FAIR
Suggested Character Quality: PURE ONE
Suggested Lifetime Scripture Verse: II Timothy 2:22 *"Flee also youthful lusts: but follow righteousness, faith, charity, peace, with them that call on the Lord out of a pure heart."* *

BLANCHARD

Literal Meaning: WHITE
Suggested Character Quality: PURE ONE
Suggested Lifetime Scripture Verse: II Timothy 2:22 *"Flee also youthful lusts: but follow righteousness, faith, charity, peace, with them that call on the Lord out of a pure heart."* *

BLANCHE

Literal Meaning: WHITE FAIR ONE
Suggested Character Quality: PURITY
Suggested Lifetime Scripture Verse: Proverbs 31:30 *"Charm is deceitful and beauty is passing, but a woman who reveres the Lord will be praised."*

BOB

Literal Meaning: BRIGHT OR SHINING WITH FAME
Suggested Character Quality: EXCELLENT WORTH
Suggested Lifetime Scripture Verse: Psalm 24:3-4 *"Who shall go up into the mountain of the Lord; who shall stand in His holy place? He who has clean hands and a pure heart, who has not lifted up his soul to falsehood, who has not sworn deceptively."*

BOBBI

Literal Meaning: SHINING WITH FAME
Suggested Character Quality: EXCELLENT WORTH
Suggested Lifetime Scripture Verse: Philippians 4:13 *"I have strength for every situation through Him who empowers me."*

BOBBY

Literal Meaning: BRIGHT OR SHINING WITH FAME
Suggested Character Quality: EXCELLENT WORTH
Suggested Lifetime Scripture Verse: Psalm 24:3-4 *"Who shall go up into the mountain of the Lord; who shall stand in His holy place? He who has clean hands and a pure heart, who has not lifted up his soul to falsehood, who has not sworn deceptively."*

BONITA

Literal Meaning: GOOD
Suggested Character Quality: A GOOD HEART
Suggested Lifetime Scripture Verse: Psalm 64:10 *"The righteous shall be glad in the Lord, and trust in Him; and all the upright in heart shall offer praise."*

BONNIE

Literal Meaning: SWEET AND GOOD
Suggested Character Quality: A GOOD HEART
Suggested Lifetime Scripture Verse: Psalm 64:10 *"The righteous shall be glad in the Lord, and trust in Him; and all the upright in heart shall offer praise."*

BOONE

Literal Meaning: BLESSING
Suggested Character Quality: BLESSING OF GOD
Suggested Lifetime Scripture Verse: Proverbs 8:32 *"Now therefore hearken unto me, O ye children: for blessed are they that keep My ways."* *

BOOTH

Literal Meaning: A BOOTH
Suggested Character Quality: SHELTERED BY GOD
Suggested Lifetime Scripture Verse: Joshua 1:9 *"Have not I commanded thee? Be strong and of a good courage; be not afraid, neither be thou dismayed: for the Lord thy God is with thee whithersoever thou goest."* *

BORIS

Literal Meaning: WARRIOR
Suggested Character Quality: LOYAL HEART
Suggested Lifetime Scripture Verse: Deuteronomy 11:1 *"Love the Lord your God, therefore, and always heed His charge. His laws, His ordinances, and His commandments. Of the Lord your God's discipline you must be ever mindful."*

BOYD

Literal Meaning: WHITE OR FAIR
Suggested Character Quality: PURE
Suggested Lifetime Scripture Verse: Psalm 19:9 *"The fear of the Lord is clean, enduring forever: the judgments of the Lord are true and righteous altogether."* *

BRAD

Literal Meaning: FROM THE BROAD MEADOW
Suggested Character Quality: ABUNDANT PROVIDER
Suggested Lifetime Scripture Verse: Psalm 23:1, 2 *"The Lord is my Shepherd; I shall not lack; He makes me to lie down in green pastures."*
Explanation: A meadow suggests prosperity, peacefulness, security; the person who provides these things for others provides abundantly.

BRADFORD

Literal Meaning: FROM THE BROAD RIVER CROSSING
Suggested Character Quality: FAITHFUL PROVIDER
Suggested Lifetime Scripture Verse: Psalm 1:3 *"And he shall be like a tree planted by the rivers of water, that bringeth forth his fruit in his season; his leaf also shall not wither; and whatsoever he doeth shall prosper."* *

BRADLEY

Literal Meaning: FROM THE BROAD MEADOW
Suggested Character Quality: ABUNDANT PROVIDER
Suggested Lifetime Scripture Verse: Psalm 23:1, 2 *"The Lord is my Shepherd; I shall not lack; He makes me to lie down in green pastures."*
Explanation: See Brad

BRADY

Literal Meaning: FROM THE BROAD ISLE
Suggested Character Quality: STRONG IN SPIRIT
Suggested Lifetime Scripture Verse: Ephesians 6:10 *"Finally, my brethren, be strong in the Lord, and in the power of His might."* *

BRANDON

Literal Meaning: FROM THE BEACON HILL
Suggested Character Quality: STRONG IN VICTORY
Suggested Lifetime Scripture Verse: Jeremiah 15:20 *"And I will make you to this people a fortified wall of bronze. They will fight against you, but they shall not prevail over you; for I am with you to save you and to deliver you, says the Lord."*
Explanation: The beacon, a shining bright light, was used to signal victory from one camp to another.

BRANT

Literal Meaning: PROUD ONE
Suggested Character Quality: RISING ABOVE
Suggested Lifetime Scripture Verse: Psalm 24:3-4 *"Who shall go up into the mountain of the Lord; who shall stand in His holy place? He who has clean hands and a pure heart, who has not lifted up his soul to falsehood, who has not sworn deceptively."*

BRECK

Literal Meaning: LARGE, COARSE FERN
Suggested Character Quality: ABUNDANT LIFE
Suggested Lifetime Scripture Verse: John 10:10b *". . . I am come that they might have life, and that they might have it more abundantly."* *

BRENDA

Literal Meaning: FIERY
Suggested Character Quality: ENTHUSIASTIC
Suggested Lifetime Scripture Verse: Psalm 119:16 *"I take great delight in Thy statutes; and I will not forget Thy word."*

BRENDON

Literal Meaning: FROM THE FIERY HILL
Suggested Character Quality: STRONG IN VICTORY
Suggested Lifetime Scripture Verse: Jeremiah 15:20 *"And I will make you to this people a fortified wall of bronze. They will fight against you, but they shall not prevail over you; for I am with you to save you and to deliver you, says the Lord."*

BRENT

Literal Meaning: STEEP HILL
Suggested Character Quality: RISING ABOVE
Suggested Lifetime Scripture Verse: Psalm 24:3-4 *"Who shall go up into the mountain of the Lord; who shall stand in His holy place? He who has clean hands and a pure heart, who has not lifted up his soul to falsehood, who has not sworn deceptively."*

BRETT

Literal Meaning: MAN OF BRITTANY
Suggested Character Quality: LOYAL
Suggested Lifetime Scripture Verse: Deuteronomy 11:1 *"Therefore thou shalt love the Lord thy God, and keep His charge, and His statutes, and His judgments and His commandments, alway."* *

BRIAN

Literal Meaning: STRENGTH, VIRTUE, HONOR
Suggested Character Quality: STRONG IN VIRTUE
Suggested Lifetime Scripture Verse: Proverbs 24:5 *"A wise man is strong, and a man of knowledge adds to his strength."*

BRICE

Literal Meaning: QUICK ONE
Suggested Character Quality: QUICK TO EXCEL
Suggested Lifetime Scripture Verse: Psalm 5:12 *"Thou, O Lord, dost bless the righteous; as with a shield Thou dost surround him with favor."*

BRIDGET

Literal Meaning: MIGHTY AND STRONG
Suggested Character Quality: STRONG HEART
Suggested Lifetime Scripture Verse: Psalm 73:26b *". . . God is the strength of my heart, and my portion forever."* *

BRITT

Literal Meaning: NATIVE OF BRITTANY
Suggested Character Quality: LOYAL
Suggested Lifetime Scripture Verse: Deuteronomy 11:1 *"Therefore thou shalt love the Lord Thy God, and keep His charge, and His statutes, and His judgments, and His commandments, alway."* *

BRITTANY

Literal Meaning: NATIVE OF BRITTANY
Suggested Character Quality: LOYAL
Suggested Lifetime Scripture Verse: Deuteronomy 11:1 *"Therefore thou shalt love the Lord they God, and keep His charge, and His statutes, and His judgments, and His commandments, alway."* *

BROCK

Literal Meaning: A BADGER
Suggested Character Quality: STRONG WARRIOR
Suggested Lifetime Scripture Verse: Micah 3:8a *"But truly I am full of power by the Spirit of the Lord . . ."* *

BROOK

Literal Meaning: FROM THE BROOK
Suggested Character Quality: REFRESHING ONE
Suggested Lifetime Scripture Verse: Proverbs 17:22a *"A merry heart doeth good like a medicine . . ."* *

BROOKS

Literal Meaning: FROM THE BROOK
Suggested Character Quality: REFRESHING ONE
Suggested Lifetime Scripture Verse: Proverbs 17:22a *"A merry heart doeth good like a medicine . . ."* *

BRUCE

Literal Meaning: DWELLER AT THE THICKET
Suggested Character Quality: SECURE ONE
Suggested Lifetime Scripture Verse: Romans 8:2 *"For the life-giving principles of the Spirit have freed you in Christ Jesus from the control of the principles of sin and death."*
Explanation: A thicket was often used to protect land and crops; therefore one who lived there would be secure.

BRYAN

Literal Meaning: STRENGTH, VIRTUE, HONOR
Suggested Character Quality: STRONG IN SPIRIT
Suggested Lifetime Scripture Verse: Psalm 31:3 *"For Thou art my rock and my fortress; for Thy name's sake lead me and guide me."*

BRYCE

Literal Meaning: QUICK ONE
Suggested Character Quality: QUICK TO EXCEL
Suggested Lifetime Scripture Verse: Psalm 5:12 *"Thou, O Lord, dost bless the righteous; as with a shield Thou dost surround him with favor."*

BUCK

Literal Meaning: A MALE DEER
Suggested Character Quality: STRONG ONE
Suggested Lifetime Scripture Verse: Psalm 18:2 *"The Lord is my rock, and my fortress, and my deliverer; my God, my strength, in whom I will trust; my buckler, and the horn of my salvation, and my high tower."* *

BUD

Literal Meaning: MESSENGER
Suggested Character Quality: MESSENGER OF GOD
Suggested Lifetime Scripture Verse: Mark 16:15 *"And He said unto them, Go yea into all the world, and preach the gospel to every creature."* *

BUDDY

Literal Meaning: MESSENGER
Suggested Character Quality: MESSENGER OF GOD
Suggested Lifetime Scripture Verse: Mark 16:15 *"And He said unto them, Go yea into all the world, and preach the gospel to every creature."* *

BUFORD

Literal Meaning: A SHALLOW STREAM WHERE OXEN CROSS
Suggested Character Quality: CONSISTENT PROVIDER
Suggested Lifetime Scripture Verse: Psalm 37:3 *"Trust in the Lord, and do good; so shalt thou dwell in the land, and verily thou shalt be fed."* *

BUNNY

Literal Meaning: GOOD
Suggested Character Quality: A GOOD HEART
Suggested Lifetime Scripture Verse: Psalm 64:10 *"The righteous shall be glad in the Lord, and trust in Him; and all the upright in heart shall offer praise."*

BURKE

Literal Meaning: CASTLE DWELLER
Suggested Character Quality: OF NOBLE CHARACTER
Suggested Lifetime Scripture Verse: Psalm 24:3, 4 *"Who shall ascend into the hill of the Lord? or who shall stand in His holy place? He that hath clean hands, and a pure heart; who hath not lifted up his soul unto vanity, nor sworn deceitfully."* *

BURT

Literal Meaning: BRIGHT; OR BOROUGH TOWN
Suggested Character Quality: ABUNDANT PROVIDER
Suggested Lifetime Scripture Verse: Psalm 23:1, 2 *"The Lord is my Shepherd; I shall not lack; He makes me to lie down in green pastures."*

BUTCH

Literal Meaning: UNKNOWN
Suggested Character Quality: RELIABLE ONE
Suggested Lifetime Scripture Verse: Ecclesiastes 9:10a *"Whatsoever thy hand findeth to do, do it with thy might . . ."**

BUZZ

Literal Meaning: UNKNOWN
Suggested Character Quality: MAN OF DISTINCTION
Suggested Lifetime Scripture Verse: Psalm 25:14 *"The secret of the Lord is with them that fear Him; and He will show them His covenant."* *

BYRON

Literal Meaning: "BEAR" — Anglo-Saxon
Suggested Character Quality: FULL OF STRENGTH
Suggested Lifetime Scripture Verse: Psalm 59:9 *"O my Strength, I will wait on Thee, for God is my stronghold."*
Explanation: "Bear" suggests physical, emotional and mental strength.

CAL

Literal Meaning: BALD
Suggested Character Quality: HUMBLE SPIRIT
Suggested Lifetime Scripture Verse: Proverbs 22:4 *"The results of humility - reverence for the Lord - are riches, honor and life."*

CALEB

Literal Meaning: BOLD ONE OR DOG
Suggested Character Quality: FAITHFULNESS
Suggested Lifetime Scripture Verse: Psalm 31:23 *"O love the Lord, all ye His saints: for the Lord preserveth the faithful, and plentifully rewardeth the proud doer."* *

CALEN

Literal Meaning: UNKNOWN
Suggested Character Quality: CALM SPIRIT
Suggested Lifetime Scripture Verse: Psalm 37:5 *"Commit thy way unto the Lord; trust also in Him; and He shall bring it to pass."* *

CALLY

Literal Meaning: BEAUTIFUL FLOWER
Suggested Character Quality: GOD'S CREATION
Suggested Lifetime Scripture Verse: Psalm 96:9a *"O worship the Lord in the beauty of holiness . . ."* *

CALVIN

Literal Meaning: BALD ONE
Suggested Character Quality: HUMBLE
Suggested Lifetime Scripture Verse: Proverbs 22:4 *"The results of humility — reverence for the Lord — are riches, honor and life."*
Explanation: The Lord often used baldness to motivate one to humility; therefore the character quality "humble" is appropriate.

CAMDEN

Literal Meaning: FROM THE CROOKED OR WINDING VALLEY
Suggested Character Quality: PEACEFUL
Suggested Lifetime Scripture Verse: Psalm 23:1, 2 *"The Lord is my shepherd; I shall not want. He maketh me to lie down in green pastures: He leadeth me beside the still waters."* *

CAMERON

Literal Meaning: BENT NOSE
Suggested Character Quality: MAN OF DISTINCTION
Suggested Lifetime Scripture Verse: I Thessalonians 5:23 *"And the very God of peace sanctify you wholly; and I pray God your whole spirit and soul and body be preserved blameless unto the coming of our Lord Jesus Christ."* *

CAMILLA

Literal Meaning: ATTENDANT AT RELIGIOUS CEREMONIES
Suggested Character Quality: GOD'S SERVANT
Suggested Lifetime Scripture Verse: Psalm 100:2 *"Serve the Lord with gladness: come before His presence with singing."* *

CAMILLE

Literal Meaning: ATTENDANT AT RELIGIOUS CEREMONIES
Suggested Character Quality: GOD'S SERVANT
Suggested Lifetime Scripture Verse: Psalm 100:2 *"Serve the Lord with gladness: come before His presence with singing."* *

CAMMY

Literal Meaning: ATTENDANT AT RELIGIOUS CEREMONIES
Suggested Character Quality: GOD'S SERVANT
Suggested Lifetime Scripture Verse: Psalm 100:2 *"Serve the Lord with gladness: come before His presence with singing."* *

CANDACE

Literal Meaning: GLITTERING, GLOWING WHITE
Suggested Character Quality: WOMAN OF HONOR
Suggested Lifetime Scripture Verse: Habakkuk 3:19 *"The Lord God is my strength; He makes my feet like hinds' feet, He makes me tread upon my high places."*

CANDICE

Literal Meaning: GLITTERING GLOWING WHITE
Suggested Character Quality: WOMAN OF HONOR
Suggested Lifetime Scripture Verse: Habakkuk 3:19 *"The Lord God is my strength; He makes my feet like hinds' feet, He makes me tread upon my high places."*

CANDIDA

Literal Meaning: BRIGHT WHITE
Suggested Character Quality: WOMAN OF HONOR
Suggested Lifetime Scripture Verse: Habakkuk 3:19 *"The Lord God is my strength; He makes my feet like hinds' feet, He makes me tread upon my high places."*

CANDY

Literal Meaning: GLITTERING, GLOWING WHITE
Suggested Character Quality: WOMAN OF HONOR
Suggested Lifetime Scripture Verse: Habakkuk 3:19 *"The Lord God is my strength; He makes my feet like hinds' feet, He makes me tread upon my high places."*

CAREY

Literal Meaning: TO SING WITH JOY
Suggested Character Quality: JOYFUL SPIRIT
Suggested Lifetime Scripture Verse: John 15:11 *"I have talked these matters over with you, so that my joy may be in you and your joy be made complete."*

CARIN

Literal Meaning: PURE
Suggested Character Quality: PURE ONE
Suggested Lifetime Scripture Verse: II Timothy 2:22 *"Flee also youthful lusts: but follow righteousness, faith, charity, peace, with them that call on the Lord out of a pure heart."* *

CARL

Literal Meaning: FARMER
Suggested Character Quality: STRONG; MANLY
Suggested Lifetime Scripture Verse: Ephesians 6:10 *"In conclusion, be strong in the Lord and in the strength of His might."*

CARLA

Literal Meaning: LITTLE WOMANLY ONE
Suggested Character Quality: STRONG; WOMANLY
Suggested Lifetime Scripture Verse: Isaiah 41:10 *"Fear not, for I am with you; be not dismayed, for I am your God! I will strengthen you; yes, I will help you; yes, I will uphold you with My vindicating right hand."*

CARLETON

Literal Meaning: FARMER'S TOWN
Suggested Character Quality: STRONG AND MANLY
Suggested Lifetime Scripture Verse: Ephesians 6:10 *"In conclusion, be strong in the Lord and in the strength of His might."*

CARLIE

Literal Meaning: STRONG
Suggested Character Quality: STRENGTH OF CHARACTER
Suggested Lifetime Scripture Verse: Isaiah 41:10 *"Fear not, for I am with you; be not dismayed, for I am your God! I will strengthen you; yes, I will help you; yes, I will uphold you with My vindicating right hand."*

CARLIN

Literal Meaning: LITTLE CHAMPION
Suggested Character Quality: STRONG; MANLY
Suggested Lifetime Scripture Verse: Ephesians 6:10 *"In conclusion, be strong in the Lord and in the strength of His might."*

CARLOS

Literal Meaning: FARMER
Suggested Character Quality: STRONG AND MANLY
Suggested Lifetime Scripture Verse: Ephesians 6:10 *"In conclusion, be strong in the Lord and in the strength of His might."*

CARLTON

Literal Meaning: FARMER'S TOWN
Suggested Character Quality: STRONG AND MANLY
Suggested Lifetime Scripture Verse: Ephesians 6:10 *"In conclusion, be strong in the Lord and in the strength of His might."*

CARLY

Literal Meaning: ONE WHO IS STRONG
Suggested Character Quality: STRENGTH OF CHARACTER
Suggested Lifetime Scripture Verse: Isaiah 41:10 *"Fear not, for I am with you; be not dismayed, for I am your God! I will strengthen you; yes, I will help you; yes, I will uphold you with My vindicating right hand."*

CARMEL

Literal Meaning: A FRUITFUL FIELD
Suggested Character Quality: VIRTUOUS HEART
Suggested Lifetime Scripture Verse: Proverbs 11:30 *"The fruit of the righteous is a tree of life; and he that winneth souls is wise."**

CARMELLA

Literal Meaning: GOD'S FRUITFUL FIELD
Suggested Character Quality: VIRTUOUS HEART
Suggested Lifetime Scripture Verse: Proverbs 11:30 *"The fruit of the righteous is a tree of life; and he that winneth souls is wise."**

CARMEN

Literal Meaning: SONG
Suggested Character Quality: SONG OF JOY
Suggested Lifetime Scripture Verse: Psalm 116:17 *"I will offer to Thee the sacrifice of thanksgiving and call on the name of the Lord."*

CARMINE

Literal Meaning: A SONG
Suggested Character Quality: LIVING IN HARMONY
Suggested Lifetime Scripture Verse: Psalm 42:11 *"Why are you bowed down, O my soul, and why do you groan within me? Hope in God, for I shall yet praise Him, my face-healer and my God."*

CAROL

Literal Meaning: WOMANLY; SONG
Suggested Character Quality: SONG OF JOY
Suggested Lifetime Scripture Verse: John 15:11 *"I have talked these matters over with you so that my joy may be in you and your joy be made complete."*

CAROLINE

Literal Meaning: LITTLE, WOMANLY ONE
Suggested Character Quality: REFRESHING JOY
Suggested Lifetime Scripture Verse: Psalm 119:16 *"I take great delight in Thy statutes; I will not forget Thy word."*

CAROLYN

Literal Meaning: LITTLE WOMANLY ONE; SONG
Suggested Character Quality: JOYFUL SPIRIT
Suggested Lifetime Scripture Verse: Jeremiah 33:11 *"The voice of joy and the voice of gladness, the voice of the bridegroom and the voice of the bride, and the voices of those who say, 'Give thanks to the Lord of hosts, for the Lord is good, for His mercy endures forever,' and who bring sacrifices of thanksgiving to the house of the Lord. For I will restore the fortunes of the land as formerly, says the Lord.'"*

CARPENTER

Literal Meaning: WOODWORKER
Suggested Character Quality: SKILLED ONE
Suggested Lifetime Scripture Verse: Ecclesiastes 9:10a *"Whatsoever thy hand findeth to do, do it with thy might ..."* *

CARRIE

Literal Meaning: STRONG; WOMANLY
Suggested Character Quality: STRONG WOMAN
Suggested Lifetime Scripture Verse: Isaiah 41:10 *"Fear not, for I am with you; be not dismayed, for I am your God! I will strengthen you; yes, I will help you; yes, I will uphold you with My vindicating right hand."*

CARSON

Literal Meaning: SON OF THE MARSHDWELLER
Suggested Character Quality: GIFT OF GOD
Suggested Lifetime Scripture Verse: Colossians 3:10 *"And have put on the new man, which is renewed in knowledge after the image of Him that created him."* *

CARTER
Literal Meaning: MAKER OF CARTS
Suggested Character Quality: INDUSTRIOUS SPIRIT
Suggested Lifetime Scripture Verse: Hebrews 13:16 *"Do not forget to do good and be generous, for with such sacrifices God is well pleased."*

CARY
Literal Meaning: STRONG AND WOMANLY
Suggested Character Quality: STRONG AND WOMANLY
Suggested Lifetime Scripture Verse: Isaiah 41:10 *"Fear not, for I am with you; be not dismayed, for I am your God! I will strengthen you; yes, I will help you; yes, I will uphold you with my vindicating right hand."*

CARYL
Literal Meaning: WOMANLY; SONG
Suggested Character Quality: SONG OF JOY
Suggested Lifetime Scripture Verse: John 15:11 *"I have talked these matters over with you so that my joy may be in you and your joy be made complete."*

CAS
Literal Meaning: TREASURE HOLDER
Suggested Character Quality: TRUSTWORTHY
Suggested Lifetime Scripture Verse: I Corinthians 4:2 *"Moreover it is required in stewards, that a man be found faithful."* *

CASEY
Literal Meaning: BRAVE, WATCHFUL
Suggested Character Quality: BRAVE PROTECTOR
Suggested Lifetime Scripture Verse: I Thessalonians 5:6 *"Therefore let us not sleep, as do others; but let us watch and be sober."* *

CASPER
Literal Meaning: TREASURE HOLDER
Suggested Character Quality: TRUSTWORTHY
Suggested Lifetime Scripture Verse: I Corinthians 4:2 *"Moreover it is required in stewards, that a man be found faithful."* *

CASSANDRA
Literal Meaning: HELPER OF MEN
Suggested Character Quality: GOD'S HELPER
Suggested Lifetime Scripture Verse: Proverbs 31:20 *She stretcheth out her hand to the poor; yea, she reacheth forth her hands to the needy."* *

CASSIE

Literal Meaning: HELPER OF MEN
Suggested Character Quality: GOD'S HELPER
Suggested Lifetime Scripture Verse: Proverbs 31:20 *"She stretcheth out her hand to the poor; yea, she reacheth forth her hands to the needy."* *

CATHERINE

Literal Meaning: PURE ONE
Suggested Character Quality: PURE ONE
Suggested Lifetime Scripture Verse: Psalm 119:7 *"I will give thanks to Thee with integrity of heart when I learn Thy righteous judgments."*

CATHLEEN

Literal Meaning: PURE
Suggested Character Quality: PURE ONE
Suggested Lifetime Scripture Verse: Psalm 119:7 *"I will praise Thee with an upright heart, when I learn Thy righteous ordinances."*

CATHY

Literal Meaning: PURE
Suggested Character Quality: PURE ONE
Suggested Lifetime Scripture Verse: Psalm 119:7 *"I will praise Thee with an upright heart, when I learn Thy righteous ordinances."*

CECIL

Literal Meaning: BLIND
Suggested Character Quality: HUMBLE SPIRIT
Suggested Lifetime Scripture Verse: Psalm 10:17 *"Lord, Thou hast heard the desire of the humble: Thou wilt prepare their heart, Thou wilt cause thine ear to hear."*
Explanation: See Cecilia

CECILE

Literal Meaning: BLIND
Suggested Character Quality: HUMBLE SPIRIT
Suggested Lifetime Scripture Verse: Psalm 10:17 *"Lord, Thou hast heard the desire of the humble: Thou wilt prepare their heart, Thou wilt cause thine ear to hear."*
Explanation: See Cecilia

CECILIA

Literal Meaning: BLIND
Suggested Character Quality: HUMBLE SPIRIT
Suggested Lifetime Scripture Verse: Psalm 10:17 *"Lord, Thou hast heard the desire of the humble: Thou wilt prepare their heart, Thou wilt cause Thine ear to hear:"* *
Explanation: Acceptance of one's condition is the first step in humility; the blind must learn this before they can be helped.

CEDRIC

Literal Meaning: CHIEFTAIN
Suggested Character Quality: BLESSED BY GOD
Suggested Lifetime Scripture Verse: Proverbs 10:22 *"The blessing of the Lord, it maketh rich, and He addeth no sorrow with it."* *

CELESTE

Literal Meaning: HEAVEN
Suggested Character Quality: WALKS WITH GOD
Suggested Lifetime Scripture Verse: Psalm 73:28 *"But it is good for me to draw near to God: I have put my trust in the Lord God, that I may declare all Thy works."* *

CELIA

Literal Meaning: BLIND
Suggested Character Quality: HUMBLE SPIRIT
Suggested Lifetime Scripture Verse: Psalm 10:17 *"Lord, Thou hast heard the desire of the humble: Thou wilt prepare their heart, Thou wilt cause thine ear to hear."* *
Explanation: See Cecilia

CHAD

Literal Meaning: WARLIKE
Suggested Character Quality: DEFENDER
Suggested Lifetime Scripture Verse: Isaiah 1:17 *"Learn to do good! Seek justice; restrain the ruthless; protect the orphan; defend the widow."*

CHANDLER

Literal Meaning: CANDLE MAKER
Suggested Character Quality: BRIGHT ONE
Suggested Lifetime Scripture Verse: Matthew 5:16 *"Let your light so shine before men, that they may see your good works, and glorify your Father which is in heaven."* *

CHANLEY

Literal Meaning: MOON
Suggested Character Quality: REFLECTOR OF LIGHT
Suggested Lifetime Scripture Verse: Psalm 119:105 *"Thy word is a lamp unto my feet, and a light unto my path."* *

CHANNING

Literal Meaning: A SINGER; CHURCH DIGNITARY
Suggested Character Quality: SING OF GOD'S PRAISES
Suggested Lifetime Scripture Verse: Psalm 9:2 *"I will be glad and rejoice in Thee: I will sing praise to Thy name, O Thou Most High."* *

CHARITY

Literal Meaning: BENEVOLENT; GRACE
Suggested Character Quality: LOVING
Suggested Lifetime Scripture Verse: I John 4:7 *"Beloved, let us love one another: for love is of God; and every one that loveth is born of God, and knoweth God."* *

CHARLENE

Literal Meaning: LITTLE WOMANLY ONE
Suggested Character Quality: WOMANLY
Suggested Lifetime Scripture Verse: Proverbs 31:10 *"Who can find a wife with strength of character? She is far more precious than jewels."*

CHARLES

Literal Meaning: STRONG; MANLY
Suggested Character Quality: STRONG; MANLY
Suggested Lifetime Scripture Verse: Joshua 1:9 *"Have I not commanded you? Be resolute and strong! Be not afraid, and be not dismayed; for the Lord your God is with you everywhere you go."*

CHARLOTTE

Literal Meaning: LITTLE WOMANLY ONE
Suggested Character Quality: FULL OF GRACE
Suggested Lifetime Scripture Verse: Psalm 23:6 *"Surely goodness and unfailing love shall follow me all the days of my life and I shall dwell in the house of the Lord forever."*

CHARMAINE

Literal Meaning: A SONG
Suggested Character Quality: SONG OF JOY
Suggested Lifetime Scripture Verse: Psalm 89:1 *"I will sing of the mercies of the Lord forever: with my mouth will I make known Thy faithfulness to all generations."* *

CHER

Literal Meaning: DEAR ONE
Suggested Character Quality: CHERISHED ONE
Suggested Lifetime Scripture Verse: Romans 8:38, 39 *"For I am persuaded, that neither death, nor life, nor angels, nor principalities, nor powers, nor things present, nor things to come, nor height, nor depth, nor any other creature, shall be able to separate us from the love of God, which is in Christ Jesus our Lord."* *

CHERI

Literal Meaning: DEAR BELOVED ONE
Suggested Character Quality: CHERISHED ONE
Suggested Lifetime Scripture Verse: Zephaniah 3:17 *"The Lord, your God, is in your midst, a mighty one who will save. He will rejoice over you with delight; He will rest you in His love; He will be joyful over you with singing."*

CHERISE

Literal Meaning: DEAR BELOVED ONE
Suggested Character Quality: CHERISHED ONE
Suggested Lifetime Scripture Verse: Zephaniah 3:17 *"The Lord, your God, is in your midst, a mighty one who will save. He will rejoice over you with delight; He will rest you in His love; He will be joyful over you with singing."*

CHERISH

Literal Meaning: BELOVED
Suggested Character Quality: CHERISHED ONE
Suggested Lifetime Scripture Verse: Romans 8:38, 39 *"For I am persuaded, that neither death, nor life, nor angels, nor principalities, nor powers, nor things present, nor things to come, nor height, nor depth, nor any other creature, shall be able to separate us from the love of God, which is in Christ Jesus our Lord."* *

CHERRY

Literal Meaning: BENEVOLENT; CHARITABLE
Suggested Character Quality: LOVING
Suggested Lifetime Scripture Verse: I John 4:7 *"Beloved, let us love one another: for love is of God; and every one that loveth is born of God, and knoweth God."* *

CHERYL

Literal Meaning: THE EPITOME OF FEMININITY
Suggested Character Quality: WOMANLY
Suggested Lifetime Scripture Verse: Proverbs 31:10 *"Who can find a virtuous woman? for her price is far above rubies."* *

CHESTER

Literal Meaning: DWELLER AT THE FORTIFIED ARMY CAMP
Suggested Character Quality: STRONG DEFENDER
Suggested Lifetime Scripture Verse: Psalm 31:3 *"For Thou art my rock and my fortress; for Thy name's sake lead me and guide me."*

CHET

Literal Meaning: DWELLER AT THE FORTIFIED ARMY CAMP
Suggested Character Quality: STRONG DEFENDER
Suggested Lifetime Scripture Verse: Psalm 31:3 *"For Thou art my rock and my fortress; for Thy name's sake lead me and guide me."*

CHIP

Literal Meaning: UNKNOWN
Suggested Character Quality: CONQUEROR
Suggested Lifetime Scripture Verse: Romans 8:37 *"Nay, in all these things we are more than conquerors through Him that loved us."* *

CHRISTA

Literal Meaning: CHRISTIAN
Suggested Character Quality: FOLLOWER OF CHRIST
Suggested Lifetime Scripture Verse: Psalm 86:11 *"Teach me, Thy way, O Lord; I will walk in Thy truth; unite my heart to revere Thy name."*

CHRISTIAN

Literal Meaning: BELIEVER IN CHRIST
Suggested Character Quality: FOLLOWER OF CHRIST
Suggested Lifetime Scripture Verse: Psalm 86:11 *"Teach me Thy way, O Lord; I will walk in Thy truth; unite my heart to revere Thy name."*

CHRISTINE

Literal Meaning: CHRISTIAN
Suggested Character Quality: FOLLOWER OF CHRIST
Suggested Lifetime Scripture Verse: Psalm 63:8 *"My soul follows close behind Thee; Thy right hand upholds me."*

CHRISTOPHER

Literal Meaning: CHRIST-BEARER
Suggested Character Quality: FOLLOWER OF CHRIST
Suggested Lifetime Scripture Verse: Psalm 86:11 *"Teach me Thy way, O Lord; I will walk in Thy truth; unite my heart to revere Thy name."*

CHRISTY

Literal Meaning: CHRISTIAN
Suggested Character Quality: FOLLOWER OF CHRIST
Suggested Lifetime Scripture Verse: Psalm 86:11 *"Teach me Thy way, O Lord; I will walk in Thy truth; unite my heart to revere Thy name."*

CHUCK

Literal Meaning: STRONG; MANLY
Suggested Character Quality: FEARLESS, STRONG
Suggested Lifetime Scripture Verse: Proverbs 28:1, 12 *"The wicked flee when there is one pursuing, but the righteous are as fearless as a young lion . . . When the righteous rejoice, great is the glory; but when the wicked rise, men hide themselves."*

CICELY

Literal Meaning: THE DIM-SIGHTED
Suggested Character Quality: HUMBLE SPIRIT
Suggested Lifetime Scripture Verse: Psalm 10:17 *"Lord, Thou hast heard the desire of the humble: Thou wilt prepare their heart, Thou wilt cause thine ear to hear."* *
Explanation: See Cecilia

CINDY

Literal Meaning: GODDESS OF THE MOON
Suggested Character Quality: REFLECTOR OF LIGHT
Suggested Lifetime Scripture Verse: Psalm 27:1 *"The Lord is my light and my salvation; whom shall I fear? The Lord is the stronghold of my life; of whom shall I be afraid?"*
Explanation: The moon reflects the light of the sun; we are to reflect God's Son.

CINNAMON

Literal Meaning: AROMATIC SPICE
Suggested Character Quality: LIVING FRAGRANCE
Suggested Lifetime Scripture Verse: II Corinthians 2:15 *"For we are unto God a sweet savor of Christ, in them that are saved, and in them that perish."* *

CLAIRE

Literal Meaning: BRIGHT, ILLUSTRIOUS
Suggested Character Quality: PURE IN GRACE
Suggested Lifetime Scripture Verse: II Timothy 2:22 *"But flee from the lusts of youth. Go in pursuit of integrity, faith, love, peace, in fellowship with those who call upon the Lord out of pure hearts."*

CLARA

Literal Meaning: BRILLIANT, BRIGHT, ILLUSTRIOUS
Suggested Character Quality: PURE IN GRACE
Suggested Lifetime Scripture Verse: II Timothy 2:22 *"But flee from the lusts of youth. Go in pursuit of integrity, faith, love, peace, in fellowship with those who call upon the Lord out of pure hearts."*

CLARENCE

Literal Meaning: FAMOUS ONE
Suggested Character Quality: STRONG IN CHARACTER
Suggested Lifetime Scripture Verse: Philippians 1:6 *"Of this I am convinced, that He who has begun a good work in you will bring it to completion in the day of Christ Jesus."*

CLARK

Literal Meaning: "LEARNED" — Latin
Suggested Character Quality: FULL OF WISDOM
Suggested Lifetime Scripture Verse: Psalm 49:3 *"My mouth shall speak wisdom; and the thoughts of my heart shall be of insight."*

CLAUDE

Literal Meaning: "LAME" — Latin
Suggested Character Quality: HUMBLE HEART
Suggested Lifetime Scripture Verse: Psalm 54:4 *"Behold, God is my ally; the Lord is with those who sustain my soul."*
Explanation: "Lame" suggests dependence. The humble person recognizes weakness and accepts it.

CLAUDETTE

Literal Meaning: LAME
Suggested Character Quality: FULL OF HUMILITY
Suggested Lifetime Scripture Verse: Psalm 5:8 *"O Lord, lead me in Thy righteousness because of those who watch me; make Thy way straight before me."*
Explanation: See Claude

CLAUDIA

Literal Meaning: LAME ONE
Suggested Character Quality: HUMBLE HEART
Suggested Lifetime Scripture Verse: Isaiah 30:15 *"For thus says the Lord God, The Holy One of Israel: In conversion and rest you shall be saved; in quietness and confidence shall be your strength."*
Explanation: All inabilities provide opportunities for God's power.

CLAUDINE

Literal Meaning: THE LAME ONE
Suggested Character Quality: HUMILITY OF SPIRIT
Suggested Lifetime Scripture Verse: Isaiah 30:15 *"For thus says the Lord God, The Holy One of Israel: In conversion and rest you shall be saved; in quietness and confidence shall be your strength."*
Explanation: See Claudia

CLAY

Literal Meaning: TOWN AT A CLAY SITE
Suggested Character Quality: IN GOD'S MOLD
Suggested Lifetime Scripture Verse: Jeremiah 18:6 *"O house of Israel, cannot I do with you as this potter did? says the Lord. Take notice, just as the clay is in the potter's hand, so are you in My hand, O house of Israel."*

CLAYTON

Literal Meaning: FROM THE CLAY ESTATE OR TOWN
Suggested Character Quality: IN GOD'S MOLD
Suggested Lifetime Scripture Verse: Jeremiah 18:6 *"O house of Israel, cannot I do with you as this potter did? says the Lord. Take notice, just as the clay is in the potter's hand, so are you in My hand, O house of Israel."*

CLEM

Literal Meaning: MERCIFUL
Suggested Character Quality: MERCIFUL SPIRIT
Suggested Lifetime Scripture Verse: Matthew 5:7 *"Blessed are the merciful: for they shall obtain mercy."* *

CLEMENT

Literal Meaning: MERCIFUL
Suggested Character Quality: MERCIFUL SPIRIT
Suggested Lifetime Scripture Verse: Matthew 5:7 *"Blessed are the merciful: for they shall obtain mercy."* *

CLEVE

Literal Meaning: OF THE CLIFF
Suggested Character Quality: VIGILANT SPIRIT
Suggested Lifetime Scripture Verse: Ephesians 6:18 *"Praying always with all prayer and supplication in the Spirit, and watching thereunto with all perserverance and supplication for all saints."* *

CLEVELAND

Literal Meaning: OF THE CLIFF LAND
Suggested Character Quality: VIGILANT SPIRIT
Suggested Lifetime Scripture Verse: Ephesians 6:18 *"Praying always with all prayer and supplication in the Spirit, and watching thereunto with all perserverance and supplication for all saints."* *

CLIFF

Literal Meaning: TOWN AT A CLIFF
Suggested Character Quality: VIGILANT
Suggested Lifetime Scripture Verse: I Corinthians 16:13 *"Be alert; stand firm in the faith; play the man; be strong."*

CLIFFORD

Literal Meaning: FROM THE CLIFF-FORD
Suggested Character Quality: VIGILANT
Suggested Lifetime Scripture Verse: I Corinthians 16:13 *"Be alert; stand firm in the faith; play the man; be strong."*
Explanation: Many times a watchman was stationed at the fording place in order to give advance warning of approaching enemies.

CLIFTON

Literal Meaning: FROM THE CLIFF TOWN
Suggested Character Quality: VIGILANT SPIRIT
Suggested Lifetime Scripture Verse: I Corinthians 16:13 *"Be alert; stand firm in the faith; play the man; be strong."*

CLINT

Literal Meaning: FROM THE HEADLAND-ESTATE OR TOWN
Suggested Character Quality: GREAT IN FORGIVENESS
Suggested Lifetime Scripture Verse: Amos 5:24 *Let justice roll on like water, and righteousness like a mighty stream."*
Explanation: Arbitrarily chosen

CLINTON

Literal Meaning: HILL TOWN
Suggested Character Quality: VIGILANT SPIRIT
Suggested Lifetime Scripture Verse: Ephesians 6:18 *"Praying always with all prayer and supplication in the Spirit, and watching thereunto with all perserverance and supplication for all saints."*

CLYDE

Literal Meaning: HEARD FROM FAR AWAY
Suggested Character Quality: OF GOOD REPORT
Suggested Lifetime Scripture Verse: Psalm 112:7 *"He need never fear any evil report; his heart will remain firm, fully trusting in the Lord."*

CODY

Literal Meaning: HELPER
Suggested Character Quality: HELPER
Suggested Lifetime Scripture Verse: Proverbs 27:9 *"Ointment and perfume rejoice the heart: so doth the sweetness of a man's friend by hearty counsel."* *

COLE

Literal Meaning: THE DOVE
Suggested Character Quality: PEACELOVING
Suggested Lifetime Scripture Verse: Matthew 10:16 *"Behold, I send you forth as sheep in the midst of wolves: be ye therefore wise as serpents, and harmless as doves."* *

COLETTE

Literal Meaning: VICTORIOUS ARMY
Suggested Character Quality: VICTORIOUS SPIRIT
Suggested Lifetime Scripture Verse: I Corinthians 15:57 *"But thanks be to God, who gives us the victory through our Lord Jesus Christ!"*

COLLEEN

Literal Meaning: GIRL, MAIDEN
Suggested Character Quality: VIRTUOUS SPIRIT
Suggested Lifetime Scripture Verse: Proverbs 2:11, 12 *"Discretion will protect you; discernment will guard you, to deliver you from the way of evil, from men speaking perverted things."*

CONLEY

Literal Meaning: UNKNOWN
Suggested Character Quality: OF SOUND MIND
Suggested Lifetime Scripture Verse: II Timothy 1:7 *"For God hath not given us the spirit of fear; but of power, and of love, and of a sound mind."* *

CONNIE

Literal Meaning: FIRMNESS; CONSTANCY
Suggested Character Quality: EARNEST DEVOTEE
Suggested Lifetime Scripture Verse: Psalm 34:1 *"I will bless the Lord at all times; His praise shall continually be in my mouth."* *

CONRAD

Literal Meaning: ABLE IN COUNSEL
Suggested Character Quality: FULL OF WISDOM
Suggested Lifetime Scripture Verse: Psalm 111:10 *"For reverence of the Lord is the beginning of wisdom. There is insight in all who observe it. His praise is everlasting."*

CONSTANCE

Literal Meaning: FIRMNESS; CONSTANCY
Suggested Character Quality: DEVOTED SPIRIT
Suggested Lifetime Scripture Verse: Psalm 34:1 *"I will bless the Lord at all times: His praise shall continually be in my mouth."* *

CONWAY

Literal Meaning: WAY OF WISDOM
Suggested Character Quality: WISE ONE
Suggested Lifetime Scripture Verse: Proverbs 1:7a *"The fear of the Lord is the beginning of knowledge . . ."* *

CORA

Literal Meaning: "MAIDEN" — Greek
Suggested Character Quality: VIRTUOUS HEART
Suggested Lifetime Scripture Verse: Psalm 31:5 *"Into Thy hand I commit my spirit; Thou hast redeemed me, Lord God of truth."*

COREY

Literal Meaning: DWELLER BY A HOLLOW OR BY A SEETHING POOL
Suggested Character Quality: PROSPEROUS ONE
Suggested Lifetime Scripture Verse: Psalm 13:6 *"Let me sing to the Lord because He has dealt generously with me."*

CORNELIA

Literal Meaning: THE CORNEL TREE; A JEWEL
Suggested Character Quality: VIRTUOUS WOMAN
Suggested Lifetime Scripture Verse: Proverbs 31:29 *"Many daughters have done virtuously, but thou excellest them all."* *

CORNELIUS

Literal Meaning: "BATTLE HORN" — Latin
Suggested Character Quality: VIGILANT SPIRIT
Suggested Lifetime Scripture Verse: Romans 12:12 *"Joyfully hoping as you endure affliction, persistent in prayer."*
Explanation: "Battle Horn" suggests the need for constant vigilance to give the right signal in battle.

CORRIE

Literal Meaning: MAIDEN
Suggested Character Quality: VIRTUOUS HEART
Suggested Lifetime Scripture Verse: Psalm 31:5 *"Into Thy hand I commit my spirit; Thou hast redeemed me, Lord God of truth."*

COURTNEY

Literal Meaning: SHORT NOSE
Suggested Character Quality: MAN OF DISCRETION
Suggested Lifetime Scripture Verse: Zechariah 7:9 *"Thus says the Lord of hosts: Render true judgment; let every one show loving-kindness and compassion to his brother."*
Explanation: Someone with a short nose would not be sticking it in other people's business; therefore, discretion is an appropriate characteristic.

COY

Literal Meaning: SHY; QUIET
Suggested Character Quality: QUIET, PEACEFUL SPIRIT
Suggested Lifetime Scripture Verse: Isaiah 32:17 *"And the work of righteousness shall be peace; and the effect of righteousness, quietness and assurance forever."* *

CRAIG

Literal Meaning: DWELLER AT THE CRAG
Suggested Character Quality: STRONG; ENDURING
Suggested Lifetime Scripture Verse: Proverbs 24:5 *"A wise man is strong, and a man of knowledge adds to his strength."*

CRAWFORD
Literal Meaning: OF THE CROWS CROSSING
Suggested Character Quality: INDUSTRIOUS
Suggested Lifetime Scripture Verse: Phillippians 4:13 *"I can do all things through Christ which strengtheneth me."* *

CRYSTAL
Literal Meaning: A CLEAR JEWEL
Suggested Character Quality: BRIGHT ONE
Suggested Lifetime Scripture Verse: I Thessalonians 5:5 *"Ye are all the children of light, and the children of the day: we are not of the night, nor of darkness."* *

CULLY
Literal Meaning: THE DOVE
Suggested Character Quality: PEACELOVING
Suggested Lifetime Scripture Verse: Matthew 10:16 *"Behold, I send you forth as sheep in the midst of wolves: be ye therefore wise as serpents, and harmless as doves."* *

CURTIS
Literal Meaning: COURTEOUS ONE
Suggested Character Quality: COURTEOUS ONE
Suggested Lifetime Scripture Verse: Zechariah 7:9 *"Thus says the Lord of hosts: Render true judgments; let every one show loving-kindness and compassion to his brother."*

CYNTHIA
Literal Meaning: THE MOON
Suggested Character Quality: REFLECTOR OF LIGHT
Suggested Lifetime Scripture Verse: Psalm 27:1 *"The Lord is my light and my salvation; whom shall I fear?"* *
Explanation: See Cindy

CYRUS
Literal Meaning: THRONE; SUN
Suggested Character Quality: OF GOOD CHARACTER
Suggested Lifetime Scripture Verse: Psalm 119:101 *"I have refrained my feet from every evil way, that I might observe Thy word."*

DALE
Literal Meaning: DWELLER IN THE VALLEY
Suggested Character Quality: COURAGEOUS
Suggested Lifetime Scripture Verse: Psalm 23:4 *"Yes, though I walk through the valley of the shadow of death, I will fear no harm; for Thou art with me: Thy rod and Thy staff, they comfort me."*

DALLAS
Literal Meaning: SKILLED
Suggested Character Quality: INDUSTRIOUS
Suggested Lifetime Scripture Verse: Colossians 3:23 *"And whatsoever ye do, do it heartily, as to the Lord, and not unto men."**

DALTON
Literal Meaning: FROM THE VALLEY, TOWN
Suggested Character Quality: PEACEFUL ONE
Suggested Lifetime Scripture Verse: Psalm 119:165 *"Great peace have they which love Thy law: and nothing shall offend them."**

DANA
Literal Meaning: A DANE
Suggested Character Quality: INDUSTRIOUS SPIRIT
Suggested Lifetime Scripture Verse: Romans 12:11 *"Never slacking in interest, serving the Lord, keeping spiritually aglow."*
Explanation: The people of Scandinavian countries are known for their hard work and diligence.

DANIEL
Literal Meaning: GOD IS MY JUDGE
Suggested Character Quality: GOD IS JUDGE
Suggested Lifetime Scripture Verse: Psalm 7:10 *"My shield depends upon God, who saves the upright in heart."*

DANNELLE
Literal Meaning: GOD IS MY JUDGE
Suggested Character Quality: GOD IS JUDGE
Suggested Lifetime Scripture Verse: Psalms 104:1 *"Bless the Lord, O my soul, O Lord my God, Thou art very great; Thou art clothed with honor and majesty."**

DANNY

Literal Meaning: GOD IS MY JUDGE
Suggested Character Quality: GOD IS JUDGE
Suggested Lifetime Scripture Verse: Psalm 7:10 *"My shield depends upon God, who saves the upright in heart."*

DAPHNE

Literal Meaning: LAUREL TREE
Suggested Character Quality: VICTORIOUS SPIRIT
Suggested Lifetime Scripture Verse: II Timothy 4:7, 8 *"I have fought a good fight, I have finished my course, I have kept the faith: Henceforth there is laid up for me a crown of righteousness, which the Lord, the righteous judge, shall give me at that day: and not to me only, but unto all them also that love His appearing."* *

DARCEY

Literal Meaning: THE DARK
Suggested Character Quality: PROTECTED BY GOD
Suggested Lifetime Scripture Verse: Psalm 46:1 *"God is our refuge and strength, a very present help in trouble."* *

DARCY

Literal Meaning: THE DARK
Suggested Character Quality: PROTECTED BY GOD
Suggested Lifetime Scripture Verse: Psalm 46:1 *"God is our refuge and strength, a very present help in trouble."* *

DAREEN

Literal Meaning: UNKNOWN
Suggested Character Quality: DEVOTED HEART
Suggested Lifetime Scripture Verse: Psalm 105:3 *"Glory ye in His holy name: let the heart of them rejoice that seek the Lord."* *

DARLA

Literal Meaning: LITTLE DEAR ONE
Suggested Character Quality: TENDERLY LOVED
Suggested Lifetime Scripture Verse: Song of Solomon 2:4 *"He has brought me into the banqueting hall, and His banner over me is love."*

DARLENE

Literal Meaning: LITTLE DEAR ONE
Suggested Character Quality: TENDERLY LOVED
Suggested Lifetime Scripture Verse: Song of Solomon 2:4 *"He has brought me into the banqueting hall, and His banner over me is love."*

DARREN
Literal Meaning: LITTLE GREAT ONE
Suggested Character Quality: BLESSED WITH BOUNTY
Suggested Lifetime Scripture Verse: Proverbs 10:22 *"It is the blessing of the Lord that brings riches and toiling will add nothing to it."*

DARRYL
Literal Meaning: BELOVED ONE
Suggested Character Quality: BELOVED
Suggested Lifetime Scripture Verse: Psalm 32:10-11 *"Many sorrows are to the ungodly, but he who trusts in the Lord shall be encircled with lovingkindness. Be glad in the Lord and exult, ye righteous; shout joyfully, ye upright in heart."*

DARWIN
Literal Meaning: DARING FRIEND
Suggested Character Quality: MAN OF ESTEEM
Suggested Lifetime Scripture Verse: John 15:13 *"Greater love hath no man than this, that a man lay down his life for his friends."* *

DAVID
Literal Meaning: BELOVED ONE
Suggested Character Quality: BELOVED
Suggested Lifetime Scripture Verse: I John 4:7 *"Beloved, let us love one another, because love springs from God and whoever loves has been born of God and knows God."*

DAVIS
Literal Meaning: BELOVED SON
Suggested Character Quality: BELOVED
Suggested Lifetime Scripture Verse: I John 4:7 *"Beloved, let us love one another, because love springs from God and whoever loves has been born of God and knows God."*

DAWN
Literal Meaning: THE DAWN OF DAY
Suggested Character Quality: JOY AND PRAISE
Suggested Lifetime Scripture Verse: Psalm 143:8 *"In the morning proclaim to me Thy covenant love, for I have put my trust in Thee. Make me understand the way I should go, for I lift up my soul to Thee."*

DAWSON
Literal Meaning: UNKNOWN
Suggested Character Quality: GIFT OF GOD
Suggested Lifetime Scripture Verse: Romans 6:23b *". . . the gift of God is eternal life through Jesus Christ our Lord."*

DEAN

Literal Meaning: DWELLER IN THE VALLEY
Suggested Character Quality: COURAGEOUS HEART
Suggested Lifetime Scripture Verse: Psalm 16:8 *"I have placed the Lord before me continually; because He is at my right hand, I shall not be moved."*

DEANNA

Literal Meaning: GODDESS; DIVINE ONE
Suggested Character Quality: GOD'S PRINCESS
Suggested Lifetime Scripture Verse: Isaiah 60:2 *"For behold, darkness shall cover the earth and a dark cloud the nations; but the Lord shall arise over you, His glory shall be seen upon you."*

DEBBY

Literal Meaning: THE BEE
Suggested Character Quality: SEEKING ONE
Suggested Lifetime Scripture Verse: Jeremiah 29:13 *"You will seek Me and find Me when you will seek Me with all your heart."*
Explanation: The bee could not live unless it went out seeking for its sustenance.

DEBORAH

Literal Meaning: THE BEE
Suggested Character Quality: SEEKING ONE
Suggested Lifetime Scripture Verse: Jeremiah 29:13 *"You will seek Me and find Me when you will seek Me with all your heart."*
Explanation: See Debby

DEBRA

Literal Meaning: THE BEE
Suggested Character Quality: SEEKING ONE
Suggested Lifetime Scripture Verse: Jeremiah 29:13 *"You will seek Me and find Me when you will seek Me with all your heart."*
Explanation: See Debby

DEE

Literal Meaning: DARK ONE
Suggested Character Quality: PROTECTED BY GOD
Suggested Lifetime Scripture Verse: Psalm 46:1 *"God is our refuge and strength, a very present help in trouble."**

DEL

Literal Meaning: OF DELOS
Suggested Character Quality: DELIGHTFUL ONE
Suggested Lifetime Scripture Verse: Psalm 37:4 *"Have your delight in the Lord and He will give you the desires of your heart."*

DELBERT

Literal Meaning: NOBLY BRIGHT
Suggested Character Quality: MAN OF HONOR
Suggested Lifetime Scripture Verse: Isaiah 33:15, 16 *"He that walketh righteously, and speaketh uprightly; he that despiseth the gain of oppressions, that shaketh his hands from holding bribes, that stoppeth his ears from hearing of blood, and shutteth his eyes from selling evil; he shall dwell on high: his place of defense shall be the munitions of rocks: bread shall be given him: his waters shall be sure."* *

DELCI

Literal Meaning: DELIGHTFUL ONE
Suggested Character Quality: DELIGHTFUL ONE
Suggested Lifetime Scripture Verse: Psalm 37:4 *Have your delight in the Lord and He will give you the desires of your heart."*

DELIA

Literal Meaning: OF DELOS
Suggested Character Quality: DELIGHTFUL ONE
Suggested Lifetime Scripture Verse: Psalm 37:4 *"Have your delight in the Lord and He shall give you the desires of your heart."*

DELMAR

Literal Meaning: OF THE SEA
Suggested Character Quality: RESOURCEFUL
Suggested Lifetime Scripture Verse: I Corinthians 9:22b *". . . I am made all things to all men, that I might by all means save some."* *

DELORES

Literal Meaning: SORROWS
Suggested Character Quality: COMPASSIONATE SPIRIT
Suggested Lifetime Scripture Verse: I Corinthians 13:13 *"There remain then, faith, hope, love, these three; but the greatest of these is love."*

DELROY

Literal Meaning: DELBERT — DAY-BRIGHT; ROY - KING
Suggested Character Quality: WISE RULER
Suggested Lifetime Scripture Verse: James 3:17 *"But the wisdom that is from above is first pure, than peaceable, gentle, and easy to be entreated, full of mercy and good fruits, without partiality, and without hypocrisy."* *

DELSIE

Literal Meaning: DELIGHTFUL ONE
Suggested Character Quality: DELIGHTFUL ONE
Suggested Lifetime Scripture Verse: Psalm 37:4 *"Have your delight in the Lord and He will give you the desires of your heart."*

DENISE

Literal Meaning: ADHERENT OF DIONYSUS, GREEK GOD OF WINE
Suggested Quality: WISE DISCERNER
Suggested Lifetime Scripture Verse: Psalm 119:140 *"Thy word is well tested; therefore Thy servant loves it."*
Explanation: The thought expressed here is that one must know how to discern between good and evil.

DENNIS

Literal Meaning: GOD OF WINE
Suggested Character Quality: DISCERNER OF EXCELLENCE
Suggested Lifetime Scripture Verse: Matthew 6:33 *"But you, seek first His kingdom and His righteousness and all these things will be added to you."*
Explanation: See Denise

DEREK

Literal Meaning: "RULE OF THE PEOPLE" — Germanic
Suggested Character Quality: FULL OF JUSTICE
Suggested Lifetime Scripture Verse: Psalm 41:1 *"Blessings are his, who considers the weak; in the day of misfortune the Lord will deliver him."*
Explanation: "Rule of the People" suggests one who exhibits justice.

DERYL

Literal Meaning: DEAR, LOVED ONE
Suggested Character Quality: BELOVED ONE
Suggested Lifetime Scripture Verse: Psalm 26:3 *"For Thy lovingkindness is before my eyes, and I have walked in Thy truth."*

DESMOND

Literal Meaning: MAN OF THE WORLD
Suggested Character Quality: RESOURCEFUL ONE
Suggested Lifetime Scripture Verse: I Corinthians 9:22b *". . . I am made all things to all men, that I might by all means save some."* *

DEVON

Literal Meaning: A POET
Suggested Character Quality: IN GOD'S LIGHT
Suggested Lifetime Scripture Verse: Psalm 36:9 *"For with Thee is the fountain of life: in Thy light shall we see light."* *

DE WAYNE

Literal Meaning: DARK COMPLECTED
Suggested Character Quality: CHEERFUL OF HEART
Suggested Lifetime Scripture Verse: Proverbs 15:13a *"A merry heart maketh a cheerful countenance . . ."* *

DEWEY

Literal Meaning: BELOVED ONE
Suggested Character Quality: BELOVED
Suggested Lifetime Scripture Verse: I John 4:9 *"In this was manifested the love of God toward us, because that God sent His only begotten Son into the world, that we might live through Him."* *

DeWITT

Literal Meaning: BLOND ONE
Suggested Character Quality: FAIR AND NOBLE
Suggested Lifetime Scripture Verse: Psalm 24:3, 4 *"Who shall ascend into the hill of the Lord? or who shall stand in His holy place? He that hath clean hands, and a pure heart; who hath not lifted up his soul unto vanity, nor sworn deceitfully."* *

DEXTER

Literal Meaning: RIGHT-HANDED; DEXTEROUS
Suggested Character Quality: INDUSTRIOUS ONE
Suggested Lifetime Scripture Verse: Ecclesiastes 9:10a *"Whatsoever thy hand findeth to do, do it with thy might . . ."* *

DIANA

Literal Meaning: DIVINE ONE
Suggested Character Quality: IN GOD'S GLORY
Suggested Lifetime Scripture Verse: Isaiah 54:10 *"For though the mountains should move and the hills should shake, My lovingkindness shall never depart from you nor the covenant of My peace be withdrawn, says the Lord, who has compassion upon you."*

DIANE

Literal Meaning: DIVINE ONE
Suggested Character Quality: IN GOD'S GLORY
Suggested Lifetime Scripture Verse: Isaiah 54:10 *"For though the mountains should move and the hills should shake, My lovingkindness shall never depart from you, nor the covenant of My peace be withdrawn, says the Lord, who has compassion upon you."*

DIANNE

Literal Meaning: GODDESS; DIVINE ONE
Suggested Character Quality: IN GOD'S GLORY
Suggested Lifetime Scripture Verse: Isaiah 54:10 *"For though the mountains should move and the hills should shake, My lovingkindness shall never depart from you, nor the covenant of My peace be withdrawn, says the Lord, who has compassion upon you."*

DICK

Literal Meaning: POWERFUL RULER
Suggested Character Quality: BRAVE; STRONG
Suggested Lifetime Scripture Verse: Isaiah 12:2 *"Behold, God is my salvation; I will trust and not be afraid, for Jehovah, the Lord, is my strength and my song; yes, He has become my salvation."*

DION

Literal Meaning: GRECIAN WINE-GOD
Suggested Character Quality: DISCERNER OF EXCELLENCE
Suggested Lifetime Scripture Verse: Matthew 6:33 *"But you, seek first His kingdom and His righteousness and all these things will be added to you."*
Explanation: See Denise

DIXIE

Literal Meaning: THE TENTH
Suggested Character Quality: WOMAN OF ESTEEM
Suggested Lifetime Scripture Verse: I Chronicles 29:12 *"Both riches and honor come to Thee, and Thou reignest over all; and in Thine hand is power and might; and in Thine hand it is to make great, and to give strength unto all."* *

DODSON

Literal Meaning: UNKNOWN
Suggested Character Quality: PRINCE OF GOD
Suggested Lifetime Scripture Verse: Proverbs 22:1 *"A good name is rather to be chosen than great riches, and loving favor rather than silver and gold."* *

DOMINICK

Literal Meaning: BELONGING TO GOD
Suggested Character Quality: BELONGING TO GOD
Suggested Lifetime Scripture Verse: Psalm 63:1a *"O God, Thou art my God; early will I seek Thee . . ."* *

DOMINIQUE

Literal Meaning: BELONGING TO THE LORD
Suggested Character Quality: BELONGING TO GOD
Suggested Lifetime Scripture Verse: Lamentations 3:25 *"The Lord is good to those who wait for Him, to the soul that seeks Him."*

DONALD

Literal Meaning: WORLD MIGHTY, WORLD RULER
Suggested Character Quality: OVERCOMER
Suggested Lifetime Scripture Verse: Revelation 2:7 *"Whoever has an ear, let him hear what the Spirit says to the churches. I shall grant the victor to eat from the tree of life that stands in the paradise of God."*

DONNA

Literal Meaning: LADY
Suggested Character Quality: DIGNITY OF CHARACTER
Suggested Lifetime Scripture Verse: Hosea 14:9 *"Whoever is wise will understand these things, and the discerning man will know them; for the ways of the Lord are right and the righteous walk in them; but transgressors stumble in them."*

DONOVAN

Literal Meaning: DARK WARRIOR
Suggested Character Quality: IN GOD'S LIGHT
Suggested Lifetime Scripture Verse: Matthew 5:16 *"Let your light so shine before men, that they may see your good works, and glorify your Father which is in heaven."* *

DORA

Literal Meaning: GIFT OF GOD
Suggested Character Quality: GIFT OF GOD
Suggested Lifetime Scripture Verse: Isaiah 30:18 *"Nevertheless the Lord longs to be gracious to you! Therefore He shall rise up to bestow mercy on you; for the Lord is a God of Justice. Blessed are they who wait for Him."*

DOREEN

Literal Meaning: "SULLEN" — Irish
Suggested Character Quality: DEVOTED HEART
Suggested Lifetime Scripture Verse: Psalm 13:5 *"But I have trusted in Thine unfailing love: my heart rejoices in Thy deliverance."*
Explanation: Sullen, in this case, has the connotation that one is serious about life; therefore, devotion would be characteristic of this person.

DORIE

Literal Meaning: GIFT OF GOD
Suggested Character Quality: GOD'S GRACIOUS GIFT
Suggested Lifetime Scripture Verse: Psalm 119:58 *"Wholeheartedly I sought Thy favor; be merciful to me according to Thy word."*

DORIS

Literal Meaning: BOUNTIFUL
Suggested Character Quality: EXCELLENT VIRTUE
Suggested Lifetime Scripture Verse: Prov. 2:11, 12 *"Discretion will protect you; discernment will guard you, to deliver you from the way of evil, from men speaking perverted things."*

DOROTHEA

Literal Meaning: GIFT OF GOD
Suggested Character Quality: GOD'S GRACIOUS GIFT
Suggested Lifetime Scripture Verse: Psalm 119:58 *"Wholeheartedly I sought Thy favor; be merciful to me according to Thy word."*

DOROTHY

Literal Meaning: GIFT OF GOD
Suggested Character Quality: GIFT OF GOD
Suggested Lifetime Scripture Verse: Psalm 119:58 *"Wholeheartedly I sought Thy favor; be merciful to me according to Thy word."*

DORSEY

Literal Meaning: UNKNOWN
Suggested Character Quality: FREE IN THE LORD
Suggested Lifetime Scripture Verse: John 8:36 *"If the Son therefore shall make you free, ye shall be free indeed."* *

DOUGLAS

Literal Meaning: FROM THE BLACK OR DARK WATER
Suggested Character Quality: SEEKER OF LIGHT
Suggested Lifetime Scripture Verse: Isaiah 60:1 *"Arise, shine; for your light has come, and the glory of the Lord has risen upon you!"*
Explanation: To escape darkness, one must seek the light.

DOYLE

Literal Meaning: DARK STRANGER
Suggested Character Quality: MAN OF DISTINCTION
Suggested Lifetime Scripture Verse: I Thessalonians 2:12 *"That ye would walk worthy of God, who hath called you unto His kingdom and glory."* *

DRAKE

Literal Meaning: MALE DUCK OR SWAN
Suggested Character Quality: COURAGEOUS SPIRIT
Suggested Lifetime Scripture Verse: Joshua 1:9 *"Have not I commanded thee? Be strong and of a good courage; be not afraid, neither be thou dismayed: for the Lord thy God is with thee whithersoever thou goest."* *

DREW

Literal Meaning: TRUSTWORTHY
Suggested Character Quality: TRUSTWORTHY
Suggested Lifetime Scripture Verse: Psalm 15:1, 2 *"Lord, who shall abide in Thy tabernacle? Who shall dwell in Thy holy hill? He that walketh uprightly, and worketh righteousness, and speaketh the truth in his heart."* *

DUANE

Literal Meaning: SONG
Suggested Character Quality: CHEERFUL OF HEART
Suggested Lifetime Scripture Verse: Habakkuk 3:18 *"Yet I will rejoice in the Lord, I will joy in the God of my salvation."* *

DUDLEY

Literal Meaning: FROM THE PEOPLE'S MEADOW
Suggested Character Quality: WALKS WITH GOD
Suggested Lifetime Scripture Verse: Psalm 23:1, 2 *"The Lord is my shepherd; I shall not want. He maketh me to lie down in green pastures: He leadeth me beside the still waters."* *

DUNCAN

Literal Meaning: "BROWN WARRIOR" — Celtic
Suggested Character Quality: LOYAL ONE
Suggested Lifetime Scripture Verse: Psalm 56:12 *"On me, O God, are Thy vows; I will give Thee thank-offerings."*
Explanation: A warrior's best quality is his loyalty to his commander and country.

DUSTIN

Literal Meaning: BRAVE FIGHTER
Suggested Character Quality: LOYAL HEART
Suggested Lifetime Scripture Verse: Psalm 34:1 *"I will bless the Lord at all times: His praise shall continually be in my mouth."* *

DUSTY

Literal Meaning: BRAVE FIGHTER
Suggested Character Quality: LOYAL HEART
Suggested Lifetime Scripture Verse: Psalm 34:1 *"I will bless the Lord at all times: His praise shall continually be in my mouth."* *

DUTCH

Literal Meaning: UNKNOWN
Suggested Character Quality: BELONGING TO GOD
Suggested Lifetime Scripture Verse: Colossians 3:12 *"Put on therefore, as the elect of God, holy and beloved, bowels of mercies, kindness, humbleness of mind, meekness, longsuffering."* *

DWIGHT

Literal Meaning: WHITE OR BLOND ONE
Suggested Character Quality: DWELLER IN TRUTH
Suggested Lifetime Scripture Verse: Psalm 15:2, 5 *"He who walks in integrity, who does what is right, and who speaks the truth in his heart; . . . He who does these things shall never be moved."*
Explanation: White corresponds with purity and honesty.

DYLAN

Literal Meaning: SON OF THE SEA
Suggested Character Quality: BELOVED ONE
Suggested Lifetime Scripture Verse: Ephesians 1:6 *"To the praise of the glory of His grace, wherein He hath made us accepted in the beloved:"* *

EARL

Literal Meaning: NOBLEMAN; CHIEF
Suggested Character Quality: MAN OF HONOR
Suggested Lifetime Scripture Verse: Isaiah 30:18 *"Nevertheless the Lord longs to be gracious to you! Therefore He shall rise up to bestow mercy on you; for the Lord is a God of justice. Blessed are they who wait for Him."*

EARNESTINE

Literal Meaning: THE EARNEST
Suggested Character Quality: ZEALOUS ONE
Suggested Lifetime Scripture Verse: Psalm 119:34 *"Give me understanding, and I shall keep Thy law; yea, I shall observe it with my whole heart."*

EBBA

Literal Meaning: FLOWING BACK TIDE
Suggested Character Quality: FULL OF LIFE
Suggested Lifetime Scripture Verse: John 6:63 *It is the Spirit that quickeneth; the flesh profiteth nothing: the words that I speak unto you, they are spirit, and they are life."**

EBENEZER

Literal Meaning: THE STONE OF HELP
Suggested Character Quality: ENDURING STRENGTH
Suggested Lifetime Scripture Verse: Psalm 28:7 *"The Lord is my strength and my shield; my heart trusted in Him, and I am helped: therefore my heart greatly rejoiceth; and with my song will I praise Him."**

EBERHARD

Literal Meaning: STRONG AS A BOAR
Suggested Character Quality: MIGHTY WARRIOR
Suggested Lifetime Scripture Verse: II Timothy 2:4 *"No man that warreth entangleth himself with the affairs of this life; that he may please Him who hath chosen him to be a soldier."**

ED

Literal Meaning: "HAPPY" — Anglo-Saxon
Suggested Character Quality: CHEERFUL ONE
Suggested Lifetime Scripture Verse: Psalm 43:4 *"Then I will go to the altar of God, to God, the joy of my exultation, and praise Thee with the harp, O God, my God."*

EDGAR

Literal Meaning: PROSPEROUS SPEARMAN
Suggested Character Quality: COURAGEOUS HEART
Suggested Lifetime Scripture Verse: I Corinthians 15:58 *"Consequently, my beloved brothers, be steadfast, immovable, at all times abounding in the Lord's service, aware that your labor in the Lord is not futile."*

EDGERTON

Literal Meaning: SPEARMAN
Suggested Character Quality: NOBLE WARRIOR
Suggested Lifetime Scripture Verse: Ephesians 6:10, 11 *"Finally, my brethren, be strong in the Lord, and in the power of His might. Put on the whole armor of God, that ye may be able to stand against the wiles of the devil."**

EDITH

Literal Meaning: RICH GIFT
Suggested Character Quality: GOD'S GIFT
Suggested Lifetime Scripture Verse: Isaiah 30:18 *"Nevertheless the Lord longs to be gracious to you! Therefore He shall rise up to bestow mercy on you; for the Lord is a God of Justice. Blessed are they who wait for Him."*

EDMUND

Literal Meaning: CHEERFUL ONE
Suggested Character Quality: CHEERFUL ONE
Suggested Lifetime Scripture Verse: Psalm 43:4 *"Then I will go to the altar of God, to God, the joy of my exultation, and praise Thee with the harp, O God, my God."*

EDNA

Literal Meaning: REJUVENATION
Suggested Character Quality: YOUTHFUL HEART
Suggested Lifetime Scripture Verse: Psalm 71:5 *"For Thou art my hope, O Lord God; Thou art my trust from my youth."**

EDWARD

Literal Meaning: PROSPEROUS GUARDIAN
Suggested Character Quality: PROSPEROUS GUARDIAN
Suggested Lifetime Scripture Verse: Psalm 37:37 *"Watch the upright and observe the righteous, for there is a future to the man of peace."*

EDWIN

Literal Meaning: "RICH FRIEND" — Anglo-Saxon
Suggested Character Quality: FRIENDLY SPIRIT
Suggested Lifetime Scripture Verse: Proverbs 18:24 *"A man has many friends for companionship, but there is a friend who sticks closer than a brother."*

EDWINA

Literal Meaning: VALUED FRIEND
Suggested Character Quality: FRIENDLY ONE
Suggested Lifetime Scripture Verse: Proverbs 17:17 *"A friend loveth at all times . . ."**

EDYTH

Literal Meaning: RICH GIFT
Suggested Character Quality: GOD'S GIFT
Suggested Lifetime Scripture Verse: Isaiah 30:18 *Nevertheless the Lord longs to be gracious to you! Therefore He shall rise up to bestow mercy on you; for the Lord is a God of Justice. Blessed are they who wait for Him."*

EFFIE

Literal Meaning: OF GOOD REPORT
Suggested Character Quality: WOMAN OF ESTEEM
Suggested Lifetime Scripture Verse: Proverbs 31:25 *"Strength and honor are her clothing; and she shall rejoice in time to come."* *

EILEEN

Literal Meaning: LIGHT
Suggested Character Quality: LIGHT
Suggested Lifetime Scripture Verse: Psalm 37:6 *"And He will bring forth thy righteousness as the light, and thy justice as the noonday."* *

ELAINE

Literal Meaning: THE LILY MAID OF ASTOLAT
Suggested Character Quality: BRIGHT ONE
Suggested Lifetime Scripture Verse: Isaiah 62:3 *"You shall be a crown of glory in the hand of the Lord and a royal diadem in the palm of your God."*

ELDER

Literal Meaning: AUTHORITY
Suggested Character Quality: MAN OF WISDOM
Suggested Lifetime Scripture Verse: Psalm 111:10 *"The fear of the Lord is the beginning of wisdom: a good understanding have all they that do His commandments: His praise endureth forever."* *

ELDON

Literal Meaning: Place Name — ALDER VALLEY
Suggested Character Quality: PROSPEROUS SPIRIT
Suggested Lifetime Scripture Verse: Psalm 37:37 *"Watch the upright and observe the righteous, for there is future to the man of peace."*

ELEANOR

Literal Meaning: LIGHT; BRIGHT ONE
Suggested Character Quality: RADIANT SPIRIT
Suggested Lifetime Scripture Verse: Isaiah 62:3 *"You shall be a crown of glory in the hand of the Lord and a royal diadem in the palm of your God."*
Explanation: The light of God causes a person to radiate His presence.

ELFRIDA

Literal Meaning: ELF; COUNSELOR
Suggested Character Quality: GOOD COUNSELOR
Suggested Lifetime Scripture Verse: Proverbs 2:6 *"For the Lord giveth wisdom: out of His mouth cometh knowledge and understanding."* *

ELI

Literal Meaning: HEIGHT OF ELEVATED
Suggested Character Quality: IN GOD'S HONOR
Suggested Lifetime Scripture Verse: Psalm 5:12 *"Thou, O Lord, dost bless the righteous; as with a shield Thou dost surround him with favor."*

ELIJAH

Literal Meaning: JEHOVAH IS GOD
Suggested Character Quality: REVERENT SPIRIT
Suggested Lifetime Scripture Verse: Proverbs 19:23 *"The fear of the Lord tendeth to life: and he that hath it shall abide satisfied; he shall not be visited with evil."* *

ELINOR

Literal Meaning: LIGHT; BRIGHT ONE
Suggested Character Quality: BRIGHT ONE
Suggested Lifetime Scripture Verse: Isaiah 62:3 *"You shall be a crown of glory in the hand of the Lord and a royal diadem in the palm of your God."*
Explanation: See Eleanor

ELISA

Literal Meaning: CONSECRATED TO GOD
Suggested Character Quality: CONSECRATED ONE
Suggested Lifetime Scripture Verse: Psalm 119:34 *"Give me understanding, and I shall observe Thy law, and keep it wholeheartedly."*

ELIZABETH

Literal Meaning: CONSECRATED TO GOD
Suggested Character Quality: CONSECRATED ONE
Suggested Lifetime Scripture Verse: Psalm 119:34 *"Give me understanding, and I shall observe Thy law, and keep it wholeheartedly."*

ERIC

Literal Meaning: EVER POWERFUL; EVER RULER
Suggested Character Quality: GODLY POWER
Suggested Lifetime Scripture Verse: Psalm 8:4, 6 *"What is man that Thou art mindful of him, or the son of man that Thou carest for him? . . . Thou givest him dominion over the works of Thy hands; Thou has placed all things under his feet."*

ERIKA

Literal Meaning: EVER POWERFUL
Suggested Character Quality: WOMAN OF ESTEEM
Suggested Lifetime Scripture Verse: Habakkuk 3:19 *"The Lord God is my strength; He makes my feet like hinds feet, He makes me tread upon my high places."*

ERIN

Literal Meaning: PEACE
Suggested Character Quality: PEACEFUL SPIRIT
Suggested Lifetime Scripture Verse: Romans 14:19 *"Let us therefore follow after the things which make for peace, and things wherewith one may edify another."* *

ERNEST

Literal Meaning: EARNEST ONE
Suggested Character Quality: VIGOROUS SPIRIT
Suggested Lifetime Scripture Verse: Psalm 119:40 *"Truly, I yearn for Thy precepts; give me life according to Thy righteousness."*

ERWIN

Literal Meaning: SEA-FRIEND
Suggested Character Quality: FRIENDLY ONE
Suggested Lifetime Scripture Verse: Proverbs 11:30 *"The fruit of the righteous is a tree of life, and a wise man wins friends."*

ESSIE

Literal Meaning: A STAR
Suggested Character Quality: BRIGHT ONE
Suggested Lifetime Scripture Verse: Psalm 37:6 *"And He shall bring forth thy righteousness as the light, and thy judgment as the noonday."* *

ESTHER

Literal Meaning: A STAR
Suggested Character Quality: HUMILITY OF SPIRIT
Suggested Lifetime Scripture Verse: Isaiah 30:15 *"For thus says the Lord God, the Holy One of Israel: In conversion and rest you shall be saved; in quietness and confidence shall be your strength."*
Explanation: The biblical Esther is noted for her outstanding humility of spirit.

ELLA

Literal Meaning: ALL
Suggested Character Quality: BRIGHT ONE
Suggested Lifetime Scripture Verse: Isaiah 62:3 *"You shall be a crown of glory in the hand of the Lord and a royal diadem in the palm of your God."*

ELLEN

Literal Meaning: BRIGHT ONE
Suggested Character Quality: RADIANT SPIRIT
Suggested Lifetime Scripture Verse: Isaiah 62:3 *"You shall be a crown of glory in the hand of the Lord and a royal diadem in the palm of your God."*
Explanation: See Eleanor

ELLERY

Literal Meaning: Place Name
Suggested Character Quality: NOBLE SPIRIT
Suggested Lifetime Scripture Verse: Job 10:12 *"Thou didst bestow upon me life and compassion; and Thy care has preserved my spirit."*

ELLIOTT

Literal Meaning: THE LORD IS GOD
Suggested Character Quality: REVERENT SPIRIT
Suggested Lifetime Scripture Verse: Proverbs 19:23 *"The fear of the Lord tendeth to life: and he that hath it shall abide satisfied; he shall not be visited with evil."* *

ELMER

Literal Meaning: NOBLE; FAMOUS
Suggested Character Quality: NOBLE HEART
Suggested Lifetime Scripture Verse: Psalm 112:5 *"It is well with him who is generous and ready to lend, the man who conducts his business with fairness."*

ELMO

Literal Meaning: AMIABLE
Suggested Character Quality: BELOVED
Suggested Lifetime Scripture Verse: I John 4:7 *"Beloved, let us love one another: for love is of God; and everyone that loveth is born of God, and knoweth God."*

ELROY

Literal Meaning: ROYAL
Suggested Character Quality: GRACIOUS AND MANLY
Suggested Lifetime Scripture Verse: Hebrews 13:9b *". . . For it is a good thing that the heart be established with grace; . . ."* *

ELSA

Literal Meaning: CONSECRATED TO GOD
Suggested Character Quality: CONSECRATED TO GOD
Suggested Lifetime Scripture Verse: Psalm 119:34 *"Give me understanding, and I shall observe Thy law, and keep it wholeheartedly."*

ELSIE

Literal Meaning: CONSECRATED TO GOD
Suggested Character Quality: CONSECRATED TO GOD
Suggested Lifetime Scripture Verse: Psalm 119:34 *"Give me understanding, and I shall observe Thy law, and keep it wholeheartedly."*

ELVA

Literal Meaning: LIKE AN ELF
Suggested Character Quality: FAIR LADY
Suggested Lifetime Scripture Verse: Psalm 29:2 *"Give unto the Lord the glory due unto His name; worship the Lord in the beauty of holiness."* *

ELWIN

Literal Meaning: ELFIN FRIEND
Suggested Character Quality: FRIENDLY
Suggested Lifetime Scripture Verse: Proverbs 11:30 *"The fruit of the righteous is a tree of life, and a wise man wins friends."*

ELWOOD

Literal Meaning: FROM THE OLD WOOD
Suggested Character Quality: FRIENDLY SPIRIT
Suggested Lifetime Scripture Verse: Proverbs 18:24 *"A man that hath friends must show himself friendly; and there is a friend that sticketh closer than a brother."* *

EMA

Literal Meaning: NURSE
Suggested Character Quality: CARING ONE
Suggested Lifetime Scripture Verse: Jude 1:21 *"Keep yourselves in the love of God, all the while awaiting the mercy of our Lord Jesus Christ for eternal life."*

EMERSON

Literal Meaning: WORK KING
Suggested Character Quality: INDUSTRIOUS LEADER
Suggested Lifetime Scripture Verse: I Corinthians 15:58 *"Therefore, my beloved brethren, be ye steadfast, unmovable, always abounding in the work of the Lord, forasmuch as ye know that your labor is not in vain in the Lord."* *

EMERY

Literal Meaning: WORK KING
Suggested Character Quality: INDUSTRIOUS LEADER
Suggested Lifetime Scripture Verse: I Corinthians 15:58 *"Therefore, beloved brethren, be ye steadfast, unmovable, always abounding in work of the Lord, forasmuch as ye know that your labor is not in vain in Lord."* *

EMIL

Literal Meaning: INDUSTRIOUS
Suggested Character Quality: DILIGENT ONE
Suggested Lifetime Scripture Verse: Psalm 37:3 *"Trust in the Lord and good; inhabit the land and practice faithfulness."*

EMILIO

Literal Meaning: THE INDUSTRIOUS
Suggested Character Quality: DILIGENT ONE
Suggested Lifetime Scripture Verse: Psalm 37:3 *"Trust in the Lord and good; inhabit the land and practice faithfulness."*

EMILY

Literal Meaning: INDUSTRIOUS
Suggested Character Quality: DILIGENT ONE
Suggested Lifetime Scripture Verse: Proverbs 31:27 *"She looks well to ways of her household and eats no bread of idleness."*

EMMA

Literal Meaning: NURSE
Suggested Character Quality: CARING ONE
Suggested Lifetime Scripture Verse: Jude 1:21 *"Keep yourselves love of God, all the while awaiting the mercy of our Lord Jesus Chr eternal life."*

EMMETT

Literal Meaning: THE INDUSTRIOUS, THE ANT
Suggested Character Quality: INDUSTRIOUS & STRONG
Suggested Lifetime Scripture Verse: Proverbs 24:5 *"A wise man i yea, a man of knowledge increaseth strength."* *

ENOS

Literal Meaning: MAN
Suggested Character Quality: CONSECRATED TO GOD
Suggested Lifetime Scripture Verse: Acts 17:28a *"For in Him w move, and have our being; . . ."* *

ETHAN

Literal Meaning: FIRM
Suggested Character Quality: STEADFAST HEART
Suggested Lifetime Scripture Verse: I Corinthians 15:58 *"Consequently, my beloved brothers, be steadfast; immovable, at all times abounding in the Lord's service, aware that your labor in the Lord is not futile."*

ETHEL

Literal Meaning: NOBLE ONE
Suggested Character Quality: DIGNITY OF CHARACTER
Suggested Lifetime Scripture Verse: I Chronicles 29:17 *"But O my God, I know that Thou dost test the heart and dost take pleasure in what is right . . ."*

EUGENE

Literal Meaning: WELL-BORN; NOBLE
Suggested Character Quality: NOBLE HERITAGE
Suggested Lifetime Scripture Verse: Psalm 16:5, 6 *"The Lord is the portion of my inheritance and of my cup; thou maintainest my lot. Yea, I have a goodly heritage."* *

EUGENIA

Literal Meaning: "NOBILITY" — Greek
Suggested Character Quality: NOBLE SPIRIT
Suggested Lifetime Scripture Verse: Psalm 62:7 *"My salvation and my glory depend on God; the rock of my defense, my refuge is in God."* *

EUNICE

Literal Meaning: HAPPY, VICTORIOUS ONE
Suggested Character Quality: JOY WITH VICTORY
Suggested Lifetime Scripture Verse: Psalm 66:2 *"Sing out to glorify His name; render Him glorious praise."*

EVA

Literal Meaning: LIFE
Suggested Character Quality: FULL OF LIFE
Suggested Lifetime Scripture Verse: Psalm 119:40 *"Truly, I yearn for Thy precepts; give me life according to Thy righteousness."*

EVAN

Literal Meaning: Equivalent of John
Suggested Character Quality: GOD'S GIFT
Suggested Lifetime Scripture Verse: Isaiah 43:10 *"You are my witnesses, says the Lord, and My servant whom I have chosen, in order that you may know and believe Me, and understand that I am He. Before Me no God was formed, nor shall there be after Me."*

EVANGELINE

Literal Meaning: BEARER OF GOOD NEWS
Suggested Character Quality: BRINGER OF TRUTH
Suggested Lifetime Scripture Verse: I Peter 3:15 *"But sanctify the Lord God in your hearts: and be ready always to give an answer to every man that asketh you a reason of the hope that is in you, with meekness and fear."* *

EVE

Literal Meaning: LIFE
Suggested Character Quality: FULL OF LIFE
Suggested Lifetime Scripture Verse: Psalm 119:40 *"Truly, I yearn for Thy precepts; give me life according to Thy righteousness."*

EVELYN

Literal Meaning: LIGHT
Suggested Character Quality: LIGHT
Suggested Lifetime Scripture Verse: Psalm 37:6 *"And He shall bring forth your righteousness as the light, and your justice as the noonday."*

EVERETT

Literal Meaning: STRONG OR BRAVE AS A BOAR
Suggested Character Quality: MIGHTY ONE
Suggested Lifetime Scripture Verse: Proverbs 24:5 *"A wise man is strong, and a man of knowledge adds to his strength."*

EVIE

Literal Meaning: LIFE OR LIVING
Suggested Character Quality: FULL OF LIFE
Suggested Lifetime Scripture Verse: II Corinthians 5:15 *"And that He died for all, that they which live should not henceforth live unto themselves, but unto Him which died for them, and rose again."**

EZEKIEL

Literal Meaning: GOD MAKES STRONG
Suggested Character Quality: STRENGTH IN GOD
Suggested Lifetime Scripture Verse: Ephesians 6:10 *"Finally, my brethren, be strong in the Lord, and in the power of His might."* *

FABIAN

Literal Meaning: PROSPEROUS FARMER
Suggested Character Quality: PROSPEROUS ONE
Suggested Lifetime Scripture Verse: Proverbs 10:22 *"The blessing of the Lord, it maketh rich, and He addeth no sorrow with it."* *

FAITH

Literal Meaning: BELIEF IN GOD; LOYALTY, FIDELITY
Suggested Character Quality: TRUSTFUL
Suggested Lifetime Scripture Verse: Psalm 54:6 *"With a freewill offering I will sacrifice to Thee; I will praise Thy name, O Lord, for it is good."*

FARRAH

Literal Meaning: UNKNOWN
Suggested Character Quality: TRUSTFUL
Suggested Lifetime Scripture Verse: Psalm 71:5 *"For Thou art my hope, O Lord God: Thou art my trust from my youth."* *

FARREL

Literal Meaning: VALOROUS
Suggested Character Quality: CHAMPION
Suggested Lifetime Scripture Verse: I Corinthians 9:25 *"And every man that striveth for the mastery is temperate in all things. Now they do it to obtain a corruptible crown; but we are incorruptible."* *

FAWN

Literal Meaning: A YOUNG DEER
Suggested Character Quality: INNOCENT ONE
Suggested Lifetime Scripture Verse: Psalm 19:14 *"Let the words of my mouth, and the meditation of my heart, be acceptable in Thy sight, O Lord, my strength, and my redeemer."* *

FAY

Literal Meaning: FAITH
Suggested Character Quality: FULL OF TRUST
Suggested Lifetime Scripture Verse: Psalm 9:10 *"Thus shall those who know Thy name trust in Thee, for Thou, O Lord, has not forsaken those who seek Thee."*

FELICIA

Literal Meaning: HAPPY
Suggested Character Quality: HAPPY ONE
Suggested Lifetime Scripture Verse: Psalm 16:11 *"Thou wilt show me the path of life: in Thy presence is fulness of joy; at Thy right hand there are pleasures forevermore."* *

FELIX

Literal Meaning: HAPPY
Suggested Character Quality: HAPPY ONE
Suggested Lifetime Scripture Verse: Psalm 16:11 *"Thou wilt show me the path of life: in Thy presence is fulness of joy; at Thy right hand there are pleasures forevermore."* *

FERDINAND

Literal Meaning: WORLD-DARING; LIFE-ADVENTURING
Suggested Character Quality: LIFE-ADVENTURING
Suggested Lifetime Scripture Verse: Proverbs 19:23 *"Reverence for the Lord leads to life; he who remains satisfied with that will not be visited by harm."*

FERGUS

Literal Meaning: MAN-CHOICE; STRONG MAN
Suggested Character Quality: STEADFAST SPIRIT
Suggested Lifetime Scripture Verse: I Corinthians 15:58 *"Consequently, my beloved brothers, be steadfast, immovable, at all times abounding in the Lord's service, aware that your labor in the Lord is not futile."*

FERN

Literal Meaning: Plant Name
Suggested Character Quality: ABUNDANT LIFE
Suggested Lifetime Scripture Verse: Isaiah 58:11 *"The Lord shall guide you continually and shall satisfy your soul in dry places; your strength shall be renewed, and you shall be like a well-watered garden, like a spring whose waters never disappoint."*

FINLEY

Literal Meaning: FAIR SOLDIER
Suggested Character Quality: SOLDIER OF CHRIST
Suggested Lifetime Scripture Verse: II Timothy 2:4 *"No man that warreth entangleth himself with the affairs of this life; that he may please Him who hath chosen him to be a soldier."* *

FLO

Literal Meaning: TO FLOWER AND TO BLOOM
Suggested Character Quality: LIVING FRAGRANCE
Suggested Lifetime Scripture Verse: II Corinthians 2:14 *"But thanks be to God, who invariably leads us triumphantly in Christ and evidences through us in every place the fragrance that results from knowing Him."* *

FLORA

Literal Meaning: A FLOWER
Suggested Character Quality: FRAGRANT SPIRIT
Suggested Lifetime Scripture Verse: II Corinthians 2:14 *"But thanks be to God, who invariably leads us on triumphantly in Christ and evidences through us in every place the fragrance that results from knowing Him."*

FLORENCE

Literal Meaning: BLOOMING, FLOUISHING, PROSPEROUS
Suggested Character Quality: SOWER OF CHEER
Suggested Lifetime Scripture Verse: Joel 2:26 *"You shall eat and be full, and be satisfied, and you shall praise the name of the Lord your God, who has done these wonders for you. My people shall never again be put to shame."*

FLOSSIE

Literal Meaning: BLOOMING, FLOURISHING
Suggested Character Quality: LIVING FRAGRANCE
Suggested Lifetime Scripture Verse: II Corinthians 2:14 *"But thanks be to God, who invariably leads us on triumphantly in Christ and evidences through us in every place the fragrance that results from knowing Him."*

FLOYD

Literal Meaning: GRAY HAIRED ONE
Suggested Character Quality: WISE ONE
Suggested Lifetime Scripture Verse: Psalm 111:10 *"For reverence of the Lord is the beginning of wisdom. There is insight in all who observe it. His praise is everlasting."*

FORD

Literal Meaning: RIVER CROSSING, (BRIDGE)
Suggested Character Quality: INTERCESSOR
Suggested Lifetime Scripture Verse: Psalm 5:2 *"Hearken unto the voice of my cry, my King, and my God: for unto Thee will I pray."*

FORREST

Literal Meaning: WOODSMAN
Suggested Character Quality: STRONG; MANLY
Suggested Lifetime Scripture Verse: Joshua 1:9 *"Have I not commanded you? Be resolute and strong! Be not afraid, and be not dismayed; for the Lord your God is with you everywhere you go."*

FRAN

Literal Meaning: FREE ONE
Suggested Character Quality: LIVING IN FREEDOM
Suggested Lifetime Scripture Verse: John 8:36 *"So if the Son liberates you, then you are really free."*

FRANCES

Literal Meaning: FREE ONE
Suggested Character Quality: LIVING IN FREEDOM
Suggested Lifetime Scripture Verse: John 8:36 *"So if the Son liberates you, then you are really free."*

FRANCIS

Literal Meaning: FREE ONE
Suggested Character Quality: LIVING IN FREEDOM
Suggested Lifetime Scripture Verse: John 8:36 *"So if the Son liberates you, then you are really free."*

FRANK

Literal Meaning: FREE MAN
Suggested Character Quality: LIVING IN FREEDOM
Suggested Lifetime Scripture Verse: John 8:36 *"So if the Son liberates you, then you are really free."*

FRANKLIN

Literal Meaning: A FREE MAN
Suggested Character Quality: FREE MAN
Suggested Lifetime Scripture Verse: John 8:36 *"So, if the Son therefore shall make you free, ye shall be free indeed."* *

FRANZ

Literal Meaning: A FREE MAN
Suggested Character Quality: FREE MAN
Suggested Lifetime Scripture Verse: John 8:36 *"So, if the Son therefore shall make you free, ye shall be free indeed."* *

FRED

Literal Meaning: PEACEFUL RULER
Suggested Character Quality: PEACEFUL
Suggested Lifetime Scripture Verse: Philippians 4:7 *"So will the peace of God, that surpasses all understanding, keep guard over your hearts and your thoughts in Christ Jesus."*

FREDERIC

Literal Meaning: PEACEFUL RULER
Suggested Character Quality: PEACEFUL
Suggested Lifetime Scripture Verse: Philippians 4:7 *"So will the peace of God, that surpasses all understanding, keep guard over your hearts, and your thoughts in Christ Jesus."*

FREDERICK

Literal Meaning: PEACEFUL RULER
Suggested Character Quality: PEACEFUL
Suggested Lifetime Scripture Verse: Philippians 4:7 *"So will the peace of God, that surpasses all understanding, keep guard over your hearts and your thoughts in Christ Jesus."*

FREMONT

Literal Meaning: PROTECTOR OF PEACE & FREEDOM
Suggested Character Quality: LIVING IN FREEDOM
Suggested Lifetime Scripture Verse: Galatians 2:20 *"I am crucified with Christ: nevertheless I live; yet not I, but Christ liveth in me: and the life which I now live in the flesh I live by faith of the Son of God, who loved me and gave Himself for me."* *

GABRIEL

Literal Meaning: MAN OF GOD
Suggested Character Quality: MAN OF GOD
Suggested Lifetime Scripture Verse: Psalm 119:73 *"Thy hands have made and prepared me; give me understanding, that I may learn Thy commandments."*

GAIL

Literal Meaning: GAY, LIVELY ONE
Suggested Character Quality: SOURCE OF JOY
Suggested Lifetime Scripture Verse: Psalm 45:7 *"Thou hast loved righteousness and hated injustice, therefore God, Thy God has anointed Thee with the oil of gladness above Thy companions."*

GALE

Literal Meaning: HAPPY, LIVELY ONE
Suggested Character Quality: JOYFUL SPIRIT
Suggested Lifetime Scripture Verse: Psalm 45:7 *"Thou hast loved righteousness and hated injustice, therefore God, Thy God has anointed Thee with the oil of gladness above Thy companions."*

GALEN

Literal Meaning: "CALM" — Greek
Suggested Character Quality: CALM SPIRIT
Suggested Lifetime Scripture Verse: Psalm 31:14 *"But I trust in Thee, O Lord; I said, 'Thou art my God.' "*

GARLAND

Literal Meaning: ENCIRCLE OR ADORN
Suggested Character Quality: VICTORIOUS SPIRIT
Suggested Lifetime Scripture Verse: I Corinthians 15:57 *"But thanks be to God, which giveth us the victory through our Lord Jesus Christ."* *

GARNETT

Literal Meaning: SEED
Suggested Character Quality: NEW LIFE
Suggested Lifetime Scripture Verse: Colossians 3:10 *"And have put on the new man, which is renewed in knowledge after the image of Him that created him."* *

GARR

Literal Meaning: BRAVE WITH THE SPEAR
Suggested Character Quality: MIGHTY WARRIOR
Suggested Lifetime Scripture Verse: Psalm 28:7 *"The Lord is my strength and my shield; my heart trusted in Him, and I am helped: therefore my heart greatly rejoiceth; and with my song will I praise Him."* *

GARRET

Literal Meaning: GENTLE
Suggested Character Quality: COURTEOUS SPIRIT
Suggested Lifetime Scripture Verse: Ephesians 4:32 *"Be kind toward one another, tenderhearted, forgiving one another, even as God has in Christ forgiven you."*

GARRETT

Literal Meaning: BRAVE WITH THE SPEAR
Suggested Character Quality: MIGHTY WARRIOR
Suggested Lifetime Scripture Verse: Psalm 28:7 *"The Lord is my strength and my shield; my heart trusted in Him, and I am helped: therefore my heart greatly rejoiceth; and with my song will I praise Him."**

GARTH

Literal Meaning: KEEPER OF A YARD OR ENCLOSURE
Suggested Character Quality: PROTECTOR
Suggested Lifetime Scripture Verse: Psalm 121:1, 2 *"I will lift up mine eyes unto the hills, from whence cometh my help. My help cometh from the Lord, which made heaven and earth."* *

GARY

Literal Meaning: SPEAR; SPEARMAN
Suggested Character Quality: MAN OF LOYALTY
Suggested Lifetime Scripture Verse: II Timothy 2:4 *"No soldier gets involved in the affairs of everyday life, so that he may please the one who enlisted him."*

GAYLE

Literal Meaning: GAY, LIVELY ONE
Suggested Character Quality: SOURCE OF JOY
Suggested Lifetime Scripture Verse: Psalm 45:7 *"Thou hast loved righteousness and hated injustice, therefore God, Thy God has anointed Thee with the oil of gladness above thy companions."*

GENA

Literal Meaning: NOBLE, WELLBORN
Suggested Character Quality: NOBLE
Suggested Lifetime Scripture Verse: Colossians 3:12 *"Put on therefore, as the elect of God, holy and beloved, bowels of mercies, kindness, humbleness of mind, meekness, longsuffering."**

GENE

Literal Meaning: WELL-BORN; NOBLE
Suggested Character Quality: WELL-BORN; NOBLE
Suggested Lifetime Scripture Verse: Psalm 91:15 *"When he calls upon me, I will answer him; I will be with him in trouble; I will rescue him and honor Him."*

GENEVA

Literal Meaning: WHITE
Suggested Character Quality: PURITY
Suggested Lifetime Character Scripture Verse: Psalm 27:4 *"One thing I have asked of the Lord; that will I look for, that I may live in the house of the Lord all the days of my life, to observe the Lord's loveliness, and to meditate in His temple."*

GENNY

Literal Meaning: WHITE WAVE
Suggested Character Quality: FAIR LADY
Suggested Lifetime Scripture Verse: Proverbs 31:26 *"She opens her mouth with wisdom and gentle teaching is on her tongue."*

GENO

Literal Meaning: WELL-BORN, NOBLE
Suggested Character Quality: WELL-BORN, NOBLE
Suggested Lifetime Scripture Verse: Psalm 91:15 *"When he calls upon me, I will answer him; I will be with him in trouble; I will rescue him and honor him."*

GENTRY

Literal Meaning: GENTLEMAN
Suggested Character Quality: GENTLE MAN
Suggested Lifetime Scripture Verse: Titus 3:2 *"To speak evil of no man, to be no brawlers, but gentle, showing all meekness unto all men."* *

GEOFF

Literal Meaning: DIVINELY PEACEFUL
Suggested Character Quality: PEACEFUL
Suggested Lifetime Scripture Verse: James 3:17 *"But the wisdom from above is first of all pure, then peaceable, courteous, congenial, full of mercy and good fruits, impartial, and sincere."*

GEOFFREY

Literal Meaning: DIVINELY PEACEFUL
Suggested Character Quality: PEACEFUL
Suggested Lifetime Scripture Verse: James 3:17 *"But the wisdom from above is first of all pure, then peaceable, courteous, congenial, full of mercy and good fruits, impartial and sincere."*

GEORGE

Literal Meaning: LAND WORKER; FARMER
Suggested Character Quality: INDUSTRIOUS
Suggested Lifetime Scripture Verse: Psalm 37:3 *"Trust in the Lord and do good; inhabit the land and practice faithfulness."*

GEORGENE

Literal Meaning: FARMER
Suggested Character Quality: INDUSTRIOUS
Suggested Lifetime Scripture Verse: Proverbs 31:27 *"She looks well to the ways of her household and eats no bread of idleness."*

GEORGIA

Literal Meaning: FARMER
Suggested Character Quality: INDUSTRIOUS ONE
Suggested Lifetime Scripture Verse: Proverbs 31:27 *"She looks well to the ways of her household and eats no bread of idleness."*

GERALD

Literal Meaning: SPEAR; MIGHTY
Suggested Character Quality: GOD'S WARRIOR
Suggested Lifetime Scripture Verse: II Corinthians 10:4 *"For the weapons of our warfare are not physical, but they are powerful with God's help for the tearing down of fortresses."*

GERALDINE

Literal Meaning: SPEAR; MIGHTY
Suggested Character Quality: APPOINTED BY GOD
Suggested Lifetime Scripture Verse: Psalm 116:13 *"I will take the cup of salvation and call on the name of the Lord."*

GERARD

Literal Meaning: SPEAR-BRAVE; SPEAR-STRONG
Suggested Character Quality: LOYAL HEART
Suggested Lifetime Scripture Verse: Deuteronomy 11:1 *"Love the Lord your God, therefore, and always heed His charge, His laws, His ordinances, and His commandments. Of the Lord your God's discipline you must be ever mindful."*

GERTRUDE

Literal Meaning: SPEAR-STRENGTH
Suggested Character Quality: COURAGEOUS SPIRIT
Suggested Lifetime Scripture Verse: Isaiah 12:2 *"Behold, God is my salvation; I will trust and not be afraid, for Jehovah, the Lord is my strength and my song; yes, He has become my salvation."*

GIDEON

Literal Meaning: THE CUTTER DOWN; FELLER OF TREES
Suggested Character Quality: MAN OF VALOR
Suggested Lifetime Scripture Verse: I John 5:4 *"For whatsoever is born of God overcometh the world: and this is the victory that overcometh the world, even our own faith."**

GIDGET

Literal Meaning: UNKNOWN
Suggested Character Quality: UNDERSTANDING HEART
Suggested Lifetime Scripture Verse: Proverbs 2:6 *"For the Lord giveth wisdom: out of His mouth cometh knowledge and understanding."* *

GILBERT

Literal Meaning: BRILLIANT PLEDGE OR HOSTAGE
Suggested Character Quality: NOBLE IN HONOR
Suggested Lifetime Scripture Verse: Amos 5:24 *"Let justice roll on like water, and righteousness like a mighty stream."*

GILES

Literal Meaning: SHIELD-BEARER
Suggested Character Quality: LOYAL HEART
Suggested Lifetime Scripture Verse: Deuteronomy 11:1 *"Love the Lord your God, therefore, and always heed His charge, His laws, His ordinances, and His commandments. Of the Lord your God's discipline you must be ever mindful."*
Explanation: The shield bearer stayed near his master ready to obey his commands.

GINA

Literal Meaning: A QUEEN
Suggested Character Quality: OF HUMBLE HEART
Suggested Lifetime Scripture Verse: Proverbs 15:33 *"Reverence of the Lord is the instruction of wisdom, for before honor must be humility."*
Explanation: One who would truly be a queen must first be humble.

GINGER

Literal Meaning: MAIDENLY
Suggested Character Quality: PURE ONE
Suggested Lifetime Scripture Verse: Psalm 119:1 *"Blessed are those whose way is upright, who walk in the law of the Lord."*

GLADYS

Literal Meaning: A PRINCESS
Suggested Character Quality: GOD'S PRINCESS
Suggested Lifetime Scripture Verse: I Peter 2:9 *"But you are a chosen race, a royal priesthood, a holy nation, a people of His acquisition, so that you may proclaim the perfections of Him who called you out of darkness into His marvelous light."*

GLEN

Literal Meaning: DWELLER IN A GLEN OR VALLEY
Suggested Character Quality: PROSPEROUS ONE
Suggested Lifetime Scripture Verse: Psalm 1:3 *"He is like a tree planted by streams of water, that yields its fruits in its season, whose leaf does not wither; and everything he does shall prosper."*
Explanation: Valley suggests a place of fertility and growth.

GLENDA

Literal Meaning: VALLEY
Suggested Character Quality: INCREASING FAITH
Suggested Lifetime Scripture Verse: Jeremiah 29:13 *"You will seek Me and find Me when you will seek Me with all your heart."*
Explanation: See Glen

GLENN

Literal Meaning: DWELLER IN THE GLEN OR VALLEY
Suggested Character Quality: PROSPEROUS ONE
Suggested Lifetime Scripture Verse: Psalm 1:3 *"He is like a tree planted by streams of water, that yields its fruits in its season, whose leaf does not wither; and everything he does shall prosper."*
Explanation: See Glen

GLENNA

Literal Meaning: DWELLER IN A VALLEY OR GLEN
Suggested Character Quality: INCREASING FAITH
Suggested Lifetime Scripture Verse: Jeremiah 29:13 *"You will seek Me and find Me when you will seek Me with all your heart."*
Explanation: See Glen

GLORIA

Literal Meaning: GLORY; GLORIOUS ONE
Suggested Character Quality: GLORY TO GOD
Suggested Lifetime Scripture Verse: Psalm 66:2 *"Sing out to glorify His name; render Him glorious praise."*

GOLDIE

Literal Meaning: GOLD
Suggested Character Quality: BRIGHT ONE
Suggested Lifetime Scripture Verse: Proverbs 4:18 *"But the path of the just is as the shining light, that shineth more and more unto the perfect day."* *

GORDON

Literal Meaning: FROM THE TRIANGULAR OR GORE-SHAPED HILL
Suggested Character Quality: ASCENDING ONE
Suggested Lifetime Scripture Verse: Psalm 24:3-4 *"Who shall go up into the mountain of the Lord; who shall stand in His holy place? He who has clean hands and a pure heart, who has not lifted up his soul to falsehood..."*
Explanation: Hills or mountains have always inspired men to seek ideals beyond themselves.

GORDY

Literal Meaning: FROM THE TRIANGULAR OR GORE-SHAPED HILL
Suggested Character Quality: ASCENDING ONE
Suggested Lifetime Scripture Verse: Psalm 24:3, 4 *"Who shall go up into the mountain of the Lord; who shall stand in His holy place? He who has clean hands and a pure heart, who has not lifted up his soul to falsehood..."*
Explanation: See Gordon

GRACE

Literal Meaning: THANKS
Suggested Character Quality: THANKFUL SPIRIT
Suggested Lifetime Scripture Verse: Psalm 7:17 *"I will give thanks to the Lord according to His righteousness, and I will sing praise to the name of the Lord most high."*

GRADY

Literal Meaning: NOBLE
Suggested Character Quality: NOBLE SPIRIT
Suggested Lifetime Scripture Verse: Proverbs 21:21 *"He that followeth after righteousness and mercy findeth life, righteousness, and honor."* *

GRAHAM

FROM THE GRAY HOME
Suggested Character Quality: OBEDIENT SPIRIT
Suggested Lifetime Scripture Verse: Deuteronomy 13:4 *"Ye shall walk after the Lord your God, and fear Him, and keep His commandments, and obey His voice, and ye shall serve Him, and cleave unto Him."* *

GRANT

Literal Meaning: GREAT ONE
Suggested Character Quality: GENEROUS HEART
Suggested Lifetime Scripture Verse: Psalm 112:4 *"Light rises for the upright in times of darkness; gracious and merciful is the good man."*

GRAY

Literal Meaning: BAILIFF
Suggested Character Quality: FULL OF WISDOM
Suggested Lifetime Scripture Verse: Proverbs 24:5 *"A wise man is strong; yea, a man of knowledge increaseth strength."* *

GREG

Literal Meaning: WATCHMAN; WATCHFUL ONE
Suggested Character Quality: WATCHFUL ONE
Suggested Lifetime Scripture Verse: I Corinthians 16:13 *"Be alert; stand firm in the faith; play the man; be strong."*

GREGORY

Literal Meaning: WATCHMAN; WATCHFUL ONE
Suggested Character Quality: WATCHFUL ONE
Suggested Lifetime Scripture Verse: I Corinthians 16:13 *"Be alert; stand firm in the faith; play the man; be strong."*

GRETCHEN

Literal Meaning: A PEARL
Suggested Character Quality: PURE ONE
Suggested Lifetime Scripture Verse: Matthew 5:8 *"Blessed are the pure in heart: for they shall see God."* *

GROVER

Literal Meaning: GROVE-DWELLER; GARDENER
Suggested Character Quality: PROSPEROUS ONE
Suggested Lifetime Scripture Verse: Philippians 1:6 *"Being confident of this very thing, that He which hath begun a good work in you will perform it until the day of Jesus Christ."* *

GUADALUPE

Literal Meaning: WOLF: CITY IN MEXICO
Suggested Character Quality: WOMAN OF GOD
Suggested Lifetime Scripture Verse: Proverbs 31:30 *"Favor is deceitful, and beauty is vain: but a woman that feareth the Lord, she shall be praised."*

GUNNAR

Literal Meaning: WARRIOR
Suggested Character Quality: GOD'S WARRIOR
Suggested Lifetime Scripture Verse: Ephesians 6:10, 11 *"Finally, my brethren, be strong in the Lord, and in the power of His might. Put on the whole armor of God, that ye may be able to stand against the wiles of the devil."* *

GUS

Literal Meaning: "STAFF" — Germanic
Suggested Character Quality: GIVER OF SUPPORT
Suggested Lifetime Scripture Verse: Proverbs 6:23 *"For to you the commandments is a lamp, the teaching a light, and the reproofs of discipline a way of life."*

GUY

Literal Meaning: WARRIOR
Suggested Character Quality: WATCHFUL ONE
Suggested Lifetime Scripture Verse: I Corinthians 16:13 *"Be alert; stand firm in the faith; play the man; be strong."*

GWEN

Literal Meaning: "WHITE" — Welsh
Suggested Character Quality: BLESSED ONE
Suggested Lifetime Scripture Verse: Psalm 18:35 *"Thou hast given me the shield of Thy salvation; Thy right hand sustains me, Thy gentleness has made me great."*
Explanation: The color white suggests receiving God's blessing.

GWENDOLYN

Literal Meaning: WHITE-BROWED ONE
Suggested Character Quality: BLESSED ONE
Suggested Lifetime Scripture Verse: Psalm 18:35 *"Thou hast given me the shield of Thy salvation; Thy right hand sustains me, Thy gentleness has made me great."*

HAL

Literal Meaning: "ARMY-POWER" — Anglo-Saxon
Suggested Character Quality: STRONG LEADER
Suggested Lifetime Scripture Verse: Joshua 1:9 *"Have I not commanded you? Be resolute and strong! Be not afraid, and be not dismayed; for the Lord your God is with you everywhere you go."*

HALEY

Literal Meaning: INGENIOUS - SCIENTIFIC
Suggested Character Quality: RESOURCEFUL ONE
Suggested Lifetime Scripture Verse: Proverbs 31:30b, 31 *"... a woman that feareth the Lord, she shall be praised. Give her of the fruit of her hands; and let her own works praise her in the gates."* *

HAMILTON

Literal Meaning: FROM THE MOUNTAIN; HOME-LOVERS ESTATE
Suggested Character Quality: MAN OF CHARACTER
Suggested Lifetime Scripture Verse: James 1:12 *"Blessed is the man that endureth temptation: for when he is tried, he shall receive the crown of life, which the Lord hath promised to them that love Him."* *

HAMPTON

Literal Meaning:FROM THE MOUNTAIN HAMLET; HOME-LOVERS ESTATE
Suggested Character Quality: MAN OF CHARACTER
Suggested Lifetime Scripture Verse: James 1:12 *"Blessed is the man that endureth temptation: for when he is tried, he shall receive the crown of life, which the Lord hath promised to them that love Him."* *

HANK

Literal Meaning: RULER OF AN ESTATE, A HOME
Suggested Character Quality: INDUSTRIOUS
Suggested Lifetime Scripture Verse: Colossians 3:23 *"Whatever you do, work heartily as for the Lord and not for men."*

HANNAH

Literal Meaning: GRACE
Suggested Character Quality: FULL OF GRACE
Suggested Lifetime Scripture Verse: Psalm 84:11 *"For the Lord God is a sun and shield; the Lord bestows mercy and honor, He holds back nothing good from those who walk uprightly."*

HANS

Literal Meaning: GOD IS GRACIOUS
Suggested Character Quality: GOD'S GRACIOUS GIFT
Suggested Lifetime Scripture Verse: Numbers 6:25 *"The Lord make His face shine upon you and be gracious to you."*

HAPPY

Literal Meaning: SHE IS MY DELIGHT (FROM THE HEBREW HEPZIBETH
Suggested Character Quality: JOYFUL SPIRIT
Suggested Lifetime Scripture Verse: Psalm 16:11 *"Thou wilt show me the path of life: in Thy presence is fulness of joy; at Thy right hand there are pleasures for evermore."* *

HARLAN

Literal Meaning: Place Name - "ARMY-LAND"
Suggested Character Quality: STRONG LEADER
Suggested Lifetime Scripture Verse: Joshua 1:9 *"Have I not commanded you? Be resolute and strong! Be not afraid, and be not dismayed; for the Lord your God is with you everywhere you go."*

HARLEY

Literal Meaning: ARMY-MEADOW
Suggested Character Quality: STRONG LEADER
Suggested Lifetime Scripture Verse: Joshua 1:9 *"Have I not commanded you? Be resolute and strong! Be not afraid, and be not dismayed; for the Lord your God is with you everywhere you go."*

HARLOWE

Literal Meaning: FROM THE HILL FORT (OLD ENGLISH)
Suggested Character Quality: MAN OF DISTINCTION
Suggested Lifetime Scripture Verse: I Chronicles 29:12 *"Both riches and honor come of Thee, and Thou reignest over all; and in Thine hand is power and might; and in Thine hand it is to make great, and to give strength unto all."* *

HARMON

Literal Meaning: HARMONY (GREEK)
Suggested Character Quality: FRIENDLY SPIRIT
Suggested Lifetime Scripture Verse: Romans 15:5, 6 *"Now the God of patience and consolation grant you to be likeminded one toward another according to Christ Jesus: That ye may with one mind and one mouth glorify God, even the Father of our Lord Jesus Christ."* *

HARMONY

Literal Meaning: HARMONY (GREEK)
Suggested Character Quality: FRIENDLY SPIRIT
Suggested Lifetime Scripture Verse: Romans 15:5, 6 *"Now the God of patience and consolation grant you to be likeminded one toward another according to Christ Jesus: That ye may with one mind and one mouth glorify God, even the Father of our Lord Jesus Christ."* *

HAROLD

Literal Meaning: "ARMY-RULER" — Old Norse
Suggested Character Quality: STRONG LEADER
Suggested Lifetime Scripture Verse: Joshua 1:9 *"Have I not commanded you? Be resolute and strong! Be not afraid, and be not dismayed; for the Lord your God is with you everywhere you go."*

HARRIET

Literal Meaning: ARMY-POWER
Suggested Character Quality: FULL OF WISDOM
Suggested Lifetime Scripture Verse: Proverbs 2:6 *"For the Lord gives wisdom; from His mouth come knowledge and discernment."*

HARRIS

Literal Meaning: SON OF HARRY (ARMY-MAN: OLD ENGLISH)
Suggested Character Quality: STRONG LEADER
Suggested Lifetime Scripture Verse: Joshua 1:9 *"Have I not commanded you? Be resolute and strong! Be not afraid, and be not dismayed; for the Lord your God is with you everywhere you go."*

HARRISON

Literal Meaning: SON OF HARRY (ARMY-MAN: OLD ENGLISH)
Suggested Character Quality: STRONG LEADER
Suggested Lifetime Scripture Verse: Joshua 1:9 *"Have I not commanded you? Be resolute and strong! Be not afraid, and be not dismayed; for the Lord your God is with you everywhere you go."*

HARVEY

Literal Meaning: "ARMY-WARRIOR" — Old German
Suggested Character Quality: LOYAL
Suggested Lifetime Scripture Verse: Romans 12:9 & 10 *"Let your love be sincere, clinging to the right with abhorrence of evil. Be joined together in a brotherhood of mutual love, trying to outdo one another in showing respect."*

HARRY

Literal Meaning: "ARMY-MAN" (OLD ENGLISH)
Suggested Character Quality: STRONG LEADER
Suggested Lifetime Scripture Verse: Joshua 1:9 *"Have I not commanded you? Be resolute and strong! Be not afraid, and be not dismayed; for the Lord your God is with you everywhere you go."*

HARTLEY

Literal Meaning: DEER MEADOW (OLD ENGLISH)
Suggested Character Quality: FULL OF LIFE
Suggested Lifetime Scripture Verse: John 7:38 *"He that believeth on Me, as the Scripture hath said, out of his belly shall flow rivers of living water."* *

HATTIE

Literal Meaning: HEAD OF THE ESTATE (FRENCH)
Suggested Character Quality: FULL OF WISDOM
Suggested Lifetime Scripture Verse: Proverbs 2:6 *"For the Lord gives wisdom; from His mouth come knowledge and discernment."*

HAYES

Literal Meaning: FROM THE HEDGE PLACE (OLD ENGLISH)
Suggested Character Quality: PROTECTOR
Suggested Lifetime Scripture Verse: Psalm 124:8 *"Our help is in the name of the Lord, who made heaven and earth."*

HAZEL

Literal Meaning: "HAZELNUT TREE" — Old English
Suggested Character Quality: QUIET SPIRIT
Suggested Lifetime Scripture Verse: Proverbs 15:33 *"Reverence of the Lord is the instruction of wisdom, for before honor must be humility."*
Explanation: The tree has always inspired men by its quiet, stately beauty.

HEATHER

Literal Meaning: "THE HEATHER FLOWER OR SHRUB" — Middle English
Suggested Character Quality: JOYFUL SPIRIT
Suggested Lifetime Scripture Verse: Isaiah 12:3 *"With joy, therefore, will you draw water from the fountains of salvation."*

HECTOR

Literal Meaning: TO HOLD FAST (GREEK)
Suggested Character Quality: STEADFAST
Suggested Lifetime Scripture Verse: I Corinthians 15:58 *"Therefore, my beloved brethren, be ye steadfast; unmovable, always abounding in the work of the Lord, forasmuch as ye know that your labor is not in vain in the Lord."**

HEIDI

Literal Meaning: "NOBLENESS" — German
Suggested Character Quality: FULL OF HONOR
Suggested Lifetime Scripture Verse: Hosea 14:9 *"Whoever is wise will understand these things, and the discerning man will know them; for the ways of the Lord are right and the righteous walk in them; but transgressors stumble in them."*

HELEN

Literal Meaning: "LIGHT; A TORCH" — Greek
Suggested Character Quality: BRIGHT ONE
Suggested Lifetime Scripture Verse: Psalm 37:6 *"He will bring forth your righteousness like the light, and your right as the noonday brightness."*

HENDERSON

Literal Meaning: HOME RULER
Suggested Character Quality: INDUSTRIOUS
Suggested Lifetime Scripture Verse: Colossians 3:23 *"Whatever you do, work heartily as for the Lord and not for men."*

HENNING

Literal Meaning: UNKNOWN
Suggested Character Quality: INDUSTRIOUS
Suggested Lifetime Scripture Verse: Colossians 3:23 *"Whatever you do, work heartily as for the Lord and not for men."*

HENRIETTA

Literal Meaning: ESTATE OR HOME RULER
Suggested Character Quality: INDUSTRIOUS
Suggested Lifetime Scripture Verse: Proverbs 31:27 *"She looks well to the ways of her household, and does not eat the bread of idleness."*

HENRY

Literal Meaning: RULER OF AN ESTATE, A HOME
Suggested Character Quality: INDUSTRIOUS
Suggested Lifetime Scripture Verse: Colossians 3:23 *"Whatever you do, work heartily as for the Lord and not for men."*

HERBERT

Literal Meaning: GLORIOUS WARRIOR
Suggested Character Quality: DILIGENT WORKER
Suggested Lifetime Scripture Verse: Colossians 3:23 *"Whatever you do, work heartily as for the Lord and not for men."*

HERMAN

Literal Meaning: "ARMY-MAN WARRIOR" — Old German
Suggested Character Quality: MAN OF DILIGENCE
Suggested Lifetime Scripture Verse: Isaiah 12:2 *"Behold, God is my salvation; I will trust and not be afraid, for Jehovah, the Lord, is my strength and my song; He has become my salvation."*

HERSCHEL

Literal Meaning: DEER (HEBREW)
Suggested Character Quality: MESSENGER OF GOD
Suggested Lifetime Scripture Verse: Isaiah 52:7 *"How beautiful upon the mountains are the feet of him that bringeth good tidings, that publisheth peace; that bringeth good tidings of good, that publisheth salvation; that saith unto Zion, Thy God reigneth."* *

HESTER

Literal Meaning: A STAR (GREEK)
Suggested Character Quality: HUMILITY OF SPIRIT
Suggested Lifetime Scripture Verse: Isaiah 30:15 *"For thus says the Lord God, the Holy One of Israel: In conversion and rest you shall be saved; in quietness and confidence shall be your strength."*
Explanation: See Esther

HILARY

Literal Meaning: CHEERFUL (GREEK)
Suggested Character Quality: CHEERFUL ONE
Suggested Lifetime Scripture Verse: Philippians 4:4 *"Rejoice in the Lord always; and again I say, Rejoice."* *

HILDA

Literal Meaning: "BATTLE-MAID" — Germanic
Suggested Character Quality: WOMAN OF STRENGTH
Suggested Lifetime Scripture Verse: Psalm 17:5 *"My steps have held closely to Thy paths; my feet have not slipped."*

HILMAR

Literal Meaning: FAMOUS; NOBLE
Suggested Character Quality: NOBLE ONE
Suggested Lifetime Scripture Verse: Psalm 37:37 *"Mark the perfect man, and behold the upright: for the end of that man is peace."* *

HINRICH

Literal Meaning: RULER OF PRIVATE PROPERTY
Suggested Character Quality: INDUSTRIOUS
Suggested Lifetime Scripture Verse: Colossians 3:23 *"Whatever you do, work heartily as for the Lord and not for men."*

HIRAM

Literal Meaning: NOBLE (HEBREW)
Suggested Character Quality: NOBLE ONE
Suggested Lifetime Scripture Verse: I John 2:5 *"But whoso keepeth His word, in him verily is the love of God perfected: hereby know we that we are in Him."* *

HOLLY

Literal Meaning: HOLY; HOLLY TREE
Suggested Character Quality: PURE SPIRIT
Suggested Lifetime Scripture Verse: I Peter 1:15 *"But as He which hath called you is holy, so be ye holy in all manner of conversation."* *

HOMER

Literal Meaning: PLEDGE; SECURITY (GREEK)
Suggested Character Quality: PROTECTOR
Suggested Lifetime Scripture Verse: Psalm 125:1 *"They that trust in the Lord shall be as mount Zion which cannot be removed, but abideth forever."* *

HOPE

Literal Meaning: "HOPE, EXPECTATION, DESIRE" — Old English
Suggested Character Quality: TRUSTFUL
Suggested Lifetime Scripture Verse: Job 11:18 *"You will feel confident, because you have hope; you will look around and lie down without fear."*

HORACE

Literal Meaning: KEEPER OF THE HOURS; LIGHT OF THE SUN
Suggested Character Quality: LOYAL AND BRAVE
Suggested Lifetime Scripture Verse: Deuteronomy 11:1 *"Love the Lord your God, therefore, and always heed His charge, His laws, His ordinances, and His commandments. Of the Lord your God's discipline you must be ever mindful."*

HOWARD

Literal Meaning: "CHIEF, GUARDIAN" — Old English
Suggested Character Quality: REASONABLE
Suggested Lifetime Scripture Verse: Isaiah 26:3 *"Thou wilt keep Him in perfect peace whose mind is stayed on Thee, because he trusts in Thee."*

HUBERT

Literal Meaning: "BRIGHT MIND" — Germanic
Suggested Character Quality: MAN OF HONOR
Suggested Lifetime Scripture Verse: Isaiah 30:18 *"Nevertheless the Lord longs to be gracious to you! Therefore He shall rise up to bestow mercy on you; for the Lord is a God of justice. Blessed are they who wait for Him."*

HUDSON

Literal Meaning: SON OF HYDE; A MEASURE OF LAND
Suggested Character Quality: GOD'S HEIR
Suggested Lifetime Scripture Verse: Galations 4:7 *"Wherefore thou art no more a servant, but a son; and if a son, then an heir of God through Christ."* *

HUEY

Literal Meaning: MIND (OLD ENGLISH)
Suggested Character Quality: MAN OF REASON
Suggested Lifetime Scripture Verse: Psalm 32:8 *"I will instruct you and train you in the way you shall go; I will counsel you with My eye on you."*

HUGH

Literal Meaning: "MIND" — Germanic
Suggested Character Quality: MAN OF REASON
Suggested Lifetime Scripture Verse: Psalm 32:8 *"I will instruct you and train you in the way you shall go; I will counsel you with My eye on you."*

HUGO

Literal Meaning: MIND
Suggested Character Quality: MAN OF REASON
Suggested Lifetime Scripture Verse: Psalm 32:8 *I will instruct you and train you in the way you shall go; I will counsel you with My eye on you."*

HUNTER

Literal Meaning: A HUNTER (OLD ENGLISH)
Suggested Character Quality: HEART FOR GOD
Suggested Lifetime Scripture Verse: I Chronicles 16:10 *"Glory ye in His holy name: let the heart of them rejoice that seek the Lord."* *
Explanation: A hunter is a pursuer. Spiritually, one should seek after and have a heart for God.

IAN

Literal Meaning: GOD'S GRACIOUS GIFT
Suggested Character Quality: GOD'S GRACIOUS GIFT
Suggested Lifetime Scripture Verse: Isaiah 43:10 *"You are My witnesses, says the Lord, and My servant whom I have chosen, in order that.you may know and believe Me, and understand that I am He. Before Me no God was formed, nor shall there be after Me."*

IDA

Literal Meaning: HAPPY; PROSPEROUS
Suggested Character Quality: JOYFUL ONE
Suggested Lifetime Scripture Verse: Psalm 28:7 *"The Lord is my strength and my shield; my heart trusted in Him, and I am helped: therefore my heart greatly rejoiceth; and with my song will I praise Him."* *

IKE

Literal Meaning: LAUGHTER
Suggested Character Quality: JOYFUL ONE
Suggested Lifetime Scripture Verse: Proverbs 3:13 *"Happy is the man that findeth wisdom, and the man that getteth understanding."* *

INEZ

Literal Meaning: VIRTUOUS, PURE
Suggested Character Quality: PURE ONE
Suggested Lifetime Scripture Verse: Psalm 29:2 *"Give unto the Lord the glory due unto His name; worship the Lord in the beauty of holiness."* *

INGA

Literal Meaning: DAUGHTER
Suggested Character Quality: CHILD OF GOD
Suggested Lifetime Scripture Verse: Romans 8:16, 17 *"The Spirit itself beareth witness with our spirit, that we are the children of God: and if children, then heirs; heirs of God, and joint - heirs with Christ, if so be that we suffer with Him, that we may be also glorified together."* *

INGER

Literal Meaning: SON
Suggested Character Quality: CHILD OF GOD
Suggested Lifetime Scripture Verse: Romans 8:16, 17 *"The Spirit itself beareth witness with our spirit, that we are the children of God: and if children, then heirs; heirs of God, and joint - heirs with Christ, if so be that we suffer with Him, that we may be also glorified together."* *

INGRID

Literal Meaning: "HERO'S DAUGHTER" — Old Norse
Suggested Character Quality: INNER BEAUTY
Suggested Lifetime Scripture Verse: Psalm 11:7 *"For the Lord is righteous; He loves acts of righteousness; His countenance beholds the upright."*

IONA

Literal Meaning: PURPLE JEWEL
Suggested Character Quality: GOD'S TREASURE
Suggested Lifetime Scripture Verse: Proverbs 31:10 *"Who can find a virtuous woman? For her price is far above rubies."* *

IRENE

Literal Meaning: "PEACE" — Greek
Suggested Character Quality: PEACEFUL SPIRIT
Suggested Lifetime Scripture Verse: John 14:27 *"Peace I bequeath to you; My peace I give to you. I do not give you gifts such as the world gives. Do not allow your hearts to be disturbed or intimidated."*

IRIS

Literal Meaning: "THE RAINBOW" — Greek
Suggested Character Quality: GOD'S PROMISE
Suggested Lifetime Scripture Verse: Psalm 18:30 *"God! perfect is His way! The word of the Lord is proven; a shield is He to all who trust in Him."*
Explanation: God gave the rainbow as a sign of His promise that He would not again destroy the earth by water.

IRMA

Literal Meaning: HONORABLE; NOBLE
Suggested Character Quality: HONORABLE
Suggested Lifetime Scripture Verse: Proverbs 31:10, 25 *"Who can find a virtuous woman? For her price is far above rubies. Strength and honor are her clothing; and she shall rejoice in time to come."* *

IRVING

Literal Meaning: "SEA FRIEND" — Old English
Suggested Character Quality: FAITHFUL FRIEND
Suggested Lifetime Scripture Verse: Galatians 6:2 *"Carry one another's burden and thus fulfill the law of Christ."*

IRWIN

Literal Meaning: SEA-FRIEND
Suggested Character Quality: FRIENDLY ONE
Suggested Lifetime Scripture Verse: Galatians 6:2 *"Carry one another's burden and thus fulfill the law of Christ."*

ISA

Literal Meaning: CONSECRATED TO GOD
Suggested Character Quality: CONSECRATED TO GOD
Suggested Lifetime Scripture Verse: Psalm 119:34 *"Give me understanding, and I shall observe Thy law, and keep it wholeheartedly."*

ISAAC

Literal Meaning:
"LAUGHTER" — Hebrew
Suggested Character Quality: CHEERFUL FAITH
Suggested Lifetime Scripture Verse: Psalm 16:11 *"Thou dost make me know the path of life; in Thy presence is fulness of joy; in Thy right hand are pleasures for evermore."*

ISABEL

Literal Meaning: CONSECRATED TO GOD
Suggested Character Quality: CONSECRATED TO GOD
Suggested Lifetime Scripture Verse: Psalm 119:34 *"Give me understanding, and I shall observe Thy law, and keep it wholeheartedly."*

ISAIAH

Literal Meaning: SALVATION OF THE LORD (HEBREW)
Suggested Character Quality: GOD IS MY HELPER
Suggested Lifetime Scripture Verse: Psalm 46:1 *"God is our refuge and strength, a very present help in trouble."* *

ISRAEL

Literal Meaning: TO FIGHT GOD
Suggested Character Quality: AUTHORITY WITH GOD
Suggested Lifetime Scripture Verse: Psalm 24:3, 4 *"Who shall ascend into the hill of the Lord? or who shall stand in His holy place? He that hath clean hands, and a pure heart; who hath not lifted up his soul unto vanity, nor sworn deceitfully."* *

ITA

Literal Meaning: THIRST
Suggested Character Quality: SEEKER OF TRUTH
Suggested Lifetime Scripture Verse: Jeremiah 29:13 *"And ye shall seek me, and find me, when ye shall search for me with all your heart."* *

IVA

Literal Meaning: GOD IS GRACIOUS
Suggested Character Quality: GOD'S GRACIOUS GIFT
Suggested Lifetime Scripture Verse: Romans 6:23 *"For the wages of sin is death, but the gift of God is eternal life in Christ Jesus our Lord."*

IVAN

Literal Meaning: GOD IS GRACIOUS
Suggested Character Quality: GOD'S GRACIOUS GIFT
Suggested Lifetime Scripture Verse: Romans 6:23 *"For the wages of sin is death, but the gift of God is eternal life in Christ Jesus our Lord."*

IVORY

Literal Meaning: WHITE
Suggested Character Quality: PURE ONE
Suggested Lifetime Scripture Verse: I Timothy 4:12b *" . . . Be thou an example of the believers, in word, in conversation, in charity, in spirit, in faith, in purity."* *

IZZY

Literal Meaning: GIFT OF ISIS (GREEK)
Suggested Character Quality: GOD'S PRINCESS
Suggested Lifetime Scripture Verse: Colossians 3:12 *"Put on therefore, as the elect of God, holy and beloved, bowels of mercies, kindness humbleness of mind, meekness, longsuffering."* *

JACK

Literal Meaning: THE SUPPLANTER
Suggested Character Quality: TRUTHFUL
Suggested Lifetime Scripture Verse: Psalm 15:2, 5 *"He who walks in integrity, who does what is right, and who speaks the truth in his heart . . . Who does not give his money for interest and who will not take a bribe against the innocent. He who does these things shall never be moved."*
Explanation: See Jacob

JACKIE

Literal Meaning: "THE SUPPLANTER" — Old French
Suggested Character Quality: TRUTHFUL
Suggested Lifetime Scripture Verse: Proverbs 3:3 *"Let not lovingkindness and faithfulness leave you; bind them about your neck, write them on the tablet of your heart."*
Explanation: See Jacob

JACKSON

Literal Meaning: SON OF JACK; GOD IS GRACIOUS
Suggested Character Quality: GOD'S GRACIOUS GIFT
Suggested Lifetime Scripture Verse: Numbers 6:25 *"The Lord make His face shine upon you and be gracious to you."*

JACOB

Literal Meaning: "THE SUPPLANTER" — Hebrew
Suggested Character Quality: TRUTHFUL
Suggested Lifetime Scripture Verse: Psalm 15:2, 5 *"He who walks in integrity, who does what is right, and who speaks the truth in his heart . . . Who does not give his money for interest and who will not take a bribe against the innocent. He who does these things shall never be moved."*
Explanation: The Lord molded the dishonesty of Jacob of the Scriptures into a man after God's heart.

JACQUELINE

Literal Meaning: THE SUPPLANTER
Suggested Character Quality: NOBLE IN TRUTH
Suggested Lifetime Scripture Verse: Proverbs 3:3 *"Let not lovingkindness and faithfulness leave you; bind them about your neck, write them on the tablet of your heart."*
Explanation: See Jacob

JAKE

Literal Meaning: "THE SUPPLANTER" — Hebrew
Suggested Character Quality: TRUTHFUL
Suggested Lifetime Scripture Verse: Psalm 15:2, 5 *"He who walks in integrity, who does what is right, and who speaks the truth in his heart. Who does not give his money for interest and who will not take a bribe against the innocent. He who does these things shall never be moved."*
Explanation: See Jacob

JAMES

Literal Meaning: "THE SUPPLANTER" — Old Spanish
Suggested Character Quality: TRUTHFUL
Suggested Lifetime Scripture Verse: Psalm 15:2, 5 *"He who walks in integrity, who does what is right and who speaks the truth in his heart . . . Who does not give his money for interest and who will not take a bribe against the innocent. He who does these things shall never be moved."*
Explanation: See Jacob

JAMIE

Literal Meaning: "THE SUPPLANTER" — Hebrew
Suggested Character Quality: TRUTHFUL
Suggested Lifetime Scripture Verse: Proverbs 3:3 *"Let not lovingkindness and faithfulness leave you; bind them about your neck, write them on the tablet of your heart."*
Explanation: See Jacob

JAMISON

Literal Meaning: THE SUPPLANTER (HEBREW, FROM JACOB)
Suggested Character Quality: TRUTHFUL
Suggested Lifetime Scripture Verse: Psalm 15:2, 5 *"He who walks in integrity, who does what is right and who speaks the truth in his heart . . . who does not give his money for interest and who will not take a bribe against the innocent. He who does these things shall never be moved."*
Explanation: See Jacob

JAN

Literal Meaning: GOD IS GRACIOUS
Suggested Character Quality: GOD'S GRACIOUS GIFT
Suggested Lifetime Scripture Verse: Isaiah 30:18 *"Nevertheless the Lord longs to be gracious to you! Therefore He shall rise up to bestow mercy on you; for the Lord is a God of justice. Blessed are they who wait for Him."*

JANE

Literal Meaning: GOD IS GRACIOUS
Suggested Character Quality: GOD'S GRACIOUS GIFT
Suggested Lifetime Scripture Verse: Isaiah 30:18 *"Nevertheless the Lord longs to be gracious to you! Therefore He shall rise up to bestow mercy on you; for the Lord is a God of Justice. Blessed are they who wait for Him."*

JANEAL
Literal Meaning: GOD IS GRACIOUS (HEBREW)
Suggested Character Quality: GOD'S GRACIOUS GIFT
Suggested Lifetime Scripture Verse: Isaiah 30:18 *"Nevertheless the Lord longs to be gracious to you! Therefore He shall rise up to bestow mercy on you; for the Lord is a God of Justice. Blessed are they who wait for Him."*

JANELL
Literal Meaning: GOD IS GRACIOUS
Suggested Character Quality: GOD'S GRACIOUS GIFT
Suggested Lifetime Scripture Verse: Isaiah 30:18 *"Nevertheless the Lord longs to be gracious to you! Therefore He shall rise up to bestow mercy on you; for the Lord is a God of Justice. Blessed are they who wait for Him."*

JANET
Literal Meaning: GOD IS GRACIOUS
Suggested Character Quality: GOD'S GRACIOUS GIFT
Suggested Lifetime Scripture Verse: Isaiah 30:18 *"Nevertheless the Lord longs to be gracious to you! Therefore He shall rise up to bestow mercy on you; for the Lord is a God of justice. Blessed are they who wait for Him."*

JANETTA
Literal Meaning: GOD IS GRACIOUS (Hebrew)
Suggested Character Quality: GOD'S GRACIOUS GIFT
Suggested Lifetime Scripture Verse: Isaiah 30:18 *"Nevertheless the Lord longs to be gracious to you! Therefore He shall rise up to bestow mercy on you; for the Lord is a God of Justice. Blessed are they who wait for Him."*

JANICE
Literal Meaning: GOD IS GRACIOUS
Suggested Character Quality: GOD'S GRACIOUS GIFT
Suggested Lifetime Scripture Verse: Isaiah 30:18 *"Nevertheless the Lord longs to be gracious to you! Therefore He shall rise up to bestow mercy on you; for the Lord is a God of justice. Blessed are they who wait for Him."*

JANNA
Literal Meaning: GOD IS GRACIOUS
Suggested Character Quality: GOD'S GRACIOUS GIFT
Suggested Lifetime Scripture Verse: Isaiah 30:18 *"Nevertheless the Lord longs to be gracious to you! Therefore He shall rise up to bestow mercy on you; for the Lord is a God of Justice. Blessed are they who wait for Him."*

JANSSEN
Literal Meaning: GOD IS GRACIOUS; SON OF JOHN
Suggested Character Quality: GOD'S GRACIOUS GIFT
Suggested Lifetime Scripture Verse: Numbers 6:25 *"The Lord make His face shine upon you and be gracious to you."*

JARRED

Literal Meaning: TO DESCEND (FROM HEBREW, JORDAN)
Suggested Character Quality: GOD'S HEIR
Suggested Lifetime Scripture Verse: Psalm 37:4 *"Delight thyself also in the Lord; and He shall give thee the desires of thine heart."* *
Explanation: To descend, as a descendant makes one an heir.

JASON

Literal Meaning: "HEALER" — Greek
Suggested Character Quality: ONE WHO HEALS
Suggested Lifetime Scripture Verse: Isaiah 61:1 *"The Spirit of the Lord God is upon me; for the Lord has anointed me to preach good tidings to the humble; He has sent Me to heal the brokenhearted; to proclaim liberty to the captives and the opening of the prison to those who are bound."*

JAY

Literal Meaning: "BLUE-JAY" — Old French
Suggested Character Quality: INTEGRITY
Suggested Lifetime Scripture Verse: Proverbs 21:3 *"To practice righteousness and justice is more acceptable to the Lord than sacrifice."*

JEAN

Literal Meaning: GOD IS GRACIOUS
Suggested Character Quality: GOD'S GRACIOUS GIFT
Suggested Lifetime Scripture Verse: Isaiah 30:18 *"Nevertheless the Lord longs to be gracious to you! Therefore He shall rise up to bestow mercy on you; for the Lord is a God of justice. Blessed are they who wait for Him."*

JEANETTE

Literal Meaning: GOD IS GRACIOUS
Suggested Character Quality: GOD'S GRACIOUS GIFT
Suggested Lifetime Scripture Verse: Isaiah 30:18 *"Nevertheless the Lord longs to be gracious to you! Therefore He shall rise up to bestow mercy on you; for the Lord is a God of justice. Blessed are they who wait for Him."*

JEFFERSON

Literal Meaning: SON OF JEFFREY; PEACE
Suggested Character Quality: PEACEFUL ONE
Suggested Lifetime Scripture Verse: James 3:17 *"But the wisdom from above is first of all pure, then peaceable, courteous, congenial, full of mercy and good fruits, without partiality, and without hypocrisy."*

JEFFREY

Literal Meaning: "DIVINELY, PEACEFUL" — Old French
Suggested Character Quality: PEACEFUL
Suggested Lifetime Scripture Verse: James 3:17 *"But the wisdom from above is first of all pure, then peaceable, courteous, congenial, full of mercy and good fruits, without partiality, and without hypocrisy."*

JENNIFER

Literal Meaning: "WHITE WAVE; WHITE PHANTOM" — Old Welsh
Suggested Character Quality: FAIR LADY
Suggested Lifetime Scripture Verse: Proverbs 31:26 *"She opens her mouth with wisdom and gentle teaching is on her tongue."*

JENNINGS

Literal Meaning: GOD IS GRACIOUS; SON OF JOHN
Suggested Character Quality: GOD'S GRACIOUS GIFT
Suggested Lifetime Scripture Verse: Numbers 6:25 *"The Lord make His face shine upon you and be gracious to you."*

JENNY

Literal Meaning: WHITE WAVE
Suggested Character Quality: FAIR LADY
Suggested Lifetime Scripture Verse: Proverbs 31:26 *"She opens her mouth with wisdom and gentle teaching is on her tongue."*

JENS

Literal Meaning: GOD IS GRACIOUS
Suggested Character Quality: GOD'S GRACIOUS GIFT
Suggested Lifetime Scripture Verse: Numbers 6:25 *"The Lord make His face shine upon you and be gracious to you."*

JEREMIAH

Literal Meaning: EXALTED BY THE LORD
Suggested Character Quality: APPOINTED BY GOD
Suggested Lifetime Scripture Verse: Isaiah 52:13 *"Behold! My servant shall work wisely. He shall arise, be exalted, and shall stand exceedingly high."*

JEREMY

Literal Meaning: "APPOINTED BY JEHOVAH" — Hebrew
Suggested Character Quality: APPOINTED BY GOD
Suggested Lifetime Scripture Verse: Isaiah 52:13 *"Behold! My servant shall work wisely. He shall rise, be exalted, and shall stand exceedingly high."*

JEROLD

Literal Meaning: No Literal Meaning found
Suggested Character Quality: APPOINTED BY GOD
Suggested Lifetime Scripture Verse: Jeremiah 15:20 *"And I will make you to this people a fortified wall of bronze. They will fight against you, but they shall not prevail over you; for I am with you to save you and to deliver you, says the Lord."*

JEROME

Literal Meaning: SACRED OR HOLY NAME
Suggested Character Quality: DEVOUT HEART
Suggested Scripture Verse: Psalm 112:1 *"Hallelujah! Oh, the bliss of the man who reveres the Lord, who greatly delights in His ordinances!"*

JERRI

Literal Meaning: SPEAR-MIGHTY
Suggested Character Quality: CONSECRATED ONE
Suggested Lifetime Scripture Verse: Lamentations 3:24 *"The Lord is my portion, says my soul, therefore do I hope in Him."*

JERROLL

Literal Meaning: SPEAR CARRIER; RULER
Suggested Character Quality: GOD'S WARRIOR
Suggested Lifetime Scripture Verse: II Corinthians 10:4 *"For the weapons of our warfare are not carnal, but mighty through God to the pulling down of strong holds."* *

JERRY

Literal Meaning: APPOINTED BY JEHOVAH
Suggested Character Quality: APPOINTED BY GOD
Suggested Lifetime Scripture Verse: Isaiah 52:13 *"Behold! My servant shall work wisely. He shall arise, be exalted, and shall stand exceedingly high."*

JESS

Literal Meaning: GOD EXISTS (HEBREW)
Suggested Character Quality: GOD EXISTS
Suggested Lifetime Scripture Verse: Psalm 31:21 *"Blessed be the Lord, for He has shown me His lovingkindness as in an entrenched city."*

JESSE

Literal Meaning: "GOD EXISTS" — Hebrew
Suggested Character Quality: GOD EXISTS
Suggested Lifetime Scripture Verse: Psalm 31:21 *"Blessed be the Lord, for He has shown me His lovingkindness as in an entrenched city."*

JESSICA

Literal Meaning: WEALTHY ONE
Suggested Character Quality: BLESSED ONE
Suggested Lifetime Scripture Verse: Psalm 119:2 *"Blessed are those who keep His testimonies, who seek Him with their whole heart."*

JESUS

Literal Meaning: SAVIOUR; HEALER
Suggested Character Quality: GOD IS SAVIOR
Suggested Lifetime Scripture Verse: Psalm 111:10 *"The fear of the Lord is the beginning of wisdom: a good understanding have all they that do His commandments: His praise endureth forever."* *

JEWEL

Literal Meaning: A PRECIOUS THING OR GEM
Suggested Character Quality: PRECIOUS ONE
Suggested Lifetime Scripture Verse: Isaiah 60:2 *"For behold, darkness shall cover the earth and a dark cloud the nations; but the Lord shall arise over you, His glory shall be seen upon you."*

JILL

Literal Meaning: YOUTHFUL ONE
Suggested Character Quality: YOUTHFUL HEART
Suggested Lifetime Scripture Verse: Psalm 71:17 *"O God, Thou hast taught me from my youth and I still declare Thy wonders."*

JILLIAN

Literal Meaning: JILL (YOUTHFUL) LILLIAN (A LILY)
Suggested Character Quality: YOUTHFUL SPIRIT
Suggested Lifetime Scripture Verse: Psalm 71:5 *"For Thou art my hope, O Lord God: Thou art my trust from my youth."* *

JOAN

Literal Meaning: GOD IS GRACIOUS
Suggested Character Quality: GOD'S GRACIOUS GIFT
Suggested Lifetime Scripture Verse: Isaiah 30:18 *"Nevertheless the Lord longs to be gracious to you! Therefore He shall rise up to bestow mercy on you; for the Lord is a God of justice. Blessed are they who wait for Him."*

JOANNA

Literal Meaning: GOD IS GRACIOUS
Suggested Character Quality: GOD'S GRACIOUS GIFT
Suggested Lifetime Scripture Verse: Isaiah 30:18 *"Nevertheless the Lord longs to be gracious to you! Therefore He shall rise up to bestow mercy on you; for the Lord is a God of justice. Blessed are they who wait for Him."*

JOANNE

Literal Meaning: GOD IS GRACIOUS
Suggested Character Quality: GOD'S GRACIOUS GIFT
Suggested Lifetime Scripture Verse: Isaiah 30:18 *"Nevertheless the Lord longs to be gracious to you! Therefore He shall rise up to bestow mercy on you; for the Lord is a God of justice. Blessed are they who wait for Him."*

JODELL

Literal Meaning: UNKNOWN
Suggested Character Quality: INCREASING FAITHFULNESS
Suggested Lifetime Scripture Verse: Ephesians 6:18 *"Praying always with all prayer and supplication in the Spirit, and watching thereunto with all perseverence and supplication for all saints."* *

JODI

Literal Meaning: PRAISED
Suggested Character Quality: PRAISED OF GOD
Suggested Lifetime Scripture Verse: Lamentations 3:25 *"The Lord is good to those who wait for Him, to the soul that seeks Him."*

JODIE

Literal Meaning: PRAISED
Suggested Character Quality: PRAISED OF GOD
Suggested Lifetime Scripture Verse: Lamentations 3:25 *"The Lord is good to those who wait for Him, to the soul that seeks Him."*

JODINA

Literal Meaning: ADMIRED; PRAISED
Suggested Character Quality: PRAISED OF GOD
Suggested Lifetime Scripture Verse: Lamentations 3:25 *"The Lord is good to those who wait for Him, to the soul that seeks Him."*

JODY

Literal Meaning: PRAISED
Suggested Character Quality: PRAISED OF GOD
Suggested Lifetime Scripture Verse: Lamentations 3:25 *"The Lord is good to those who wait for Him, to the soul that seeks Him."*

JOE

Literal Meaning: HE SHALL ADD
Suggested Character Quality: INCREASING FAITHFULNESS
Suggested Lifetime Scripture Verse: Proverbs 16:21 *"The wise in heart will be called a discerning man, and pleasant speech will increase learning."*

JOEL

Literal Meaning: THE LORD IS GOD
Suggested Character Quality: DECLARER OF GOD
Suggested Lifetime Scripture Verse: Matthew 5:16 *"Similarly let your light shine among the people so that they observe your good works and give glory to your heavenly Father."*

JOHAN

Literal Meaning: GOD'S GRACIOUS GIFT
Suggested Character Quality: GOD'S GRACIOUS GIFT
Suggested Lifetime Scripture Verse: Numbers 6:25 *"The Lord make His face shine upon you and be gracious to you."*

JOHN

Literal Meaning: GOD IS GRACIOUS
Suggested Character Quality: GOD'S GRACIOUS GIFT
Suggested Lifetime Scripture Verse: Numbers 6:25 *"The Lord make His face shine upon you and be gracious to you."*

JON

Literal Meaning: GOD IS GRACIOUS
Suggested Character Quality: GOD'S GRACIOUS GIFT
Suggested Lifetime Scripture Verse: Numbers 6:25 *"The Lord make His face shine upon you and be gracious to you."*

JONAS

Literal Meaning: DOVE
Suggested Character Quality: PEACEFUL
Suggested Lifetime Scripture Verse: Psalm 23:1-2 *"The Lord is my Shepherd; I shall not lack; He makes me to lie down in green pastures."*

JONATHAN

Literal Meaning: GOD IS GRACIOUS
Suggested Character Quality: GOD'S GRACIOUS GIFT
Suggested Lifetime Scripture Verse: Numbers 6:25 *"The Lord make His face shine upon you and be gracious to you."*

JONETTA

Literal Meaning: No Literal Meaning Found
Suggested Character Quality: GIFT OF GOD
Suggested Lifetime Scripture Verse: Isaiah 30:18 *"Nevertheless the Lord longs to be gracious to you! Therefore He shall rise up to bestow mercy on you; for the Lord is a God of justice. Blessed are they who wait for Him."*

JORDAN

Literal Meaning: DESCENDING
Suggested Character Quality: GOD'S HEIR
Suggested Lifetime Scripture Verse: Psalm 37:4 *"Delight thyself also in the Lord; and He shall give thee the desires of thine heart."* *
Explanation: See Jarred

JORDANNA

Literal Meaning: DESCENDING
Suggested Character Quality: GOD'S HEIR
Suggested Lifetime Scripture Verse: Psalm 37:4 *"Delight thyself also in the Lord; and He shall give thee the desires of thine heart."* *
Explanation: See Jarred

JOSEPH

Literal Meaning: HE SHALL ADD
Suggested Character Quality: INCREASING FAITHFULNESS
Suggested Lifetime Scripture Verse: Proverbs 16:21 *"The wise in heart will be called a discerning man, and pleasant speech will increase learning."*

JOSEPHINE

Literal Meaning: "HE SHALL ADD" — Hebrew
Suggested Character Quality: INCREASING FAITHFULNESS
Suggested Lifetime Scripture Verse: Psalm 25:1-2 *"To Thee; O Lord, I lift up my soul; my God, in Thee I trust, let me not be ashamed, let not my enemies triumph over me."*

JOSHUA

Literal Meaning: GOD OF SALVATION
Suggested Character Quality: GOD IS SAVIOR
Suggested Lifetime Scripture Verse: Psalm 119:174 *"I have longed for Thy salvation, O Lord; and Thy law is my delight."* *

JOY

Literal Meaning: JOYFUL ONE
Suggested Character Quality: JOYFUL
Suggested Lifetime Scripture Verse: Psalm 16:11 *"Thou dost make me know the path of life; in Thy presence is fulness of joy; in Thy right hand are pleasures for evermore."*

JOYCE

Literal Meaning: JOYFUL ONE
Suggested Character Quality: JOYFUL
Suggested Lifetime Scripture Verse: Psalm 16:11 *"Thou dost make me know the path of life; in Thy presence is fulness of joy; in Thy right hand are pleasures for evermore."*

JOYLYNN

Literal Meaning: JOYFUL ONE
Suggested Character Quality: OVERFLOWING JOY
Suggested Lifetime Scripture Verse: Isaiah 55:12 *"For you shall go out with joy and be led forth in peace, the mountains and the hills breaking out in song before you and all the trees of the field clapping their hands."*

JUANITA

Literal Meaning: GOD'S GRACIOUS GIFT
Suggested Character Quality: GOD'S GRACIOUS GIFT
Suggested Lifetime Scripture Verse: Isaiah 30:18 *"Nevertheless the Lord longs to be gracious to you! Therefore He shall rise up to bestow mercy on you; for the Lord is a God of justice. Blessed are they who wait for Him."*

JUDITH

Literal Meaning: PRAISED
Suggested Character Quality: PRAISED OF GOD
Suggested Lifetime Scripture Verse: Lamentations 3:25 *"The Lord is good to those who wait for Him, to the soul that seeks Him."*

JUDSON

Literal Meaning: PRAISED; SON OF JUDE
Suggested Character Quality: GOD'S HEIR
Suggested Lifetime Scripture Verse: Galations 4:7 *"Wherefore thou art no more a servant, but a son; and if a son, then an heir of God through Christ."* *

JUDY

Literal Meaning: PRAISED OF GOD
Suggested Character Quality: PRAISED OF GOD
Suggested Lifetime Scripture Verse: Lamentations 3:25 *"The Lord is good to those who wait for Him, to the soul that seeks Him."*

JULE

Literal Meaning: YOUTHFUL ONE
Suggested Character Quality: YOUTHFUL ONE
Suggested Lifetime Scripture Verse: Psalm 71:5 *"For Thou art my hope, O Lord God: Thou art my trust from my youth."* *

JULIA

Literal Meaning: YOUTHFUL ONE
Suggested Character Quality: YOUTHFUL ONE
Suggested Lifetime Scripture Verse: Psalm 71:5 *"For Thou art my hope, O Lord God: Thou are my trust from my youth."* *

JULIAN

Literal Meaning: "BELONGING TO JULIUS" — Latin
Suggested Character Quality: YOUTHFUL HEART
Suggested Lifetime Scripture Verse: Psalm 103:2, 5 *"Bless the Lord, O my soul, and forget not all His benefits . . . Who satisfies you throughout life with good things so that your youth is like the eagle's."*

JULIANA

Literal Meaning: YOUTHFUL
Suggested Character Quality: YOUTHFUL HEART
Suggested Lifetime Scripture Verse: Psalm 71:17 *"O God, Thou hast taught me from my youth and I still declare Thy wonders."*

JULIANNE

Literal Meaning: YOUTHFUL ONE
Suggested Character Quality: YOUTHFUL HEART
Suggested Lifetime Scripture Verse: Psalm 71:17 *"O God, Thou hast taught me from my youth and I still declare Thy wonders."*

JULIE

Literal Meaning: YOUTHFUL ONE
Suggested Character Quality: YOUTHFUL ONE
Suggested Lifetime Scripture Verse: Psalm 71:5 *"For Thou art my hope, O Lord God: Thou art my trust from my youth."* *

JULIEANNE

Literal Meaning: YOUTHFUL ONE
Suggested Character Quality: YOUTHFUL HEART
Suggested Lifetime Scripture Verse: Psalm 71:17 *"O God, Thou hast taught me from my youth and I still declare Thy wonders."*

JULIET

Literal Meaning: YOUTHFUL
Suggested Character Quality: YOUTHFUL HEART
Suggested Lifetime Scripture Verse: Psalm 71:5 *"For Thou art my hope, O Lord God: Thou art my trust from my youth."*

JULIUS

Literal Meaning: YOUTHFUL
Suggested Character Quality: YOUTHFUL HEART
Suggested Lifetime Scripture Verse: Psalm 103:2, 5 *"Bless the Lord, O my soul, and forget not all His benefits . . . who satisfies you throughout life with good things, so that your youth is renewed like the eagles."*

JUNE

Literal Meaning: BORN IN JUNE
Suggested Character Quality: BENEVOLENT HEART
Suggested Lifetime Scripture Verse: Matthew 5:42 *"Give to the one who begs from you and do not refuse the borrower."*

JUSTIN

Literal Meaning: JUST
Suggested Character Quality: FULL OF JUSTICE
Suggested Lifetime Scripture Verse: Psalm 119:66 *"Teach me good taste and knowledge, for I have confidence in Thy commandments."*

KANDI

Literal Meaning: UNKNOWN
Suggested Character Quality: WOMAN OF HONOR
Suggested Lifetime Scripture Verse: Habakkuk 3:19 *"The Lord God is my strength; He makes my feet like hinds' feet, He makes me tread upon my high places."*

KANDICE

Literal Meaning: UNKNOWN
Suggested Character Quality: WOMAN OF HONOR
Suggested Lifetime Scripture Verse: Habakkuk 3:19 *"The Lord God is my strength; He makes my feet like hinds' feet, He makes me tread upon my high places."*

KARA

Literal Meaning: DEAR, BELOVED ONE
Suggested Character Quality: PURITY
Suggested Lifetime Scripture Verse: Proverbs 31:30 *"Charm is deceitful · and beauty is passing, but a woman who reveres the Lord will be praised."*

KAREN

Literal Meaning: PURE ONE
Suggested Character Quality: PURE ONE
Suggested Lifetime Scripture Verse: Psalm 40:8 *"I delight to do Thy will, my God — Thy law is deep within my heart."*

KARI

Literal Meaning: PURE ONE
Suggested Character Quality: PURE ONE
Suggested Lifetime Scripture Verse: Psalm 119:7 *"I will give thanks to Thee with integrity of heart when I learn Thy righteous judgments."*

KARIN

Literal Meaning: PURE ONE
Suggested Character Quality: PURE ONE
Suggested Lifetime Scripture Verse: Psalm 40:8 *"I delight to do Thy will, my God — Thy law is deep within my heart."*

KARINE

Literal Meaning: PURE ONE
Suggested Character Quality: PURE ONE
Suggested Lifetime Scripture Verse: Psalm 40:8 *"I delight to do Thy will, my God — Thy law is deep within my heart."*

KARL

Literal Meaning: FARMER
Suggested Character Quality: STRONG, MANLY
Suggested Lifetime Scripture Verse: Joshua 1:9 *"Have I not commanded you? Be resolute and strong! Be not afraid, and be not dismayed; for the Lord your God is with you everywhere you go."*

KARLA

Literal Meaning: LITTLE WOMANLY ONE
Suggested Character Quality: STRONG, WOMANLY
Suggested Lifetime Scripture Verse: Isaiah 41:10 *"Fear not, for I am with you; be not dismayed, for I am your God! I will strengthen you, yes, I help you; yes, I will uphold you with My vindicating right hand."*

KASSANDRA

Literal Meaning: UNKNOWN
Suggested Character Quality: COMPASSIONATE
Suggested Lifetime Scripture Verse: Proverbs 31:20 *"She stretcheth out her hand to the poor; yea, she reacheth forth her hands to the needy."* *

KATHERINE

Literal Meaning: PURE ONE
Suggested Character Quality: PURE ONE
Suggested Lifetime Scripture Verse: Psalm 119:7 *"I will give thanks to Thee with integrity of heart when I learn Thy righteous judgments."*

KATHI

Literal Meaning: PURE ONE
Suggested Character Quality: PURE ONE
Suggested Lifetime Scripture Verse: Psalm 119:7 *"I will give thanks to Thee with integrity of heart when I learn Thy righteous judgments."*

KATHIE

Literal Meaning: PURE
Suggested Character Quality: PURE ONE
Suggested Lifetime Scripture Verse: Psalm 119:7 *"I will give thanks to Thee with integrity of heart when I learn Thy righteous judgments."*

KATHRINE

Literal Meaning: PURE ONE
Suggested Character Quality: PURITY
Suggested Lifetime Scripture Verse: Psalm 119:7 *"I will give thanks to Thee with integrity of heart when I learn Thy righteous judgments."*

KATHRYN

Literal Meaning: PURE ONE
Suggested Character Quality: PURE ONE
Suggested Lifetime Scripture Verse: Psalm 119:7 *"I will give thanks to Thee with integrity of heart when I learn Thy righteous judgments."*

KATHLEEN

Literal Meaning: PURE
Suggested Character Quality: PURE ONE
Suggested Lifetime Scripture Verse: Psalm 119:7 *"I will give thanks to Thee with integrity of heart when I learn Thy righteous judgments."*

KATHY

Literal Meaning: PURE
Suggested Character Quality: PURE ONE
Suggested Lifetime Scripture Verse: Psalm 119:7 *"I will give thanks to Thee with integrity of heart when I learn Thy righteous judgments."*

KATRINA

Literal Meaning: PURE
Suggested Character Quality: PURE ONE
Suggested Lifetime Scripture Verse: Psalm 119:7 *"I will give thanks to Thee with integrity of heart when I learn Thy righteous judgments."*

KAY

Literal Meaning: PURE
Suggested Character Quality: PURE ONE
Suggested Lifetime Scripture Verse: Psalm 119:7 *"I will give thanks to Thee with integrity of heart when I learn Thy righteous judgments."*

KEELER

Literal Meaning: LITTLE COMPANION; HANDSOME
Suggested Character Quality: GOD'S HELPER
Suggested Lifetime Scripture Verse: Proverbs 28:20a *"A faithful man shall abound with blessings . . ."* *

KEITH

Literal Meaning: FROM THE BATTLE PLACE
Suggested Character Quality: SECURE ONE
Suggested Lifetime Scripture Verse: Isaiah 12:2 *"Behold, God is my salvation; I will trust and not be afraid, for Jehovah, the Lord, is my strength and my song; yes, He has become my salvation."*

KELLEY

Literal Meaning: WARRIOR
Suggested Character Quality: EXCELLENT VIRTUE
Suggested Lifetime Scripture Verse: Psalm 51:6 *"Surely, Thou desirest truth in the inner self, and Thou makest me to understand hidden wisdom."*

KELLY

Literal Meaning: WARRIOR
Suggested Character Quality: EXCELLENT VIRTUE
Suggested Lifetime Scripture Verse: Psalm 51:6 *"Surely, Thou desirest truth in the inner self, and Thou makest me to understand hidden wisdom."*

KENDALL

Literal Meaning: FROM THE CLEAR-RIVER VALLEY OR BRIGHT VALLEY
Suggested Character Quality: STRONG, MANLY
Suggested Lifetime Scripture Verse: Joshua 1:9 *"Have I not commanded you? Be resolute and strong! Be not afraid, and be not dismayed; for the Lord your God is with you everywhere you go."*

KENDRA

Literal Meaning: No Literal Meaning Found
Suggested Character Quality: THE KNOWING WOMAN
Suggested Lifetime Scripture Verse: Proverbs 2:6 *"For the Lord gives wisdom; from His mouth come knowledge and discernment."*

KENNARD

Literal Meaning: BOLD; STRONG (OLD ENGLISH)
Suggested Character Quality: BOLD ONE
Suggested Lifetime Scripture Verse: Isaiah 12:2 *"Behold, God is my salvation; I will trust, and not be afraid: for the Lord Jehovah is my strength and my song; He also has become my salvation."* *

KENNEDY

Literal Meaning: HELMETED CHIEF
Suggested Character Quality: WISE LEADER
Suggested Lifetime Scripture Verse: Proverbs 3:5, 6 *"Trust in the Lord with all thine heart; and lean not unto thine own understanding. In all thy ways acknowledge Him, and He shall direct thy paths."* *

KENNETH

Literal Meaning: HANDSOME ONE
Suggested Character Quality: GRACIOUS; MANLY
Suggested Lifetime Scripture Verse: Psalm 37:37 *"Watch the upright and observe the righteous, for there is a future to the man of peace."*

KENT

Literal Meaning: WHITE, BRIGHT
Suggested Character Quality: GRACIOUS; MANLY
Suggested Scripture Verse: Psalm 37:37 *"Watch the upright and observe the righteous, for there is a future to the man of peace."*

KERBY

Literal Meaning: CHURCH TOWN
Suggested Character Quality: WORSHIPFUL SPIRIT
Suggested Lifetime Scripture Verse: Jonah 2:9 *"But I will sacrifice to Thee with the voice of thanksgiving; what I have vowed, I will make good. Deliverance is the Lord's."*

KERMIT

Literal Meaning: FREE MAN
Suggested Character Quality: FREE MAN
Suggested Lifetime Scripture Verse: I Corinthians 7:22 *"It comes to this: the slave who is called by the Lord is the Lord's freedman; similarly he who is called while he is free is a slave of Christ."*

KERN

Literal Meaning: CHILD WITH COAL BLACK HAIR
Suggested Character Quality: MAN OF DISTINCTION
Suggested Lifetime Scripture Verse: Proverbs 12:2a *"A good man obtaineth favor of the Lord . . ."* *

KERRI

Literal Meaning: DARK ONE
Suggested Character Quality: SEEKER OF LIGHT
Suggested Lifetime Scripture Verse: Psalm 27:8 *"In Thy behalf my heart proclaims, Seek ye My face; Thy face, Lord, I will seek."*
Explanation: One in darkness searches for the light.

KERRY

Literal Meaning: DARK ONE
Suggested Character Quality: SEEKER OF LIGHT
Suggested Lifetime Scripture Verse: Psalm 27:8 *"In Thy behalf my heart proclaims, Seek ye My face; Thy face, Lord, I will seek."*
Explanation: See Kerri

KERT

Literal Meaning: UNKNOWN
Suggested Character Quality: ABLE TO COUNSEL
Suggested Lifetime Scripture Verse: Proverbs 27:9 *"Ointment and perfume rejoice the heart: so doth the sweetness of a man's friend by hearty counsel."* *

KERWIN

Literal Meaning: DARK FRIEND (IRISH)
Suggested Character Quality: BOLD; TRUTHFUL
Suggested Lifetime Scripture Verse: Zechariah 8:16 *"These are the things that ye shall do; Speak ye every man the truth to his neighbor; execute the judgment of truth and peace in your gates."* *

KEVIN

Literal Meaning: GENTLE, LOVABLE
Suggested Character Quality: KIND ONE
Suggested Lifetime Scripture Verse: Ephesians 4:32 *"Be kind toward one another, tenderhearted, forgiving one another, even as God has in Christ forgiven you."*

KIM

Literal Meaning: CHIEF; RULER
Suggested Character Quality: DIGNITY OF CHARACTER
Suggested Lifetime Scripture Verse: Amos 5:14 *"Seek good and not evil, that you may live; so shall the Lord, the God of Hosts, be with you, as you say."*

KIMBALL

Literal Meaning: WARRIOR; CHIEF
Suggested Character Quality: STRONG, ENDURING
Suggested Lifetime Scripture Verse: Proverbs 24:5 *"A wise man is strong, and a man of knowledge adds to his strength."*

KIMBERLY

Literal Meaning: FROM THE ROYAL FORTRESS MEADOW
Suggested Character Quality: NOBLE ONE
Suggested Lifetime Scripture Verse: Proverbs 31:25 *"Strength and dignity clothe her and she laughs at the future."*

KIMMEL

Literal Meaning: NOBLE OR GLORIOUS LEADER
Suggested Character Quality: DIGNITY OF CHARACTER
Suggested Lifetime Scripture Verse: Amos 5:14 *"Seek good and not evil, that you may live; so shall the Lord, the God of Hosts, be with you, as you say."*

KING

Literal Meaning: RULER; CHIEF
Suggested Character Quality: VICTORIOUS
Suggested Lifetime Scripture Verse: I Corinthians 15:57 *"But thanks be to God, which giveth us the victory through our Lord Jesus Christ."* *

KINSEY

Literal Meaning: UNKNOWN
Suggested Character Quality: VICTORIOUS SPIRIT
Suggested Lifetime Scripture Verse: I Corinthians 15:57 *"But thanks be to God, which giveth us the victory through our Lord Jesus Christ."* *

KIP

Literal Meaning: DWELLER AT THE POINTED HILL
Suggested Character Quality: PEACEFUL MEDITATOR
Suggested Lifetime Scripture Verse: Psalm 104:34 *"My meditation of Him shall be sweet: I will be glad in the Lord."* *

KIRBY

Literal Meaning: CHURCH TOWN
Suggested Character Quality: WORSHIPFUL SPIRIT
Suggested Lifetime Scripture Verse: Jonah 2:9 *"But I will sacrifice to Thee with the voice of thanksgiving; what I have vowed, I will make good. Deliverance is the Lord's."*

KIRK

Literal Meaning: DWELLER AT THE CHURCH
Suggested Character Quality: WORSHIPFUL SPIRIT
Suggested Lifetime Scripture Verse: Jonah 2:9 *"But I will sacrifice to Th with the voice of thanksgiving; what I have vowed, I will make go Deliverance is the Lord's."*

KIRSTEN

Literal Meaning: CHRISTIAN
Suggested Character Quality: FOLLOWER OF CHRIST
Suggested Lifetime Scripture Verse: Psalm 63:8 *"My soul follows behind Thee; Thy right hand upholds me."*

KIT

Literal Meaning: PURE
Suggested Character Quality: PURE ONE
Suggested Lifetime Scripture Verse: Psalm 119:7 *"I will give t Thee with integrity of heart when I learn Thy righteous judgmen*

KNUTE

Literal Meaning: KNOT (SCANDINAVIAN)
Suggested Character Quality: STEADFAST AND STRONG
Suggested Lifetime Scripture Verse: Ephesians 6:13 *"Wherefor you the whole armor of God, that ye may be able to withstan day, and having done all, to stand."* *

KORY

Literal Meaning: LIVES BY A HOLLOW OR MISTY POOL
Suggested Character Quality: PROSPEROUS ONE
Suggested Lifetime Scripture Verse: Psalm 13:6 *"Let me sing to the Lord because He has dealt generously with me."*

KRIS

Literal Meaning: CHRISTIAN
Suggested Character Quality: FOLLOWER OF CHRIST
Suggested Lifetime Scripture Verse: Psalm 63:8 *"My soul follows close behind Thee; Thy right hand upholds me."*

KRISTA

Literal Meaning: CHRISTIAN
Suggested Character Quality: FOLLOWER OF CHRIST
Suggested Lifetime Scripture Verse: Psalm 63:8 *"My soul follows close behind Thee; Thy right hand upholds me."*

KRISTI

Literal Meaning: CHRISTIAN
Suggested Character Quality: FOLLOWER OF CHRIST
Suggested Lifetime Scripture Verse: Psalm 63:8 *"My soul follows close behind Thee; Thy right hand upholds me."*

KRISTIN

Literal Meaning: CHRISTIAN
Suggested Character Quality: FOLLOWER OF CHRIST
Suggested Lifetime Scripture Verse: Psalm 63:8 *"My soul follows close behind Thee; Thy right hand upholds me."*

KRISTINA

Literal Meaning: CHRISTIAN
Suggested Character Quality: FOLLOWER OF CHRIST
Suggested Lifetime Scripture Verse: Psalm 63:8 *"My soul follows close behind Thee; Thy right hand upholds me."*

KRISTINE

Literal Meaning: CHRISTIAN
Suggested Character Quality: FOLLOWER OF CHRIST
Suggested Lifetime Scripture Verse: Psalm 63:8 *"My soul follows close behind Thee; Thy right hand upholds me."*

KRISTY

Literal Meaning: CHRISTIAN
Suggested Character Quality: FOLLOWER OF CHRIST
Suggested Lifetime Scripture Verse: Psalm 63:8 *"My soul follows close behind Thee; Thy right hand upholds me."*

KURT

Literal Meaning: BOLD COUNSELOR
Suggested Character Quality: ABLE TO COUNSEL
Suggested Lifetime Scripture Verse: Isaiah 1:17 *"Learn to do good! Seek justice; restrain the ruthless; protect the orphan; defend the widow."*

KURTIS

Literal Meaning: COURTEOUS ONE
Suggested Character Quality: COURTEOUS ONE
Suggested Lifetime Scripture Verse: Zechariah 7:9 *"Thus says the Lord of hosts: render true judgment; let everyone show loving-kindness and compassion to his brother."*

KYLE

Literal Meaning: FROM THE STRAIT
Suggested Character Quality: INTEGRITY
Suggested Lifetime Scripture Verse: Psalm 91:4 *"He will cover you with His feathers, and under His wings you will find protection; His faithfulness is a shield and armor."*

LACY

Literal Meaning: RESEMBLING LACE
Suggested Character Quality: BEAUTIFUL SPIRIT
Suggested Lifetime Scripture Verse: I Chronicles 16:29 *"Give unto the Lord the glory due unto His name: bring an offering, and come before Him: worship the Lord in the beauty of holiness."* *

LAD

Literal Meaning: LAD OR ATTENDANT
Suggested Character Quality: WATCHFUL ONE
Suggested Lifetime Scripture Verse: Psalm 31:1 *"In Thee, O Lord, do I put my trust; let me never be ashamed: deliver me in Thy righteousness."* *

LANA

Literal Meaning: FAIR
Suggested Character Quality: FAIR COUNTENANCE
Suggested Lifetime Scripture Verse: Ephesians 4:32 *"Be kind toward one another, tender-hearted, forgiving one another, even as God has in Christ forgiven you."*
Explanation: A person's countenance is determined by his inward attitude.

LANAE

Literal Meaning: UNKNOWN
Suggested Character Quality: LOVING AND KIND
Suggested Lifetime Scripture Verse: Ephesians 5:2 *"And walk in love, as Christ also hath loved us, and hath given Himself for us an offering and a sacrifice to God for a sweetsmelling savor."* *

LANCE

Literal Meaning: ONE WHO SERVES (LATIN)
Suggested Character Quality: SERVANT OF GOD
Suggested Lifetime Scripture Verse: Deuteronomy 13:4 *"Ye shall walk after the Lord your God, and fear Him, and keep His commandments, and obey His voice, and ye shall serve Him, and cleave unto Him."* *

LANELLE

Literal Meaning: LIGHT
Suggested Character Quality: BRIGHT ONE
Suggested Lifetime Scripture Verse: Ephesians 5:8b *". . . But now are ye light in the Lord: walk as children of light."* *

LANETTE

Literal Meaning: A LITTLE LANE (ANGLO-SAXON)
Suggested Character Quality: FRIEND
Suggested Lifetime Scripture Verse: John 15:14 *"Ye are my friends, if ye do whatsoever I command you."* *

LANG

Literal Meaning: LONG; TALL
Suggested Character Quality: ENDURING SPIRIT
Suggested Lifetime Scripture Verse: James 5:11 *"Behold, we count them happy which endure. Ye have heard of the patience of Job, and have seen the end of the Lord; that the Lord is very pitiful, and of tender mercy."* *

LANNIE

Literal Meaning: PROBLEMS OF WAR; A SWORD
Suggested Character Quality: MIGHTY WARRIOR
Suggested Lifetime Scripture Verse: II Timothy 2:4 *"No man that warreth entangleth himself with the affairs of this life; that he may please Him who hath chosen him to be a soldier."* *

LANNY

Literal Meaning: A SWORD
Suggested Character Quality: MIGHTY WARRIOR
Suggested Lifetime Scripture Verse: II Timothy 2:4 *"No man that warreth entangleth himself with the affairs of this life; that he may please Him who hath chosen him to be a soldier."* *

LARA

Literal Meaning: THE BRIGHT; FAMOUS
Suggested Character Quality: CHEERFUL HEART
Suggested Lifetime Scripture Verse: Philippians 4:4 *"Rejoice in the Lord always: and again I say Rejoice."* *

LARAE

Literal Meaning: RIGHT, FAMOUS
Suggested Character Quality: CHEERFUL HEART
Suggested Lifetime Scripture Verse: Philippians 4:4 *"Rejoice in the Lord always: and again I say Rejoice."* *

LARISSA

Literal Meaning: THE CHEERFUL (LATIN)
Suggested Character Quality: CHEERFUL HEART
Suggested Lifetime Scripture Verse: Philippians 4:4 *"Rejoice in the Lord always: and again I say Rejoice."* *

LARK

Literal Meaning: SINGING LARK OR SKYLARK
Suggested Character Quality: A MERRY HEART
Suggested Lifetime Scripture Verse: John 15:11 *"I have talked these matters over with you so that My joy may be in you and your joy be made complete."*

LARRY

Literal Meaning: LAUREL-CROWNED ONE
Suggested Character Quality: VICTOR
Suggested Lifetime Scripture Verse: I Corinthians 15:57 *"But thanks be to God, who gives us the victory through our Lord Jesus Christ!"*
Explanation: See Lora

LARS

Literal Meaning: LAUREL-CROWNED ONE
Suggested Character Quality: VICTORIOUS SPIRIT
Suggested Lifetime Scripture Verse: I Corinthians 15:57 *"But thanks be to God, who gives us victory through our Lord Jesus Christ."*
Explanation: See Lora

LAURA

Literal Meaning: A CROWN OF LAUREL-LEAVES
Suggested Character Quality: VICTORIOUS SPIRIT
Suggested Lifetime Scripture Verse: Lamentations 3:25 *"The Lord is good to those who wait for Him, to the soul that seeks Him."*
Explanation: See Lora

LAUREL

Literal Meaning: A CROWN OF LAUREL-LEAVES
Suggested Character Quality: VICTORIOUS SPIRIT
Suggested Lifetime Scripture Verse: II Corinthians 2:14 *"But thanks be to God, who invariably leads us on triumphantly in Christ and evidences through us in every place the fragrance that results from knowing Him."*
Explanation: See Lora

LAURETTA

Literal Meaning: A CROWN OF LAUREL-LEAVES
Suggested Character Quality: VICTORIOUS SPIRIT
Suggested Lifetime Scripture Verse: II Corinthians 2:14 *"But thanks be to God, who invariably leads us on triumphantly in Christ and evidences through us in every place the fragrance that results from knowing Him."*
Explanation: See Lora

LAURIE

Literal Meaning: A CROWN OF LAUREL-LEAVES
Suggested Character Quality: VICTORIOUS SPIRIT
Suggested Lifetime Scripture Verse: I Corinthians 15:57 *"But thanks be to God, who gives us the victory through our Lord Jesus Christ!"*
Explanation: See Lora

LAURINE

Literal Meaning: A CROWN OF LAUREL LEAVES
Suggested Character Quality: VICTORIOUS SPIRIT
Suggested Lifetime Scripture Verse: I John 5:4 *"For whatsoever is born of God overcometh the world: and this is the victory that overcometh the world, even our faith."* *

Explanation: See Lora

LAURIS

Literal Meaning: A CROWN OF LAUREL LEAVES
Suggested Character Quality: VICTORIOUS SPIRIT
Suggested Lifetime Scripture Verse: I John 5:4 *"For whatsoever is born of God overcometh the world: and this is the victory that overcometh the world, even our faith."* *

Explanation: See Lora

LAVERNE

Literal Meaning: SPRING-LIKE
Suggested Character Quality: BORN ANEW
Suggested Lifetime Scripture Verse: II Timothy 2:22 *"Flee also youthful lusts: but follow righteousness, faith, charity, peace, with them that call on the Lord out of a pure heart."* *

Explanation: See La Vonne

LA VONNE

Literal Meaning: SPRING-LIKE
Suggested Character Quality: ABUNDANT LIFE
Suggested Lifetime Scripture Verse: Psalm 52:8 *"But I am like a green olive tree in the house of God; I trust in God's lovingkindness forever and ever."*

Explanation: Spring is the time of new life.

LAWREN

Literal Meaning: LAUREL-CROWNED ONE
Suggested Character Quality: VICTORIOUS
Suggested Lifetime Scripture Verse: I Corinthians 15:57 *"But thanks be to God, who gives us the victory through our Lord Jesus Christ!"*

Explanation: See Lora

LAWRENCE

Literal Meaning: LAUREL-CROWNED ONE
Suggested Character Quality: VICTOR
Suggested Lifetime Scripture Verse: I Corinthians 15:57 *"But thanks be to God, who gives us the victory through our Lord Jesus Christ!"*

Explanation: See Lora

LAWSON

Literal Meaning: THE LAUREL; CROWN OF GLORY
Suggested Character Quality: CROWNED ONE
Suggested Lifetime Scripture Verse: I Corinthians 9:25 *"And every man that striveth for the mastery is temperate in all things. Now they do it to obtain a corruptible crown; but we are incorruptible."* *

LAYNE

Literal Meaning: A COUNTRY ROAD
Suggested Character Quality: PEACEFUL SPIRIT
Suggested Lifetime Scripture Verse: Psalm 37:37 *"Mark the perfect man, and behold the upright: for the end of that man is peace."* *

LEAH

Literal Meaning: WEARY ONE
Suggested Character Quality: CONTENTED ONE
Suggested Lifetime Scripture Verse: Psalm 73:28 *"But as for me, drawing near to God is good for me; I have the Lord my refuge, so that I may announce all Thy works."*

LEANN

Literal Meaning: FROM THE MEADOW
Suggested Character Quality: CONTENTED ONE
Suggested Lifetime Scripture Verse: I Timothy 6:6 *"But godliness with contentment is great gain."* *

LEE

Literal Meaning: FROM THE PASTURE MEADOW
Suggested Character Quality: CONTENTED ONE
Suggested Lifetime Scripture Verse: Psalm 13:6 *"Let me sing to the Lord because He has dealt generously with me."*

LEIF

Literal Meaning: LOVED ONE
Suggested Character Quality: BELOVED ONE
Suggested Lifetime Scripture Verse: Galations 2:20 *"I am crucified with Christ: nevertheless I live; yet not I, but Christ liveth in me: and the life which I now live in the flesh I live by the faith of the Son of God, who loved me, and gave Himself for me."* *

LEIGH

Literal Meaning: WEARY ONE
Suggested Character Quality: CONTENTED ONE
Suggested Lifetime Scripture Verse: Psalm 73:28 *"But as for me, drawing near to God is good for me; I have made the Lord my refuge, so that I may announce all Thy works."*

LEIGHTON

Literal Meaning: FROM THE MEADOW FARM
Suggested Character Quality: PEACEFUL SPIRIT
Suggested Lifetime Scripture Verse: Psalm 23:1, 2 *"The Lord is my shepherd; I shall not want. He maketh me to lie down in green pastures: He leadeth me beside the still waters."* *

LENA

Literal Meaning: LIGHT
Suggested Character Quality: BRIGHT ONE
Suggested Lifetime Scripture Verse: Psalm 18:28 *"For Thou wilt light my candle: the Lord my God will enlighten my darkness."* *

LENNY

Literal Meaning: LION; STRONG
Suggested Character Quality: FEARLESS AND STRONG
Suggested Lifetime Scripture Verse: Proverbs 28:1, 12 *"The wicked flee when there is no one pursuing, but the righteous are as fearless as a young lion. When the righteous rejoice, great is the glory; but when the wicked rise, men hide themselves."*

LENORA

Literal Meaning: BRIGHT ONE
Suggested Character Quality: BRIGHT ONE
Suggested Lifetime Scripture Verse: Psalm 37:6 *"He will bring forth your righteousness like the light, and your right as the noonday brightness."*

LENORE

Literal Meaning: BRIGHT ONE
Suggested Character Quality: BRIGHT ONE
Suggested Lifetime Scripture Verse: Psalm 37:6 *"He will bring forth your righteousness like the light, and your right as the noonday brightness."*

LEO

Literal Meaning: LION
Suggested Character Quality: COURAGEOUS
Suggested Lifetime Scripture Verse: Proverbs 28:1, 12 *"The wicked flee when there is no one pursuing, but the righteous are as fearless as a young lion. When the righteous rejoice, great is the glory; but when the wicked rise, men hide themselves."*

LEON

Literal Meaning: LION-LIKE
Suggested Character Quality: COURAGEOUS
Suggested Lifetime Scripture Verse: Proverbs 28:1, 12 *"The wicked flee when there is no one pursuing, but the righteous are as fearless as a young lion. When the righteous rejoice, great is the glory; but when the wicked rise, men hide themselves."*

LEONA
Literal Meaning: LION
Suggested Character Quality: WOMAN OF COURAGE
Suggested Lifetime Scripture Verse: Isaiah 12:2 *"Behold, God is my salvation; I will trust and not be afraid, for Jehovah, the Lord, is my strength and my song . . ."*

LEONARD
Literal Meaning: LION-BRAVE
Suggested Character Quality: FEARLESS AND STRONG
Suggested Lifetime Scripture Verse: Proverbs 28:1, 12 *"The wicked flee when there is no one pursuing, but the righteous are as fearless as a young lion. When the righteous rejoice, great is the glory; but when the wicked rise, men hide themselves."*

LEONE
Literal Meaning: LION
Suggested Character Quality: WOMAN OF COURAGE
Suggested Lifetime Scripture Verse: Isaiah 12:2 *"Behold, God is my salvation; I will trust, and will not be afraid; for the Lord God is my strength and my song, and He has become my salvation."*

LEONTINE
Literal Meaning: THE LION-LIKE (LATIN)
Suggested Character Quality: COURAGEOUS
Suggested Lifetime Scripture Verse: Psalm 31:24 *"Be of good courage, and He shall strengthen your heart, all ye that hope in the Lord."* *

LEORA
Literal Meaning: LIGHT
Suggested Character Quality: BRIGHT ONE
Suggested Lifetime Scripture Verse: Proverbs 4:18 *"But the path of the just is as the shining light, that shineth more and more unto the perfect day."* *

LEOTA
Literal Meaning: LIGHT
Suggested Character Quality: BRINGER OF LIGHT
Suggested Lifetime Scripture Verse: Matthew 5:14 *"Ye are the light of the world. A city that is set on an hill cannot be hid."* *

LEROY
Literal Meaning: THE KING (FRENCH)
Suggested Character Quality: NOBLE ONE
Suggested Lifetime Scripture Verse: Psalm 24:3, 4 *"Who shall ascend into the hill of the Lord? or who shall stand in His holy place? He that hath clean hands, and a pure heart; who hath not lifted up his soul unto vanity, nor sworn deceitfully."* *

LESLEY (F)

Literal Meaning: DWELLER AT THE GRAY FORTRESS
Suggested Character Quality: CALM SPIRIT
Suggested Lifetime Scripture Verse: Lamentations 3:26 *"It is good if one hopes and quietly waits for the salvation of the Lord."*
Explanation: One who dwells at a fortress would feel safe and secure, therefore, calm.

LESLEY (M)

Literal Meaning: DWELLER AT THE GRAY FORTRESS
Suggested Character Quality: CALM ONE
Suggested Lifetime Scripture Verse: Lamentations 3:26 *"It is good if one hopes and quietly waits for the salvation of the Lord."*
Explanation: See Lesley (F)

LESLIE (F)

Literal Meaning: DWELLER AT THE GRAY FORTRESS
Suggested Character Quality: CALM SPIRIT
Suggested Lifetime Scripture Verse: Lamentations 3:26 *"It is good if one hopes and quietly waits for the salvation of the Lord."*
Explanation: See Lesley (F)

LESLIE (M)

Literal Meaning: DWELLER AT THE GRAY FORTRESS
Suggested Character Quality: CALM SPIRIT
Suggested Lifetime Scripture Verse: Lamentations 3:26 *"It is good if one hopes and quietly waits for the salvation of the Lord."*
Explanation: See Lesley (F)

LESTER

Literal Meaning: FROM THE SHINING CAMP
Suggested Character Quality: STRONG WARRIOR
Suggested Lifetime Scripture Verse: Psalm 18:32, 39a *"It is God that girdeth me with strength, and maketh my way perfect. For Thou hast girded me with strength unto the battle . . ."* *

LETA

Literal Meaning: JOY-DELIGHT
Suggested Character Quality: JOYFUL SPIRIT
Suggested Lifetime Scripture Verse: Psalm 16:11 *"Thou wilt show me the path of life: in Thy presence is fulness of joy; at Thy right hand there are pleasures for evermore."* *

LEVI

Literal Meaning: JOINED IN HARMONY (HEBREW)
Suggested Character Quality: JOYFUL SPIRIT
Suggested Lifetime Scripture Verse: Psalm 13:5, 6 *"But I have trusted in Thy mercy; my heart shall rejoice in Thy salvation. I will sing unto the Lord because He hath dealt bountifully with me."* *

LEW

Literal Meaning: RENOWNED WARRIOR (GERMANIC)
Suggested Character Quality: VICTORIOUS
Suggested Lifetime Scripture Verse: I Corinthians 15:57 *"But thanks to God, who gives us the victory through our Lord Jesus Christ!"*

LEWIS

Literal Meaning: RENOWNED WARRIOR (GERMANIC)
Suggested Character Quality: VICTORIOUS
Suggested Lifetime Scripture Verse: I Corinthians 15:57 *"But thanks be to God, who gives us the victory through our Lord Jesus Christ!"*

LIBBY

Literal Meaning: CONSECRATED TO GOD
Suggested Character Quality: CONSECRATED TO GOD
Suggested Lifetime Scripture Verse: Psalm 29:2 *"Give unto the Lord the glory due unto His name; worship the Lord in the beauty of holiness."* *

LILA

Literal Meaning: "DARK AS NIGHT" (ARABIC)
Suggested Character Quality: PEACEFUL AND QUIET
Suggested Lifetime Scripture Verse: Matthew 5:9 *"Blessed are the gentle, for they shall inherit the earth."*
Explanation: What is best about the night? The hurry and bustle of day are left behind. Quiet and peacefulness prepare one for rest.

LILAC

Literal Meaning: INDIGO BLUE; FLOWER (PERSIAN)
Suggested Character Quality: LIVING FRAGRANCE
Suggested Lifetime Scripture Verse: II Corinthians 2:15 *"For we are unto God a sweet savor of Christ, in them that are saved, and in them that perish."* *

LILLIAN

Literal Meaning: "THE LILY" (LATIN)
Suggested Character Quality: PURE HEART
Suggested Lifetime Scripture Verse: Psalm 19:14 *"Let the words of my mouth and the thoughts of my heart be pleasing in Thy sight, O Lord, my rock and my redeemer."*
Explanation: The lily has long been a symbol of purity.

LILLY

Literal Meaning: THE LILY-EMBLEM OF PURITY
Suggested Character Quality: PURE HEART
Suggested Lifetime Scripture Verse: I Timothy 1:5 *"Now the end of the commandment is charity out of a pure heart, and of a good conscience, and of faith unfeigned."* *
Explanation: See Lillian

LILY

Literal Meaning: THE LILY-EMBLEM OF PURITY
Suggested Character Quality: PURE HEART
Suggested Lifetime Scripture Verse: I Timothy 1:5 *"Now the end of the commandment is charity out of a pure heart, and of a good conscience, and of faith unfeigned."* *
Explanation: See Lillian

LINCOLN

Literal Meaning: FROM THE COLONY BY THE POOL
Suggested Character Quality: REFRESHING ONE
Suggested Lifetime Scripture Verse: Ephesians 4:23, 24 *"And be renewed in the spirit of your mind; and that ye put on the new man, which after God is created in righteousness and true holiness."* *

LINDA

Literal Meaning: PRETTY ONE
Suggested Character Quality: BEAUTY
Suggested Lifetime Scripture Verse: Psalm 29:2 *"Ascribe to the Lord the glory of His name; worship the Lord in sacred adornment."*

LINDAHL

Literal Meaning: FROM THE WATERFALLS
Suggested Character Quality: REFRESHING ONE
Suggested Lifetime Scripture Verse: Psalm 103:2-5 *"Bless the Lord, O my soul, and forget not all His benefits: Who forgiveth all thine iniquities; Who healeth all thy diseases; Who redeemeth thy life from destruction; Who crowneth thee with lovingkindness and tender mercies; Who satisfieth thy mouth with good things; so that thy youth is renewed like the eagle's."* *

LINDI

Literal Meaning: BEAUTIFUL
Suggested Character Quality: BEAUTIFUL SPIRIT
Suggested Lifetime Scripture Verse: Psalm 29:2 *"Give unto the Lord the glory due unto His name; worship the Lord in the beauty of holiness."* *

LINDSAY

Literal Meaning: LINDEN-TREE ISLAND
Suggested Character Quality: REFRESHING ONE
Suggested Lifetime Scripture Verse: Romans 12:2 *"And be not conformed to this world: but be ye transformed by the renewing of your mind, that ye may prove what is that good, and acceptable, and perfect, will of God."* *

LINDSEY

Literal Meaning: LINDEN-TREE ISLAND
Suggested Character Quality: REFRESHING ONE
Suggested Lifetime Scripture Verse: Romans 12:2 *"And be not conformed to this world: but be ye transformed by the renewing of your mind, that ye may prove what is that good, and acceptable, and perfect, will of God."* *

LINDY

Literal Meaning: BEAUTIFUL
Suggested Character Quality: BEAUTIFUL SPIRIT
Suggested Lifetime Scripture Verse: Psalm 29:2 *"Give unto the Lord the glory due unto His name; worship the Lord in the beauty of holiness."* *

LINEA

Literal Meaning: THE LIME TREE
Suggested Character Quality: FRUITFUL
Suggested Lifetime Scripture Verse: Galatians 5:22, 23 *"But the fruit of the Spirit is love, joy, peace, longsuffering, gentleness, goodness, faith, meekness, temperance,: against such there is no law."* *

LINNY

Literal Meaning: THE LIME TREE
Suggested Character Quality: FRUITFUL
Suggested Lifetime Scripture Verse: Galatians 5:22, 23 *"But the fruit of the Spirit is love, joy, peace, longsuffering, gentleness, goodness, faith, meekness, temperance: against such there is no law."* *

LIONEL

Literal Meaning: LION
Suggested Character Quality: COURAGEOUS
Suggested Lifetime Scripture Verse: Proverbs 28:1, 12 *"The wicked flee when there is no one pursuing, but the righteous are as fearless as a young lion. When the righteous rejoice, great is the glory, but when the wicked rise, men hide themselves."*

LISA

Literal Meaning: CONSECRATED ONE
Suggested Character Quality: CONSECRATED ONE
Suggested Lifetime Scripture Verse: Psalm 119:34 *"Give me understanding, and I shall observe Thy law, and keep it wholeheartedly."*

LISETTE

Literal Meaning: CONSECRATED TO GOD
Suggested Character Quality: CONSECRATED TO GOD
Suggested Lifetime Scripture Verse: Psalm 119:34 *"Give me understanding, and I shall observe Thy law, and keep it wholeheartedly."*

LISHA

Literal Meaning: CONSECRATED OF GOD
Suggested Character Quality: CONSECRATED OF GOD
Suggested Lifetime Scripture Verse: Psalm 119:34 *"Give me understanding, and I shall observe Thy law, and keep it wholeheartedly."*

LISSA

Literal Meaning: HONEY; THE HONEY BEE
Suggested Character Quality: SWEET SPIRIT
Suggested Lifetime Scripture Verse: Proverbs 16:24 *"Pleasant words are as an honeycomb, sweet to the soul, and health to the bones."* *

LITA

Literal Meaning: A VINEYARD OR FRUITFUL FIELD (FROM CARMELITA)
Suggested Character Quality: FRUITFUL
Suggested Lifetime Scripture Verse: Philippians 1:11 *"Being filled with the fruits of righteousness, which are by Jesus Christ, unto the glory and praise of God."* *

LIV

Literal Meaning: THE OLIVE
Suggested Character Quality: PEACEFUL
Suggested Lifetime Scripture Verse: Isaiah 26:3 *"Thou wilt keep him in perfect peace, whose mind is stayed on Thee . . ."* *
Explanation: The olive branch is a symbol of peace.

LIZ

Literal Meaning: CONSECRATED TO GOD
Suggested Character Quality: CONSECRATED TO GOD
Suggested Lifetime Scripture Verse: Psalm 119:34 *"Give me understanding, and I shall observe Thy law, and keep it wholeheartedly."*

LIZABETH

Literal Meaning: CONSECRATED TO GOD
Suggested Character Quality: CONSECRATED TO GOD
Suggested Lifetime Scripture Verse: Psalm 119:34 *"Give me understanding, and I shall observe Thy law, and keep it wholeheartedly."*

LIZANN

Literal Meaning: CONSECRATED ONE
Suggested Character Quality: CONSECRATED HEART
Suggested Lifetime Scripture Verse: Psalm 119:34 *"Give me understanding, and I shall observe Thy law, and keep it wholeheartedly."*

LIZZIE

Literal Meaning: CONSECRATED TO GOD
Suggested Character Quality: CONSECRATED TO GOD
Suggested Lifetime Scripture Verse: Psalm 119:34 *"Give me understanding, and I shall observe Thy law, and keep it wholeheartedly."*

LLOYD

Literal Meaning: GRAY-HAIRED ONE
Suggested Character Quality: WISE ONE
Suggested Lifetime Scripture Verse: Psalm 111:10 *"For reverence of the Lord is the beginning of wisdom. There is insight in all who observe it. His praise is everlasting."*

LOGAN

Literal Meaning: FROM THE STILL WATERS
Suggested Character Quality: PEACEFUL
Suggested Lifetime Scripture Verse: Romans 12:18 *"If it be possible, as much as lieth in you, live peaceably with all men."* *

LOIS

Literal Meaning: FAMOUS WARRIOR-MAID
Suggested Character Quality: VICTORIOUS
Suggested Lifetime Scripture Verse: II Corinthians 2:14 *"But thanks be to God, who invariably leads us on triumphantly in Christ and evidences through us in every place the fragrance that results from knowing Him."*
Explanation: See Lou

LOLA

Literal Meaning: LITTLE WOMANLY ONE
Suggested Character Quality: COMPASSIONATE SPIRIT
Suggested Lifetime Scripture Verse: I Corinthians 13:13 *"There remain then, faith, hope, love, these three; but the greatest of these is love."*

LOMA

Literal Meaning: No Literal Meaning Found
Suggested Character Quality: TENDERHEARTED
Suggested Lifetime Scripture Verse: Matthew 5:42 *"Give to the one who begs from you and do not refuse the borrower."*

LON

Literal Meaning: STRONG; PREPARED FOR BATTLE
Suggested Character Quality: MIGHTY WARRIOR
Suggested Lifetime Scripture Verse: Ephesians 6:10, 11 *"Finally, my brethren, be strong in the Lord, and in the power of His might. Put on the whole armor of God, that ye may be able to stand against the wiles of the devil."* *

LONA

Literal Meaning: THE LONE OR SOLITARY (MIDDLE ENGLISH)
Suggested Character Quality: QUIET SPIRIT
Suggested Lifetime Scripture Verse: I Peter 3:3, 4 *"Whose adorning let it not be that outward adorning of plaiting the hair, and of wearing of gold, or of putting on of apparel; But let it be the hidden man of the heart, in that which is not corruptible, even the ornament of a meek and quiet spirit, which is in the sight of God of great price."* *

LONDA

Literal Meaning: STRONG AND WOMANLY (FROM LOLANDA)
Suggested Character Quality: STRONG AND WOMANLY
Suggested Lifetime Scripture Verse: Psalm 27:1 *"The Lord is my light and my salvation; whom shall I fear? the Lord is the strength of my life; of whom shall I be afraid?"* *

LONELLE

Literal Meaning: STRONG; PREPARED FOR BATTLE
Suggested Character Quality: MIGHTY WARRIOR
Suggested Lifetime Scripture Verse: Psalm 27:14 *"Wait on the Lord: be of good courage, and He shall strengthen thine heart: wait, I say, on the Lord."* *

LONNA

Literal Meaning: STRONG; PREPARED FOR BATTLE
Suggested Character Quality: STRONG
Suggested Lifetime Scripture Verse: Colossians 1:10, 11 *"That ye might walk worthy of the Lord unto all pleasing, being fruitful in every good work, and increasing in the knowledge of God; strengthened with all might, according to His glorious power, unto all patience and longsuffering with joyfulness."* *

LONNIE

Literal Meaning: STRONG; PREPARED FOR BATTLE
Suggested Character Quality: MIGHTY WARRIOR
Suggested Lifetime Scripture Verse: Ephesians 6:10, 11 *"Finally, my brethren, be strong in the Lord, and in the power of His might. Put on the whole armor of God, that ye may be able to stand against the wiles of the devil."* *

LORA

Literal Meaning: A CROWN OF LAUREL LEAVES
Suggested Character Quality: VICTORIOUS SPIRIT
Suggested Lifetime Scripture Verse: Isaiah 12:2 *"Behold, God is my salvation; I will trust and will not be afraid; for the Lord God is my strength and my song, and He has become my salvation."*
Explanation: The crown of laurel leaves was given to the victor of the race.

LORELEI

Literal Meaning: SIREN OF THE RHINE; ALLURING (GERMAN)
Suggested Character Quality: BENEFICIAL GRACE
Suggested Lifetime Scripture Verse: Psalm 45:2 *"Thou art fairer than the children of men: grace is poured into thy lips: therefore God hath blessed thee forever."*

LOREN

Literal Meaning: LAUREL
Suggested Character Quality: VICTORIOUS
Suggested Lifetime Scripture Verse: I Corinthians 15:57 *"But thanks be to God, who gives us the victory through our Lord Jesus Christ!"*
Explanation: The laurel was used as a symbol of victory.

LORENA

Literal Meaning: THE LAUREL
Suggested Character Quality: VICTORIOUS HEART
Suggested Lifetime Scripture Verse: Isaiah 12:2 *"Behold, God is my salvation; I will trust, and will not be afraid; for the Lord God is my strength and my song, and He has become my salvation."*
Explanation: See Lora

LORETTA

Literal Meaning: BATTLE MAID
Suggested Character Quality: VICTORIOUS SPIRIT
Suggested Lifetime Scripture Verse: II Corinthians 2:14 *"But thanks be to God, who invariably leads us on triumphantly in Christ and evidences through us in every place the fragrance that results from knowing Him."*

LORI

Literal Meaning: A CROWN OF LAUREL LEAVES
Suggested Character Quality: VICTORIOUS SPIRIT
Suggested Lifetime Scripture Verse: Isaiah 12:2 *"Behold, God is my salvation; I will trust, and will not be afraid; for the Lord God is my strength and my song and He has become my salvation."*
Explanation: See Lora

LORNA

Literal Meaning: A CROWN OF LAUREL LEAVES
Suggested Character Quality: VICTORIOUS SPIRIT
Suggested Lifetime Scripture Verse: Isaiah 12:2 *"Behold, God is my salvation; I will trust, and will not be afraid; for the Lord God is my strength and my song, and He has become my salvation."*
Explanation: See Lora

LORRAINE

Literal Meaning: PLACE OF LOTHAR
Suggested Character Quality: WOMAN OF COURAGE
Suggested Lifetime Scripture Verse: Isaiah 12:2 *"Behold, God is my salvation; I will trust, and will not be afraid; for the Lord God is my strength and my song, and He has become my salvation."*
Explanation: Arbitrarily chosen

LOU

Literal Meaning: FAMOUS WARRIOR-MAID
Suggested Character Quality: VICTORIOUS
Suggested Lifetime Scripture Verse: II Corinthians 2:14 *"But thanks to God, who invariably leads us triumphantly in Christ and evidences through us in every place the fragrance that results from knowing Him."*
Explanation: Warriors are usually famous for their victories.

LOU ANN

Literal Meaning: FAMOUS WARRIOR-MAID; GRACE
Suggested Character Quality: VICTORIOUS
Suggested Lifetime Scripture Verse: I Corinthians 15:57 *"But thanks be to God, who gives us victory through our Lord Jesus Christ."*
Explanation: See Lou

LOUETTA

Literal Meaning: FAMOUS WARRIOR-MAID
Suggested Character Quality: VICTORIOUS
Suggested Lifetime Scripture Verse: II Corinthians 2:14 *"But thanks be to God, who invariably leads us on triumphantly in Christ and evidences through us in every place the fragrance that results from knowing Him."*
Explanation: See Lou

LOUIS

Literal Meaning: FAMOUS WARRIOR
Suggested Character Quality: VICTORIOUS
Suggested Lifetime Scripture Verse: I Corinthians 15:57 *"But thanks be to God, who gives us the victory through our Lord Jesus Christ!"*

LOUISA

Literal Meaning: FAMOUS WARRIOR-MAID
Suggested Character Quality: VICTORIOUS
Suggested Lifetime Scripture Verse: II Corinthians 2:14 *"But thanks be to God, who invariably leads us on triumphantly in Christ and evidences through us in every place the fragrance that results from knowing Him."*
Explanation: See Lou

LOUISE

Literal Meaning: FAMOUS WARRIOR-MAID
Suggested Character Quality: VICTORIOUS
Suggested Lifetime Scripture Verse: II Corinthians 2:14 *"But thanks be to God, who invariably leads us on triumphantly in Christ and evidences through us in every place the fragrance that results from knowing Him."*
Explanation: See Lou

LOWELL

Literal Meaning: LITTLE BELOVED ONE
Suggested Character Quality: BELOVED ONE
Suggested Lifetime Scripture Verse: I John 4:7 *"Beloved, let us love one another, because love springs from God and whoever loves has been born of God and knows God."*

LUANN

Literal Meaning: GRACEFUL BATTLE-MAID
Suggested Character Quality: VICTORIOUS SPIRIT
Suggested Lifetime Scripture Verse: I Corinthians 15:57 *"But thanks be to God, who gives us the victory through our Lord Jesus Christ!"*
Explanation: See Lou

LUANNE

Literal Meaning: GRACEFUL BATTLE-MAID
Suggested Character Quality: VICTORIOUS SPIRIT
Suggested Lifetime Scripture Verse: I Corinthians 15:57 *"But thanks be to God, who gives us victory through our Lord Jesus Christ!"*
Explanation: See Lou

LUCAS

Literal Meaning: BRINGING LIGHT (LATIN)
Suggested Character Quality: ENLIGHTING ONE
Suggested Lifetime Scripture Verse: Matthew 5:16 *"Let your light so shine before men, that they may see your good works, and glorify your Father which is in heaven."* *

LUCETTA

Literal Meaning: LIGHT; BRINGER OF LIGHT
Suggested Character Quality: BRINGER OF LIGHT
Suggested Lifetime Scripture Verse: Psalm 27:1 *"The Lord is my light and my salvation; whom shall I fear? the Lord is the stronghold of my life; of whom shall I be afraid?"*

LUCIA

Literal Meaning: LIGHT; BRINGER OF LIGHT (LATIN)
Suggested Character Quality: BRINGER OF LIGHT
Suggested Lifetime Scripture Verse: Psalm 27:1 *"The Lord is my light and my salvation; whom shall I fear? the Lord is the stronghold of my life; of whom shall I be afraid?"*

LUCILE

Literal Meaning: LIGHT; BRINGER OF LIGHT
Suggested Character Quality: BRINGER OF LIGHT
Suggested Lifetime Scripture Verse: Psalm 27:1 *"The Lord is my light and my salvation; whom shall I fear? The Lord is the stronghold of my life; of whom shall I be afraid."*

LUCILLE

Literal Meaning: LIGHT; BRINGER OF LIGHT
Suggested Character Quality: BRINGER OF LIGHT
Suggested Lifetime Scripture Verse: Psalm 27:1 *"The Lord is my light and my salvation; whom shall I fear? The Lord is the stronghold of my life; of whom shall I be afraid."*

LUCY

Literal Meaning: LIGHT; BRINGER OF LIGHT
Suggested Character Quality: BRINGER OF LIGHT
Suggested Lifetime Scripture Verse: Psalm 27:1 *"The Lord is my light and my salvation; whom shall I fear? The Lord is the stronghold of my life; of whom shall I be afraid."*

LUDWIG

Literal Meaning: RENOWNED IN BATTLE
Suggested Character Quality: MIGHTY WARRIOR
Suggested Lifetime Scripture Verse: Psalm 20:7 *"Some trust in chariots, and some in horses: but we will remember the name of the Lord our God."* *
Explanation: See Luella

LUELLA

Literal Meaning: RENOWNED WARRIOR
Suggested Character Quality: VICTORIOUS SPIRIT
Suggested Lifetime Scripture Verse: I Corinthians 15:57 *"But thanks be to God, who gives us victory through our Lord Jesus Christ!"*
Explanation: A renowned warrior is a victorious one.

LUETTA

Literal Meaning: FAMOUS WARRIOR
Suggested Character Quality: VICTORIOUS
Suggested Lifetime Scripture Verse: II Corinthians 2:14 *"But thanks be to God, who invariably leads us on triumphantly in Christ and evidences through us in every place the fragrance that results from knowing Him."*
Explanation: See Luella

LUKE

Literal Meaning: LIGHT; BRINGER OF LIGHT OR KNOWLEDGE
Suggested Character Quality: ENLIGHTENED ONE
Suggested Lifetime Scripture Verse: Isaiah 28:26 *"His God correctly instructs and teaches him."*

LUTHER

Literal Meaning: ILLUSTRIOUS WARRIOR
Suggested Character Quality: VICTORIOUS SPIRIT
Suggested Lifetime Scripture Verse: I Corinthians 15:57 *"But thanks be to God, who gives us the victory through our Lord Jesus Christ."*

LUVERNE

Literal Meaning: SPRINGLIKE
Suggested Character Quality: ABUNDANT LIFE
Suggested Lifetime Scripture Verse: Job 10:12 *"Thou has granted me life and favor, and Thy visitation hath preserved my spirit."* *

LYDIA

Literal Meaning: "A WOMAN OF LYDIA" (LATIN)
Suggested Character Quality: WORSHIPPER OF GOD
Suggested Lifetime Scripture Verse: Psalm 17:6 *"I have called on Thee, O God, for Thou wilt answer me. Incline Thine ear to me; hear my words."*
Explanation: The Lydia of the Bible was noted as a worshipper of God.

LYLE

Literal Meaning: FROM THE ISLAND (OLD FRENCH)
Suggested Character Quality: SOJOURNER
Suggested Lifetime Scripture Verse: II Corinthians 5:1 *"For we know that if our earthly house of this tabernacle were dissolved, we have a building of God, a house not made with hands, eternal in the heavens."* *

LYNDA

Literal Meaning: PRETTY ONE
Suggested Character Quality: INNER BEAUTY
Suggested Lifetime Scripture Verse: Psalm 29:2 *"Ascribe to the Lord the glory of His name, worship the Lord in sacred adornment."*

LYNDON

Literal Meaning: DWELLER AT THE LIME TREE, OR LINDEN-TREE HILL
Suggested Character Quality: ENCOURAGING ONE
Suggested Lifetime Scripture Verse: Proverbs 27:(9 *"Ointment and perfume rejoice the heart: so doth the sweetness of a man's friend by hearty counsel."* *

LYNETTE

Literal Meaning: FROM THE POOL OR WATERFALL
Suggested Character Quality: REFRESHING ONE
Suggested Lifetime Scripture Verse: John 7:38 *"He who believes in Me, just as the scripture says, streams of water will flow from his innermost being."*

LYNN

Literal Meaning: FROM THE POOL OR WATERFALL
Suggested Character Quality: REFRESHING ONE
Suggested Lifetime Scripture Verse: John 7:38 *"He who believes in Me, just as the scripture says, streams of water will flow from his innermost being."*

LYNNE

Literal Meaning: FROM THE POOL OR WATERFALL
Suggested Character Quality: REFRESHING ONE
Suggested Lifetime Scripture Verse: John 7:38 *"He who believes in Me, just as the scripture says, streams of water will flow from his innermost being."*

MABEL

Literal Meaning: LOVABLE
Suggested Character Quality: LOVING HEART
Suggested Lifetime Scripture Verse: Psalm 42:1 *"As a deer pants for water brooks so my soul longs for Thee, O God."*

MacARTHUR

Literal Meaning: ARTHUR - INTEGRITY
Suggested Character Quality: MAN OF INTEGRITY
Suggested Lifetime Scripture Verse: Psalm 37:37 *"Mark the perfect man, and behold the upright: for the end of that man is peace."* *

MACK

Literal Meaning: SON
Suggested Character Quality: FULL HONOR
Suggested Lifetime Scripture Verse: John 12:26 *"If any man serve me, let him follow me; and where I am, there shall also my servant be: if any man serve me, him will my Father honor."* *

MacKENZIE

Literal Meaning: WISE LEADER (IRISH)
Suggested Character Quality: WOMAN OF JUSTICE
Suggested Lifetime Scripture Verse: Proverbs 4:18 *"But the path of the just is as the shining light, that shineth more and more unto the perfect day."* *

MADELINE

Literal Meaning: WOMAN OF MAGDALA
Suggested Character Quality: TRANSFORMED HEART
Suggested Lifetime Scripture Verse: Colossians 3:10 *". . . Put on the new self who is being renewed in a full knowledge in the likeness of Him who created him."*
Explanation: The woman of Magdala, Mary, was remembered for the transformation that Jesus worked in her life.

MADONNA

Literal Meaning: MY LADY
Suggested Character Quality: GENTLE
Suggested Lifetime Scripture Verse: James 3:17 *"But the wisdom that is from above is first pure, then peaceable, gentle, and easy to be entreated, full of mercy and good fruits, without partiality, and without hypocrisy."* *

MAE

Literal Meaning: THE GREAT (LATIN)
Suggested Character Quality: ESTEEMED ONE
Suggested Lifetime Scripture Verse: II Corinthians 9:8 *"And God is able to make all grace abound toward you; that ye, always having all sufficiency in all things, may abound to every good work."* *

MAGGI

Literal Meaning: A PEARL
Suggested Character Quality: A PEARL
Suggested Lifetime Scripture Verse: Matthew 5:8 *"Blessed are the pure in heart: for they shall see God."* *

MAGGIE

Literal Meaning: A PEARL
Suggested Character Quality: A PEARL
Suggested Lifetime Scripture Verse: Matthew 5:8 *"Blessed are the pure in heart: for they shall see God."* *

MALCOLM

Literal Meaning: DISCIPLE OF COLUMBIA
Suggested Character Quality: TEACHABLE SPIRIT
Suggested Lifetime Scripture Verse: Psalm 16:7 *"I will bless the Lord who has counseled me; even in the night my emotions admonish me."*
Explanation: A disciple is one who wishes to learn.

MALLERY

Literal Meaning: STRONG
Suggested Character Quality: STRONG
Suggested Lifetime Scripture Verse: Isaiah 26:4 *"Trust ye in the Lord forever: for in the Lord Jehovah is everlasting strength."* *

MALONE

Literal Meaning: THE DARK (GREEK)
Suggested Character Quality: UNFAILINGLY KIND
Suggested Lifetime Scripture Verse: Romans 12:10 *"Be kindly affectioned one to another with brotherly love; in honor preferring one another."* *

MAME

Literal Meaning: MYRRH; BITTER
Suggested Character Quality: LIVING FRAGRANCE
Suggested Lifetime Scripture Verse: II Corinthians 2:15 *"For we are unto God a sweet savour of Christ, in them that are saved, and in them that perish."* *
Explanation: See Miriam

MANDA

Literal Meaning: WORTHY OF LOVE
Suggested Character Quality: BELOVED
Suggested Lifetime Scripture Verse: I John 4:7 *"Beloved, let us love another, because love springs from God and whoever loves has been born of God and knows God."*

MANDY

Literal Meaning: WORTHY OF LOVE
Suggested Character Quality: BELOVED
Suggested Lifetime Scripture Verse: I John 4:7 *"Beloved, let us love one another, because love springs from God and whoever loves has been born of God and knows God."*

MANFRED

Literal Meaning: MAN OF PEACE
Suggested Character Quality: PEACELOVING
Suggested Lifetime Scripture Verse: Romans 12:18 *"If it be possible, as much as lieth in you, live peaceably with all men."* *

MANLEY

Literal Meaning: VIRILE OR MANLY
Suggested Character Quality: MAN OF GOD
Suggested Lifetime Scripture Verse: I Timothy 6:11 *"But thou, O man of God, flee these things; and follow after righteousness, godliness, faith, love, patience, meekness."* *

MANNING

Literal Meaning: SON OF THE HERO
Suggested Character Quality: MAN OF GOD
Suggested Lifetime Scripture Verse: I Timothy 4:8b *". . . godliness is profitable unto all things, having promise of the life that now is, and of that which is to come."* *

MANUAL

Literal Meaning: GOD WITH US
Suggested Character Quality: GOD WITH US
Suggested Lifetime Scripture Verse: Psalm 5:12 *"For Thou, O Lord, dost bless the righteous; as with a shield Thou dost surround him with favor."*

MARA

Literal Meaning: MYRRH
Suggested Character Quality: LIVING FRAGRANCE
Suggested Lifetime Scripture Verse: Psalm 116:17 *"I will offer to Thee the sacrifice of thanksgiving and call on the name of the Lord."*
Explanation: See Miriam

MARC

Literal Meaning: GOD OF WAR
Suggested Character Quality: MIGHTY WARRIOR
Suggested Lifetime Scripture Verse: Psalm 29:1 *"Give to the Lord, O you sons of the mighty, give to the Lord glory and strength."*

MARCELLA

Literal Meaning: MARTIAL ONE
Suggested Character Quality: STRENGTH OF CHARACTER
Suggested Lifetime Scripture Verse: Psalm 28:7 *"The Lord is my strength and my shield; my heart trusted in Him, and I am helped: therefore my heart greatly rejoiceth; and with my song will I praise Him."* *

MARCIA

Literal Meaning: GOD OF WAR
Suggested Character Quality: A BRAVE HEART
Suggested Lifetime Scripture Verse: Psalm 9:1 *"I will praise the Lord with my whole heart; I will tell of all Thy marvelous works."*

MARCO

Literal Meaning: A WARRIOR
Suggested Character Quality: MIGHTY WARRIOR
Suggested Lifetime Scripture Verse: Psalm 29:1 *"Give to the Lord, O you sons of the mighty, give to the Lord glory and strength."*

MARCOS

Literal Meaning: A WARRIOR
Suggested Character Quality: MIGHTY WARRIOR
Suggested Lifetime Scripture Verse: Psalm 29:1 *"Give to the Lord, O you sons of the mighty, give to the Lord glory and strength."*

MARCUS

Literal Meaning: A WARRIOR
Suggested Character Quality: MIGHTY WARRIOR
Suggested Lifetime Scripture Verse: Psalm 29:1 *"Give to the Lord, O you sons of the mighty, give to the Lord glory and strength."*

MARCY

Literal Meaning: GOD OF WAR
Suggested Character Quality: A BRAVE HEART
Suggested Lifetime Scripture Verse: Psalm 9:1 *"I will praise the Lord with my whole heart; I will tell of all Thy marvelous works."*

MAREN
Literal Meaning: MYRRH
Suggested Character Quality: EXPRESSION OF WORSHIP
Suggested Lifetime Scripture Verse: Psalm 34:1 *"I will bless the Lord at all times: His praise shall continually be in my mouth."* *
Explanation: See Miriam.

MARGARET
Literal Meaning: A PEARL
Suggested Character Quality: A PEARL
Suggested Lifetime Scripture Verse: Matthew 5:8 *"Blessed are the pure in heart: for they shall see God."* *

MARGI
Literal Meaning: A PEARL
Suggested Character Quality: A PEARL
Suggested Lifetime Scripture Verse: Matthew 5:8 *"Blessed are the pure in heart: for they shall see God."* *

MARGIE
Literal Meaning: A PEARL
Suggested Character Quality: A PEARL
Suggested Lifetime Scripture Verse: Matthew 5:8 *"Blessed are the pure in heart: for they shall see God."* *

MARGO
Literal Meaning: A PEARL
Suggested Character Quality: A PEARL
Suggested Lifetime Scripture Verse: Matthew 5:8 *"Blessed are the pure in heart: for they shall see God."* *

MARGOT
Literal Meaning: A PEARL
Suggested Character Quality: A PEARL
Suggested Lifetime Scripture Verse: Matthew 5:8 *"Blessed are the pure in heart: for they shall see God."* *

MARIA
Literal Meaning: MYRRH
Suggested Character Quality: LIVING FRAGRANCE
Suggested Lifetime Scripture Verse: Psalm 116:17 *"I will offer to Thee the sacrifice of thanksgiving and call on the name of the Lord."*
Explanation: See Miriam

MARIAN

Literal Meaning: MYRRH
Suggested Character Quality: LIVING FRAGRANCE
Suggested Scripture Verse: Psalm 116:7 *"I will offer to Thee the sacrifice of thanksgiving and call on the name of the Lord."*
Explanation: See Miriam

MARIANNE

Literal Meaning: MYRRH
Suggested Character Quality: LIVING FRAGRANCE
Suggested Lifetime Scripture Verse: Psalm 116:17 *"I will offer to Thee the sacrifice of thanksgiving and call on the name of the Lord."*
Explanation: See Miriam

MARIBETH

Literal Meaning: MYRRH
Suggested Character Quality: LIVING FRAGRANCE
Suggested Lifetime Scripture Verse: Psalm 116:17 *"I will offer to Thee the sacrifice of thanksgiving and call on the name of the Lord."*
Explanation: See Miriam

MARIE

Literal Meaning: MYRRH
Suggested Character Quality: LIVING FRAGRANCE
Suggested Lifetime Scripture Verse: Psalm 116:17 *"I will offer to Thee the sacrifice of thanksgiving and call on the name of the Lord."*
Explanation: See Miriam

MARIEL

Literal Meaning: MYRRH
Suggested Character Quality: LIVING FRAGRANCE
Suggested Lifetime Scripture Verse: Psalm 116:17 *"I will offer to Thee the sacrifice of thanksgiving and call on the name of the Lord."*
Explanation: See Miriam

MARIETTA

Literal Meaning: MYRRH
Suggested Character Quality: LIVING FRAGRANCE
Suggested Lifetime Scripture Verse: Psalm 116:17 *"I will offer to Thee the sacrifice of thanksgiving and call on the name of the Lord."*
Explanation: See Miriam

MARILEE

Literal Meaning: MYRRH
Suggested Character Quality: LIVING FRAGRANCE
Suggested Lifetime Scripture Verse: Psalm 116:17 *"I will offer to Thee the sacrifice of thanksgiving and call on the name of the Lord."*
Explanation: See Miriam

MARILOU

Literal Meaning: MYRRH
Suggested Character Quality: LIVING FRAGRANCE
Suggested Lifetime Scripture Verse: Psalm 116:17 *"I will offer to Thee the sacrifice of thanksgiving and call on the name of the Lord."*
Explanation: See Miriam

MARILYN

Literal Meaning: MYRRH
Suggested Character Quality: LIVING FRAGRANCE
Suggested Lifetime Scripture Verse: Psalm 116:17 *"I will offer to Thee the sacrifice of thanksgiving and call on the name of the Lord."*
Explanation: See Miriam

MARIO

Literal Meaning: MARTIAL ONE (LATIN)
Suggested Character Quality: STRENGTH OF CHARACTER
Suggested Lifetime Scripture Verse: Ephesians 3:16 *"That He would grant you, according to the riches of His glory, to be strengthened with might by His Spirit in the inner man."* *

MARISA

Literal Meaning: OF THE SEA
Suggested Character Quality: A BRAVE HEART
Suggested Lifetime Scripture Verse: Psalm 31:24 *"Be of good courage, and He shall strengthen your heart, all ye that hope in the Lord."*

MARITA

Literal Meaning: MYRRH
Suggested Character Quality: LIVING FRAGRANCE
Suggested Lifetime Scripture Verse: Psalm 116:17 *"I will offer to Thee the sacrifice of thanksgiving and call on the name of the Lord."*
Explanation: See Miriam

MARJORIE

Literal Meaning: A PEARL
Suggested Character Quality: PURE OF HEART
Suggested Lifetime Scripture Verse: Matthew 5:8 *"Blessed are the pure in heart: for they shall see God."* *

MARK

Literal Meaning: WARLIKE ONE
Suggested Character Quality: MIGHTY WARRIOR
Suggested Lifetime Scripture Verse: Psalm 29:1 *"Give to the Lord, O you sons of the mighty, give to the Lord glory and strength."*

MARLENE

Literal Meaning: MYRRH
Suggested Character Quality. LIVING FRAGRANCE
Suggested Lifetime Scripture Verse: Psalm 116:17 *"I will offer to Thee the sacrifice of thanksgiving and call on the name of the Lord."*
Explanation: See Miriam

MARLIN

Literal Meaning: LITTLE FALCON, OR HAWK
Suggested Character Quality: VIGILANT ONE
Suggested Lifetime Scripture Verse: Psalm 130:6 *"My soul waiteth for the Lord more than they that watch for the morning: I say, more than they that watch for the morning."* *

MARLOW

Literal Meaning: FROM THE WATER BY THE HILL
Suggested Character Quality: REFRESHING ONE
Suggested Lifetime Scripture Verse: Psalm 147:1 *"Praise ye the Lord: for it is good to sing praises unto our God: for it is plesant; and praise is comely."* *

MARNI

Literal Meaning: OF THE SEA
Suggested Character Quality: REJOICES IN GOD
Suggested Lifetime Scripture Verse: Psalm 9:1 *"I will praise Thee, O Lord, with my whole heart; I will show forth all Thy marvellous works."* *

MARSHA

Literal Meaning: WARLIKE
Suggested Character Quality: STRENGTH OF CHARACTER
Suggested Lifetime Scripture Verse: Psalms 27:14 *"Wait on the Lord: be of good courage, and He shall strengthen thine heart: wait, I say, on the Lord."* *

MARSHALL

Literal Meaning: STEWARD
Suggested Character Quality: LOYAL ONE
Suggested Lifetime Scripture Verse: Proverbs 3:5-6 *"Trust in the Lord with all your heart and lean not on your own understanding; in all your ways acknowledge Him, and He will direct your paths."*

MARTHA

Literal Meaning: A LADY
Suggested Character Quality: WOMAN OF DISCRETION
Suggested Lifetime Scripture Verse: Proverbs 15:33 *"Reverence of the Lord is the instruction of wisdom, for before honor must be humility."*

MARTIN

Literal Meaning: WARLIKE ONE
Suggested Character Quality: LOYAL SPIRIT
Suggested Lifetime Scripture Verse: Psalm 112:7 *"He need never fear any evil report; his heart will remain firm, fully trusting in the Lord."*

MARTY

Literal Meaning: WARLIKE ONE
Suggested Character Quality: LOYAL SPIRIT
Suggested Lifetime Scripture Verse: Psalm 112:7 *"He need never fear any evil report; his heart will remain firm, fully trusting in the Lord."*

MARV

Literal Meaning: FAMOUS FRIEND
Suggested Character Quality: FRIENDLY SPIRIT
Suggested Lifetime Scripture Verse: Proverbs 18:24 *"A man has many friends for companionship, but there is a friend who sticks closer than a brother."*

MARVEL

Literal Meaning: WONDERFUL
Suggested Character Quality: A MIRACLE
Suggested Lifetime Scripture Verse: Psalm 9:1 *"I will praise the Lord with my whole heart; I will tell of all Thy marvelous works."*

MARVIN

Literal Meaning: "FAMOUS FRIEND" — Anglo-Saxon
Suggested Character Quality: FRIENDLY SPIRIT
Suggested Lifetime Scripture Verse: Proverbs 18:24 *"A man has many friends for companionship, but there is a friend who sticks closer than a brother."*

MARVINE

Literal Meaning: FAMOUS FRIEND
Suggested Character Quality: FRIENDLY SPIRIT
Suggested Lifetime Scripture Verse: John 15:14, 17 *"Ye are my friends, if ye do whatsoever I command you. These things I command you, that ye love one another."* *

MARY

Literal Meaning: MYRRH
Suggested Character Quality: LIVING FRAGRANCE
Suggested Lifetime Scripture Verse: Psalm 116:17 *"I will offer to Thee the sacrifice of thanksgiving and call on the name of the Lord."*
Explanation: See Miriam

MARYBETH

Literal Meaning: MYRRH; HOUSE OF GOD
Suggested Character Quality: EXPRESSION OF WORSHIP
Suggested Lifetime Scripture Verse: Psalm 29:2 *"Give unto the Lord the glory due unto His name; worship the Lord in the beauty of holiness."* *
Explanation: See Miriam

MARYELLEN

Literal Meaning: MYRRH; BRIGHT
Suggested Character Quality: BRIGHT FRAGRANCE
Suggested Lifetime Scripture Vesre: II Corinthians 2:14 *"Now thanks be unto God, which always causeth us to triumph in Christ, and maketh manifest the savour of His knowledge by us in every place."*
Explanation: See Miriam

MARY KAY

Literal Meaning: MYRRH; PURE
Suggested Character Quality: PURE IN HEART
Suggested Lifetime Scripture Verse: James 3:17 *"But the wisdom that is from above is first pure, then peaceable, gentle, and easy to be entreated, full of mercy and good fruits, without partiality, and without hypocrisy."* *

MASON

Literal Meaning: WORKER IN STONE
Suggested Character Quality: STRONG ONE
Suggested Lifetime Scripture Verse: Colossians 1:11 *"Strengthened with all might, according to His glorious power, unto all patience and longsuffering with joyfulness."* *

MATILDA

Literal Meaning: POWERFUL IN BATTLE
Suggested Character Quality: VICTORIOUS SPIRIT
Suggested Lifetime Scripture Verse: I Corinthians 15:57 *"But thanks be to God, which giveth us the victory through our Lord Jesus Christ."* *

MATT

Literal Meaning: GIFT OF THE LORD
Suggested Character Quality: GIFT OF THE LORD
Suggested Lifetime Scripture Verse: Numbers 6:25 *"The Lord make His face shine upon you and be gracious to you."*

MATTHEW

Literal Meaning: GIFT OF JEHOVAH
Suggested Character Quality: GIFT OF THE LORD
Suggested Lifetime Scripture Verse: Numbers 6:25 *"The Lord make His face shine upon you and be gracious to you."*

MAUDE

Literal Meaning: MIGHTY BATTLE MAIDEN
Suggested Character Quality: VICTORIOUS SPIRIT
Suggested Lifetime Scripture Verse: I Corinthians 15:57 *"But thanks be to God, which giveth us the victory through our Lord Jesus Christ."* *

MAUREEN

Literal Meaning: MYRRH; DARK ONE
Suggested Character Quality: FRAGRANCE OF GOD'S GRACE
Suggested Lifetime Scripture Verse: Psalm 84:11 *"For the Lord God is a sun and shield: the Lord will give grace and glory: no good thing will He withhold from them that walk uprightly."* *
Explanation: See Miriam

MAURICE

Literal Meaning: THE DARK
Suggested Character Quality: COURAGEOUS
Suggested Lifetime Scripture Verse: Psalm 27:14 *"Wait on the Lord: be of good courage, and He shall strengthen thine heart: wait, I say, on the Lord."* *

MAVIS

Literal Meaning: JOY; SINGING THRUSH
Suggested Character Quality: JOYOUS ONE
Suggested Lifetime Scripture Verse: Psalm 105:2, 3 *"Sing unto Him, sing psalms unto Him: talk ye of all His wondrous works. Glory ye in His holy name: let the heart of them rejoice that seek the Lord."* *

MAX

Literal Meaning: GREATEST
Suggested Character Quality: FULL OF HONOR
Suggested Lifetime Scripture Verse: Psalm 112:6, 7 *"Such a man will never be laid low, for the just shall be held in remembrance forever. He need never fear any evil report; his heart will remain firm, fully trusting in the Lord."*

MAXINE

Literal Meaning: GREATEST
Suggested Character Quality: ESTEEMED ONE
Suggested Lifetime Scripture Verse: Isaiah 62:3 *"Thou shalt also be a crown of glory in the hand of the Lord, and a royal diadem in the hand of thy God."* *

MAXWELL

Literal Meaning: GREAT
Suggested Character Quality: FULL OF HONOR
Suggested Lifetime Scripture Verse: Psalm 112:6, 7 *"Such a man will never be laid low, for the just shall be held in remembrance forever. He need never fear any evil report; his heart will remain firm, fully trusting in the Lord."*

MAY

Literal Meaning: GREAT ONE
Suggested Character Quality: ESTEEMED ONE
Suggested Lifetime Scripture Verse: Proverbs 31:31 *"Acknowledge the product of her hands; let her works praise her in the gates."*

MAYNARD

Literal Meaning: INTENSE STRENGTH
Suggested Character Quality: STEADFAST SPIRIT
Suggested Lifetime Scripture Verse: I Corinthians 15:58 *"Consequently, my beloved brothers, be steadfast, immovable, at all times abounding in the Lord's service, aware that your labors in the Lord is not futile."*

MEG

Literal Meaning: A PEARL
Suggested Character Quality: A PEARL
Suggested Lifetime Scripture Verse: Matthew 5:8 *"Blessed are the pure in heart: for they shall see God."* *

MEGAN

Literal Meaning: MIGHTY (IRISH)
Suggested Character Quality: STRONG IN HEART
Suggested Lifetime Scripture Verse: Psalm 18:2 *"The Lord is my rock, and my fortress, and my deliverer; my God, my strength, in whom I will trust; my buckler, and the horn of my salvation, and my high tower."* *

MEL

Literal Meaning: CHIEF
Suggested Character Quality: RELIABLE
Suggested Lifetime Scripture Verse: Micah 6:8 *"He has declared to you, O man, what is good, and what does the Lord require of you but to do justice, and to love mercy and to walk humbly with your God?"*

MELANIE

Literal Meaning: DARK
Suggested Character Quality: RESOLUTE COURAGE
Suggested Lifetime Scripture Verse: Nahum 1:7 *"The Lord is good, a stronghold in the day of trouble; He knows those who commit themselves to Him."*
Explanation: Arbitrarily chosen

MELBA

Literal Meaning: A HANDMAIDEN
Suggested Character Quality: SERVANT SPIRIT
Suggested Lifetime Scripture Verse: Colossians 3:23, 24 *And whatsoever ye do, do it heartily, as to the Lord, and not unto men; Knowing that of the Lord ye shall receive the reward of the inheritance: for ye serve the Lord Christ."* *

MELINDA

Literal Meaning: BEAUTIFUL, PRETTY
Suggested Character Quality: GRACIOUS SPIRIT
Suggested Lifetime Scripture Verse: Hebrews 12:28 *"Let us, therefore, be grateful that the kingdom we have received cannot be shaken, and so let us serve God acceptably with reverence and awe."*

MELODY

Literal Meaning: SONG
Suggested Character Quality: JOYFUL LIFE
Suggested Lifetime Scripture Verse: Isaiah 12:3 *"With joy, therefore, will you draw water from the fountains of salvation."*

MELVIN

Literal Meaning: CHIEF
Suggested Character Quality: RELIABLE
Suggested Lifetime Scripture Verse: Micah 6:8 *"He has declared to you, O man, what is good, and what does the Lord require of you but to do justice, and to love mercy and to walk humbly with your God?"*

MELYNA

Literal Meaning: YELLOW-COLORED
Suggested Character Quality: BRIGHT AND HAPPY
Suggested Lifetime Scripture Verse: Philippians 4:4 *"Rejoice in the Lord alway: and again I say, Rejoice."* *

MEREDITH

Literal Meaning: GUARDIAN FROM THE SEA
Suggested Character Quality: BLESSED OF GOD
Suggested Lifetime Scripture Verse: Isaiah 48:17 *"Thus says the Lord, your Redeemer, the Holy One of Israel: I am the Lord your God, who teaches for your profit, who leads you in the way you should go."*

MERLE

Literal Meaning: BLACKBIRD
Suggested Character Quality: FREE SPIRIT
Suggested Lifetime Scripture Verse: John 8:32 *"And ye shall know the truth, and the truth shall make you free."* *

MERLIN
Literal Meaning: SEA
Suggested Character Quality: GENEROUS SPIRIT
Suggested Lifetime Scripture Verse: Psalm 40:10 *"Thy righteousness I have not hid away in my heart; Thy faithfulness and Thy salvation I have proclaimed; I have not concealed Thy lovingkindness and Thy truth from the great assembly."*
Explanation: The sea suggests deepness and openness, "generosity."

MERRI
Literal Meaning: HAPPY, JOYFUL
Suggested Character Quality: CHEERFUL HEART
Suggested Lifetime Scripture Verse: Isaiah 12:3 *"With joy, therefore, will you draw water from the fountains of salvation."*

MERRILL
Literal Meaning: FAMOUS ONE (OLD FRENCH)
Suggested Character Quality: BRIGHT WITH JOY
Suggested Lifetime Scripture Verse: Proverbs 4:18 *"But the path of the just is as the shining light, that shineth more and more unto the perfect day."* *

MERV
Literal Meaning: FAMOUS FRIEND (OLD ENGLISH)
Suggested Character Quality: FRIEND
Suggested Lifetime Scripture Verse: Romans 13:8 *"Owe no man anything, but to love one another: for he that loveth another hath fulfilled the law."* *

MERVIN
Literal Meaning: FAMOUS FRIEND (OLD ENGLISH)
Suggested Character Quality: FRIEND
Suggested Lifetime Scripture Verse: Romans 13:8 *"Owe no man anything, but to love one another: for he that loveth another hath fulfilled the law."* *

MERYL
Literal Meaning: MYRRH; THE FRAGRANT
Suggested Character Quality: LIVING FRAGRANCE
Suggested Lifetime Scripture Verse: II Corinthians 2:15 *"For we are unto God a sweet savour of Christ, in them that are saved, and in them that perish."*
Explanation: See Miriam

MIA
Literal Meaning: MINE
Suggested Character Quality: BELONGING TO GOD
Suggested Lifetime Scripture Verse: Lamentations 3:25 *"The Lord is good to those who wait for Him, to the soul that seeks Him."*
Explanation: God calls us His own.

MICHAEL

Literal Meaning: WHO IS LIKE GOD
Suggested Character Quality: GODLINESS
Suggested Lifetime Scripture Verse: I Timothy 4:8 ". . . *Godliness is beneficial in every way; it holds promise for this present and for the future life.*"

MICHELE

Literal Meaning: WHO IS LIKE GOD
Suggested Character Quality: GODLINESS
Suggested Lifetime Scripture Verse: Isaiah 26:7 *"For the just the way is level. Thou, Upright One, makest smooth the path of the righteous."*

MICHELLE

Literal Meaning: WHO IS LIKE GOD
Suggested Character Quality: GODLY WOMAN
Suggested Lifetime Scripture Verse: Isaiah 26:7 *"For the just the way is level. Thou, Upright One, makest smooth the path of the righteous."*

MICK

Literal Meaning: GODLIKE
Suggested Character Quality: GODLINESS
Suggested Lifetime Scripture Verse: I Timothy 4:8 *"Because while physical training is of a little benefit, godliness is beneficial in every way; it holds promise for this present and for the future life."*

MICKEY

Literal Meaning: GODLIKE
Suggested Character Quality: GODLINESS
Suggested Lifetime Scripture Verse: I Timothy 4:8 *"Because while physical training is of a little benefit, godliness is beneficial in every way; it holds promise for this present and for the future life."*

MIKE

Literal Meaning: GODLIKE
Suggested Character Quality: GODLINESS
Suggested Lifetime Scripture Verse: I Timothy 4:8 *"Because while physical training is of a little benefit, godliness is beneficial in every way; it holds promise for this present and for the future life."*

MILDRED

Literal Meaning: MILD COUNSELOR
Suggested Character Quality: GENTLE ONE
Suggested Lifetime Scripture Verse: Colossians 3:12 *"Therefore, as God's chosen, set apart and enjoying His love, clothe yourselves with tenderness of heart, kindliness, humility, gentleness, patient endurance."*

MILES

Literal Meaning: SOLDIER
Suggested Character Quality: STRONG WARRIOR
Suggested Lifetime Scripture Verse: II Timothy 2:4 *"No man that warreth entangleth himself with the affairs of this life; that he may please Him who hath chosen him to be a soldier."* *

MILLIE

Literal Meaning: MILD POWER
Suggested Character Quality: GENTLE SPIRIT
Suggested Lifetime Scripture Verse: Colossians 3:12 *"Therefore, as God's chosen, set apart and enjoying His love, clothe yourselves with tenderness of heart, kindliness, humility, gentleness, patient endurance."*

MILO

Literal Meaning: MILL OR MILESTONE (LATIN)
Suggested Character Quality: INDUSTRIOUS ONE
Suggested Lifetime Scripture Verse: Psalm 128:2 *"For thou shalt eat the labor of thine hands: happy shalt thou be, and it shall be well with thee."* *

MILTON

Literal Meaning: DWELLER AT THE MILL-TOWN
Suggested Character Quality: PROSPEROUS ONE
Suggested Lifetime Scripture Verse: Psalm 13:6 *"Let me sing to the Lord because He has dealt generously with me."*

MIRIAM

Literal Meaning: MYRRH
Suggested Character Quality: LIVING FRAGRANCE
Suggested Lifetime Scripture Verse: Psalm 116:17 *"I will offer to Thee the sacrifice of thanksgiving and call on the name of the Lord."*
Explanation: Myrrh was an incense used in the worship of God.

MITCH

Literal Meaning: WHO IS LIKE GOD
Suggested Character Quality: GODLINESS
Suggested Lifetime Scripture Verse: I Timothy 4:8 *". . . Godliness is beneficial in every way; it holds promise for this present and for the future life."*

MITCHELL

Literal Meaning: WHO IS LIKE GOD
Suggested Character Quality: GODLINESS
Suggested Lifetime Scripture Verse: I Timothy 4:8 *". . . Godliness is beneficial in every way; it holds promise for this present and for the future life."*

MITZI

Literal Meaning: MYRRH
Suggested Character Quality: LIVING FRAGRANCE
Suggested Lifetime Scripture Verse: Psalm 116:17 *"I will offer to Thee the sacrifice of thanksgiving and call on the name of the Lord."*
Explanation: See Miriam

MOLLY

Literal Meaning: MYRRH
Suggested Character Quality: LIVING FRAGRANCE
Suggested Lifetime Scripture Verse: Psalm 116:17 *"I will offer to Thee the sacrifice of thanksgiving and call on the name of the lord."*
Explanation: See Miriam

MONICA

Literal Meaning: ADVISE
Suggested Character Quality: WOMAN OF WISDOM
Suggested Lifetime Scripture Verse: Proverbs 2:6 *"For the Lord gives wisdom; from His mouth come knowledge and discernment."*

MONTE

Literal Meaning: MOUNTAIN HUNTER
Suggested Character Quality: MIGHTY WARRIOR
Suggested Lifetime Scripture Verse: Ephesians 6:10 *"Finally, my brethren, be strong in the Lord, and in the power of His might."* *

MONTGOMERY

Literal Meaning: MOUNTAIN HUNTER
Suggested Character Quality: MIGHTY WARRIOR
Suggested Lifetime Scripture Verse: Ephesians 6:10 *"Finally, my brethren, be strong in the Lord, and in the power of His might."* *

MORGAN

Literal Meaning: DWELLER BY THE SEA
Suggested Character Quality: ABUNDANT PROVIDER
Suggested Lifetime Scripture Verse: Ephesians 4:28 *". . . Let him labor, working with his hands the thing which is good, that he may have to give to him that needeth."* *

MORRIS

Literal Meaning: DARK-COMPLEXIONED ONE
Suggested Characte Quality: SINCERE DEVOTION
Suggested Lifetime Scripture Verse: Psalm 112:1 *"Praise ye the Lord. Blessed is the man that feareth the Lord, that delighteth greatly in His commandments."*
Explanation: Arbitrarily chosen.

MORT

Literal Meaning: FROM THE QUIET WATER
Suggested Character Quality: REFRESHING ONE
Suggested Lifetime Scripture Verse: Matthew 5:6 *"Blessed are they which do hunger and thirst after righteousness: for they shall be filled."* *

MOSES

Literal Meaning: SAVED
Suggested Character Quality: DELIVERED BY GOD
Suggested Lifetime Scripture Verse: Psalm 50:23 *"He who offers a sacrifice of praise honors Me: to him who prepares his way I will show the salvation of God."*

MURIEL

Literal Meaning: SEA-BRIGHT
Suggested Character Quality: BRIGHT WITH JOY
Suggested Lifetime Scripture Verse: Isaiah 12:3 *"With joy, therefore, will you draw water from the fountains of salvation."*

MURRAY

Literal Meaning: "MERRY" — English
Suggested Character Quality: CHEERFUL SPIRIT
Suggested Lifetime Scripture Verse: Psalm 18:49 *"Therefore I will extol Thee among the nations, O Lord, and will sing praises to Thy name."*

MYRA

Literal Meaning: THE WONDERFUL
Suggested Character Quality: FAIR LADY
Suggested Lifetime Scripture Verse: Proverbs 31:30 *"Favor is deceitful, and beauty is vain: but a woman that feareth the Lord, she shall be praised."* *

MYRNA

Literal Meaning: "POLITE, GENTLE" — Gaelic
Suggested Character Quality: GENTLE SPIRIT
Suggested Lifetime Scripture Verse: Psalm 52:8 *"But I am like a green olive tree in the house of God; I trust in God's lovingkindness for ever and ever."*

MYRON

Literal Meaning: FRAGRANT OINTMENT
Suggested Character Quality: STRONG
Suggested Lifetime Scripture Verse: Proverbs 24:5 *"A wise man is strong; yea, a man of knowledge increaseth strength."* *

MYRTLE

Literal Meaning: THE MYRTLE
Suggested Character Quality: FULL OF PRAISE
Suggested Lifetime Scripture Verse: Isaiah 55:12 *"For you shall go out with joy and be led forth in peace, the mountains and the hills breaking out in song before you and all the trees of the field clapping their hands."*
Explanation: The Myrtle tree was often used to signify thanksgiving in biblical times.

NADINE

Literal Meaning: HOPE
Suggested Character Quality: HOPEFUL ONE
Suggested Lifetime Scripture Verse: Isaiah 26:4 *"Trust in the Lord forever, for the Lord God is the Rock of Ages."*

NAN

Literal Meaning: GRACE
Suggested Character Quality: GRACIOUS ONE
Suggested Lifetime Scripture Verse: Hebrews 12:28 *"Let us have grace whereby we may serve God acceptably with reverence and godly fear."* *

NANCY

Literal Meaning: GRACE
Suggested Character Quality: GRACIOUS ONE
Suggested Lifetime Scripture Verse: Hebrews 12:28 *"Let us have grace, whereby we may serve God acceptably with reverence and godly fear."*

NANETTE

Literal Meaning: GRACE
Suggested Character Quality: FULL OF GRACE
Suggested Lifetime Scripture Verse: Hebrews 12:28 *"Let us have grace, whereby we may serve God acceptably with reverence and godly fear."* *

NAOMI

Literal Meaning: THE PLEASANT ONE
Suggested Character Quality: PLEASANT SPIRIT
Suggested Lifetime Scripture Verse: Proverbs 16:24 *"Pleasant words are as a honeycomb, sweet to the soul and healing to the bones."*

NATALIE

Literal Meaning: "BIRTHDAY OF CHRIST" — Latin
Suggested Character Quality: JOYOUS CELEBRATION
Suggested Lifetime Scripture Verse: Psalm 9:2 *"I will be glad and rejoice in Thee, I will sing praise to Thy name, O most High."*
Explanation: The season of Christ's birthday is characterized by joy.

NATE

Literal Meaning: A GIFT
Suggested Character Quality: GIVEN OF GOD
Suggested Lifetime Scripture Verse: Isaiah 43:10 *"You are My witnesses, says the Lord, and My servant whom I have chosen, in order that you may know and believe Me, and understand that I am He. Before Me no God was formed, nor shall there be after Me."* *

NATHAN

Literal Meaning: A GIFT
Suggested Character Quality: GIVEN OF GOD
Suggested Lifetime Scripture Verse: Isaiah 43:10 *"You are My witnesses, says the Lord, and My servant whom I have chosen, in order that you may know and believe Me, and understand that I am He. Before Me no God was formed, nor shall there be after Me."*

NATHANIEL

Literal Meaning: A GIFT
Suggested Character Quality: GIVEN OF GOD
Suggested Lifetime Scripture Verse: Isaiah 43:10 *"You are My witnesses, says the Lord, and My servant whom I have chosen, in order that you may know and believe Me, and understand that I am He. Before Me no God was formed, nor shall there be after Me."*

NEAL

Literal Meaning: CHAMPION
Suggested Character Quality: CHAMPION
Suggested Lifetime Scripture Verse: Philippians 3:14 *"I push on to the goal for the prize of God's heavenly call in Christ Jesus."*

NED

Literal Meaning: PROTECTOR OF PROPERTY; PROTECTOR OF THE RICH
Suggested Character Quality: PROSPEROUS GUARDIAN
Suggested Lifetime Scripture Verse: Psalm 37:37 *"Watch the upright and observe the righeous, for there is a future to the man of peace."*

NEELY

Literal Meaning: LIGHT
Suggested Character Quality: BRINGER OF LIGHT
Suggested Lifetime Scripture Verse: Psalm 18:28 *"For Thou wilt light my candle: the Lord my God will enlighten my darkness."* *

NEIL

Literal Meaning: CHAMPION
Suggested Character Quality: CHAMPION
Suggested Lifetime Scripture Verse: Philippians 3:14 *"I push on to the goal for the prize of God's heavenly call in Christ Jesus."*

NEISHA

Literal Meaning: BOLD
Suggested Character Quality: BOLD ONE
Suggested Lifetime Scripture Verse: Proverbs 28:1 *"The wicked flee when no man pursueth: but the righteous are bold as a lion."* *

NEL

Literal Meaning: LIGHT
Suggested Character Quality: BRIGHT ONE
Suggested Lifetime Scripture Verse: Psalm 37:6 *"And He shall bring forth thy righteousness as the light, and thy judgment as the noonday."* *

NELDA

Literal Meaning: FROM A HOME AT THE ELDER TREE
Suggested Character Quality: FULL OF LIFE
Suggested Lifetime Scripture Verse: Psalm 36:7 & 9 *"How excellent is Thy lovingkindness, O God! Therefore the children of men put their trust under the shadow of Thy wings. For with Thee is the fountain of life: in Thy light shall we see light."* *

NELLY

Literal Meaning: LIGHT
Suggested Character Quality: BRIGHT ONE
Suggested Lifetime Scripture Verse: Psalm 37:6 *"And He shall bring forth thy righteousness as the light, and thy judgment as the noonday."* *

NELS

Literal Meaning: CHAMPION'S SON
Suggested Character Quality: CHAMPION
Suggested Lifetime Scripture Verse: Philippians 3:14 *"I push on to the goal for the prize of God's heavenly call in Christ Jesus."*

NELSON

Literal Meaning: SON OF NEIL
Suggested Character Quality: CHAMPION
Suggested Lifetime Scripture Verse: Philippians 3:14 *"I push on to the goal for the prize of God's heavenly call in Christ Jesus."*

NELVINA

Literal Meaning: LIGHT
Suggested Character Quality: LIGHT BEARER
Suggested Lifetime Scripture Verse: Psalm 37:6 *"And He shall bring forth thy righteousness as the light, and thy judgment as the noonday."* *

NEOLA

Literal Meaning: THE NEW (LATIN)
Suggested Character Quality: YOUTHFUL ONE
Suggested Lifetime Scripture Verse: Psalm 103:2, 5 *"Bless the Lord, O my soul, and forget not all His benefits: Who satisfieth thy mouth with good things; so that thy youth is renewed like the eagle's."* *

NESTOR

Literal Meaning: AGED WISDOM (GREEK)
Suggested Character Quality: WISE DISCERNER
Suggested Lifetime Scripture Verse: Psalm 111:10 *"The fear of the Lord is the beginning of wisdom: a good understanding have all they that do His commandments: his praise endureth forever."* *

NETHA

Literal Meaning: UNKNOWN
Suggested Character Quality: PURE ONE
Suggested Lifetime Scripture Verse: II Timothy 2:22 *"Flee also youthful lusts: but follow righteousness, faith, charity, peace, with them that call on the Lord out of pure heart."* *

NETTIE

Literal Meaning: SUPER EXCELLENT; THE BRIGHT, PURE AND NEAT
Suggested Character Quality: FAIR LADY
Suggested Lifetime Scripture Verse: Psalm 9:1 *"I will praise Thee, O Lord, with my whole heart; I will show forth all Thy marvelous works."* *

NEVA

Literal Meaning: SNOW; EXTREME WHITENESS
Suggested Character Quality: PURE ONE
Suggested Lifetime Scripture Verse: Titus 1:15a *"Unto the pure all things are pure . . ."* *

NEVILLE

Literal Meaning: FROM THE NEW TOWN
Suggested Character Quality: INDUSTRIOUS
Suggested Lifetime Scriture Verse: Acts 20:35 *"I have showed you all things, how that so laboring ye ought to support the weak, and to remember the words of the Lord Jesus, how He said, it is more blessed to give than to receive."* *

NEWELL

Literal Meaning: A KERNEL OR SEED
Suggested Character Quality: FRUITFUL ONE
Suggested Lifetime Scripture Verse: Psalm 1:3 *"And he shall be like a tree planted by the rivers of water, that bringeth forth his fruit in his season; his leaf also shall not wither; and whatsoever he doeth shall prosper."* *

NICHOLAS

Literal Meaning: "VICTORY OF THE PEOPLE" — Greek
Suggested Character Quality: VICTORIOUS HEART
Suggested Lifetime Scripture Verse: Psalm 18:46 *"The Lord lives; blessed be my rock, and exalted be the God of my salvation."*

NICK

Literal Meaning: "VICTORY OF THE PEOPLE" — Greek
Suggested Character Quality: VICTORIOUS SPIRIT
Suggested Lifetime Scripture Verse: Psalm 18:46 *"The Lord lives; blessed be my rock, and exalted be the God of my salvation."*

NICO

Literal Meaning: VICTORIOUS PEOPLE (GREEK)
Suggested Character Quality: VICTORIOUS SPIRIT
Suggested Lifetime Scripture Verse: Psalm 18:46 *"The Lord lives; blessed be my rock, and exalted be the God of my salvation."*

NICOLE

Literal Meaning: VICTORY OF THE PEOPLE
Suggested Character Quality: VICTORIOUS HEART
Suggested Lifetime Scripture Verse: Job 23:11 *"My feet have stayed steady in His path; I have kept His way and have never swerved aside."*

NIGEL

Literal Meaning: DARK; BLACK
Suggested Character Qualty: COURAGEOUS SPIRIT
Suggested Lifetime Scripture Verse: Philippians 4:13 *"I can do all things through Christ which strengtheneth me."* *

NILES

Literal Meaning: CHAMPION
Suggested Character Quality: CHAMPION
Suggested Lifetime Scripture Verse: Philippians 3:14 *"I push on to the goal for the prize of God's heavenly call in Christ Jesus."*

NILSA

Literal Meaning: CHAMPION
Suggested Character Quality: VICTORIOUS SPIRIT
Suggested Lifetime Scripture Verse: I John 5:4 *"For whatsoever is born of God overcometh the world: and this is the victory that overcometh the world, even our faith."* *

NINA

Literal Meaning: LITTLE GIRL (SPANISH)
Suggested Character Quality: CHILD OF GOD
Suggested Lifetime Scripture Verse: Ephesians 5:1, 2 *"Be ye therefore followers of God as dear children: and walk in love, as Christ also hath loved us, and hath given Himself for us an offering and a sacrifice to God for a sweetsmelling savor."* *

NINETTE

Literal Meaning: LITTLE GIRL (FRENCH)
Suggested Character Quality: CHILD OF GOD
Suggested Lifetime Scripture Verse: Ephesians 5:1, 2 *"Be ye therefore followers of God as dear children: and walk in love, as Christ also hath loved us, and hath given Himself for us an offering and a sacrifice to God for a sweetsmelling savor."* *

NISSA

Literal Meaning: AN ELF (SCANDINAVIAN)
Suggested Character Quality: FRIENDLY
Suggested Lifetime Scripture Verse: I John 4:7 *"Beloved, let us love one another: for love is of God; and everyone that loveth is born of God, and knoweth God."* *

NITA

Literal Meaning: GRACE
Suggested Character Quality: GRACIOUS ONE
Suggested Lifetime Scripture Verse: Isaiah 30:18 *"Nevertheless the Lord longs to be gracious to you! Therefore He shall rise up to bestow mercy on you; for the Lord is a God of Justice. Blessed are they who wait for Him."*

NOAH

Literal Meaning: REST; COMFORT (HEBREW)
Suggested Character Quality: COMFORTER
Suggested Lifetime Scripture Verse: I Thessalonians 5:14 *"Now we exhort you, brethren, warn them that are unruly, comfort the feebleminded, support the weak, be patient toward all men."* *

NOBLE

Literal Meaning: WELL-KNOWN AND NOBLE
Suggested Character Quality: MAN OF HONOR
Suggested Lifetime Scripture Verse: Psalm 112:6 *"Such a man will never be laid low, for the just shall be held in remembrance for ever."*

NOEL

Literal Meaning: "BIRTHDAY OF CHRIST" — French
Suggested Character Quality: JOYFUL CELEBRATION
Suggested Lifetime Scripture Verse: Psalm 9:1 *"I will praise the Lord with my whole heart; I will tell of all Thy marvelous works."*

NOLAN

Literal Meaning: NOBLE (IRISH)
Suggested Character Quality: NOBLE
Suggested Lifetime Scripture Verse: II Timothy 4:8 *"Henceforth there is laid up for me a crown of righteousness, which the Lord, the righteous judge, shall give me that day: and not to me only, but unto all them also that love His appearing.'* *

NOLE

Literal Meaning: PEACE
Suggested Character Quality: PEACEFUL
Suggested Lifetime Scripture Verse: Colossians 3:15 *"And let the peace of God rule in your hearts, to the which also ye are called in one body; and be ye thankful."* *

NOLEEN

Literal Meaning: FAMOUS-WELL KNOWN
Suggested Character Quality: ESTEEMED ONE
Suggested Lifetime Scripture Verse: Matthew 20:27 *"And whosoever will be chief amoung you, let him be your servant."* *

NORA

Literal Meaning: NOBLE
Suggested Character Quality: FULL OF HONOR
Suggested Lifetime Scripture Verse: Lamentations 3:26 *"It is good if one hopes and quietly waits for the salvation of the Lord."*

NORBERT

Literal Meaning: BRILLIANT ONE
Suggested Character Quality: IN GOD'S LIGHT
Suggested Lifetime Scripture Verse: Psalm 16:8 *"I have placed the Lord before me continually; because He is at my right hand, I shall not be moved."*

NORMA

Literal Meaning: A RULE; A PATTERN OR PRECEPT
Suggested Character Quality: EXAMPLES OF GODLINESS
Suggested Lifetime Scripture Verse: I Timothy 4:8 *". . . Godliness is beneficial in every way; it holds promise for this present and for the future life "*

NORMAN

Literal Meaning: A NORTHMAN
Suggested Character Quality: STRONG; MANLY
Suggested Lifetime Scripture Verse: Joshua 1:9 *"Have I not commanded you? Be resolute and stong! Be not afraid, and be not dismayed; for the Lord your God is with you everywhere you go."*

NORRIS

Literal Meaning: NURSE — Occupational Name
Suggested Character Quality: HELPFUL SPIRIT
Suggested Lifetime Scripture Verse: Romans 15:14 *"I myself am convinced about you, my brothers, that you are full of goodness, amply furnished with knowledge, and competent to advise one another."*

NORTON

Literal Meaning: COMES FROM THE NORTH TOWN
Suggested Character Quality: WALKS WITH GOD
Suggested Lifetime Scripture Verse: I Thessalonians 2:12 *"That ye would walk worthy of God, who hath called you unto His kingdom and glory."* *

NOVA

Literal Meaning: THE NEW
Suggested Character Quality: BORN ANEW
Suggested Lifetime Scripture Verse: I John 4:7 *"Beloved, let us love one another: for love is God; and everyone that loveth is born of God, and knoweth God."* *

NOVIS

Literal Meaning: CHASING A BUTTERFLY
Suggested Character Quality: FAIR LADY
Suggested Lifetime Scripture Verse: Proverbs 31:31 *"Give her of the fruit of her hands; and let her own works praise her in the gates."*

ODEAN

Literal Meaning: VALLEY
Suggested Character Quality: ABUNDANT LIFE
Suggested Lifetime Scripture Verse: John 10:7, 10 *"Then said Jesus unto them again . . . The thief cometh not, but for to steal, and to kill, and to destroy: I am come that they might have life, and that they might have it more abundantly."* *

ODEN

Literal Meaning: WEALTHY MAN
Suggested Character Quality: RICH IN BLESSINGS
Suggested Lifetime Scripture Verse: Proverbs 10:22 *"The blessing of the Lord, it maketh rich, and He addeth no sorrow with it."* *

ODIN

Literal Meaning: WEALTHY MAN
Suggested Character Quality: RICH IN BLESSINGS
Suggested Lifetime Scripture Verse: Proverbs 10:22 *"The blessing of the Lord, it maketh rich, and He addeth no sorrow with it."* *

OKE

Literal Meaning: IN THE MIDDLE OF THE SEA
Suggested Character Quality: GENEROUS SPIRIT
Suggested Lifetime Scripture Verse: Proverbs 19:17 *"He that hath pity upon the poor lendeth unto the Lord; and that which he hath given will he pay him again."* *
Explanation: The sea suggests deepness and openess; generosity.

OLA

Literal Meaning: ANCESTOR; PEACE
Suggested Character Quality: PEACEFUL
Suggested Lifetime Scripture Verse: Colossians 3:15 *"And let the peace of God rule in your hearts, to the which also ye are called in one body; and be ye thankful."* *

OLAF

Literal Meaning: ANCESTOR; PEACE
Suggested Character Quality: FULL WISDOM
Suggested Lifetime Scripture Verse: James 3:17 *"But the wisdom that is from above is first pure, then peaceable, gentle, and easy to be entreated, full of mercy and good fruits, without partiality, and without hypocrisy."* *

OLEDA

Literal Meaning: GLADNESS
Suggested Character Quality: JOYFUL SPIRIT
Suggested Lifetime Scripture Verse: Psalm 105:3 *"Glory ye in His holy name: let the heart of them rejoice that seek the Lord."* *

OLENDA

Literal Meaning: LIGHT
Suggested Character Quality: BRINGER OF LIGHT
Suggested Lifetime Scripture Verse: I Thessalonians 5:5 *"Ye are all the children of light, and the children of the day: we are not of the night, nor of darkness."* *

OLETA

Literal Meaning: GLADNESS
Suggested Character Quality: JOYFUL SPIRIT
Suggested Lifetime Scripture Verse: Psalms 105:3 *"Glory ye in His holy name: let the heart of them rejoice that seek that Lord."* *

OLGA

Literal Meaning: PEACE
Suggested Character Quality: PEACEFUL
Suggested Lifetime Scripture Verse: Isaiah 32:17 *"And the work of righteousness shall be peace; and the effect of righteousness quietness and assurance forever."* *

OLIVE

Literal Meaning: OLIVE TREE OR OLIVE BRANCH
Suggested Character Quality: PEACEFUL SPIRIT
Suggested Lifetime Scripture Verse: Proverbs 16:24 *"Pleasant words are as an honeycomb, sweet to the soul, and health to the bones."* *

OLIVER

Literal Meaning: "OLIVE TREE" — Latin
Suggested Character Quality: PEACEFUL HEART
Suggested Lifetime Scripture Verse: Philippians 4:7 *"So will the peace of God, that surpasses all understanding, keep guard over your hearts and your thoughts in Christ Jesus."*

OLIVIA

Literal Meaning: OLIVE BRANCH
Suggested Character Quality: PEACEFUL SPIRIT
Suggested Lifetime Scripture Verse: Proverbs 16:24 *"Pleasant words are as an honeycomb, sweet to the soul, and health to the bones."* *

OLLIE

Literal Meaning: OLIVE; PEACE
Suggested Character Quality: PEACEFUL HEART
Suggested Lifetime Scripture Verse: Philippians 4:7 *"So will the peace of God, that surpasses all understanding, keep guard over your hearts and your thoughts in Christ Jesus."*

OMAR

Literal Meaning: FIRST SON; MOST HIGH; RICHNESS
Suggested Character Quality: NOBLE SPIRIT
Suggested Lifetime Scripture Verse: Ephesians 4:24 *"And that ye put on the new man, which after God is created in righteousness and true holiness."* *

OPAL

Literal Meaning: A PRECIOUS STONE
Suggested Character Quality: EXCELLENT CHARACTER
Suggested Lifetime Scripture Verse: Colossians 3:12 *"Put on therefore, as the elect of God, holy and beloved, bowels of mercies, kindness, humbleness of mind, meekness, longsuffering."* *

ORA

Literal Meaning: GOLDEN
Suggested Character Quality: GOOD HEART
Suggested Lifetime Scripture Verse: Ephesians 4:32 *"Be kind toward one another, tenderhearted, forgiving one another, even as God has in Christ forgiven you."*
Explanation: A heart of gold is a good heart.

ORAN

Literal Meaning: THE PINE
Suggested Character Quality: STEADFAST ENDURANCE
Suggested Lifetime Scripture Verse: I Corinthians 15:58 *"Be steadfast, immovable, at all times abounding in the Lord's service, aware that your labor in the Lord is not futile."*

ORDELIA

Literal Meaning: ELF IN JUDGMENT
Suggested Character Quality: WISE
Suggested Lifetime Scripture Verse: Proverbs 31:26 *"She openeth her mouth with wisdom; and in her tongue is the law of kindness."* *

ORDELL

Literal Meaning: UNKNOWN
Suggested Character Quality: BELOVED ONE
Suggested Lifetime Scripture Verse: I John 2:5 *"But whoso keepeth His word, in him verily is the love of God perfected: hereby know we that we are in Him."* *

ORELL

Literal Meaning: THE LISTENER
Suggested Character Quality: COMPASSIONATE
Suggested Lifetime Scripture Verse: I Peter 3:8 *"Finally, be ye all of one mind, having compassion one of another, love as brethren, be pitiful, be courteous."* *

ORIN

Literal Meaning: PINE
Suggested Character Quality: STEADFAST ENDURANCE
Suggested Lifetime Scripture Verse: I Corinthians 15:58 *"Be steadfast, immovable, at all times abounding in the Lord's service, aware that your labor in the Lord is not futile."*

ORINDA

Literal Meaning: MAGIC POWER
Suggested Character Quality: STRONG IN SPIRIT
Suggested Lifetime Scripture Verse: Isaiah 26:4 *"Trust ye in the Lord forever: for in the Lord Jehovah is everlasting strength."* *

ORLANDA

Literal Meaning: FAME OF THE LAND
Suggested Character Quality: STRONG & WOMANLY
Suggested Lifetime Scripture Verse: Psalm 138:3 *"In the day when I cried Thou answeredst me, and strengthendst me with strength in my soul."* *

ORLANDO

Literal Meaning: FAME OF THE LAND
Suggested Character Quality: STRONG; MANLY
Suggested Lifetime Scripture Verse: Psalm 18:2 *"The Lord is my rock, and my fortress, and my deliverer; my God, my strength, in whom I will trust; my buckler, and the horn of my salvation, and my high tower."* *

ORLEAN

Literal Meaning: THE GOLDEN
Suggested Character Quality: PRICELESS ONE
Suggested Lifetime Scripture Verse: Proverbs 31:10 *"Who can find a virtuous woman? for her price is far above rubies."* *

ORLENA

Literal Meaning: GOLDEN
Suggested Character Quality: PRICELESS ONE
Suggested Lifetime Scripture Verse: Proverbs 31:10 *"Who can find a virtuous woman? for her price is far above rubies."* *

ORLIN

Literal Meaning: ORSON: BEAR, LINN: WATERFALLS
Suggested Character Quality: STRONG ONE
Suggested Lifetime Scripture Verse: Proverbs 24:5 *"A wise man is strong; yea, a man of knowledge increaseth strength."* *

ORMA

Literal Meaning: FAMOUS
Suggested Character Quality: STRENGTH OF CHARACTER
Suggested Lifetime Scripture Verse: Proverbs 31:25 *"Strength and honor are her clothing; and she shall rejoice in time to come."* *

ORMAN

Literal Meaning: SHIP MAN; FAMED MAN
Suggested Character Quality: STRONG ONE
Suggested Lifetime Scripture Verse: Psalm 18:1 *"I will love Thee, O Lord, my strength."* *

ORVILLE

Literal Meaning: FROM THE GOLDEN ESTATE
Suggested Character Quality: MAN OF RENOWN
Suggested Lifetime Scripture Verse: Psalm 104:1 *"Bless the Lord, O my soul. O Lord my God, Thou art very great; Thou art clothed with honor and majesty."* *

ORVIN

Literal Meaning: SPEAR — FRIEND, GOD FRIEND
Suggested Character Quality: FAITHFUL FRIEND
Suggested Lifetime Scripture Verse: Proverbs 27:9 *"Ointment and perfume rejoice the heart: so doth the sweetness of man's friend by hearty counsel."* *

ORVIS

Literal Meaning: UNKNOWN
Suggested Character Quality: PEACEFUL SPIRIT
Suggested Lifetime Scripture Verse: Psalm 23:1, 2 *"The Lord is my shepherd; I shall not want. He maketh me to lie down in green pastures: He leadeth me beside the still waters."* *

OSCAR

Literal Meaning: DIVINE SPIRIT
Suggested Character Quality: BLESSED IN SERVICE
Suggested Lifetime Scripture Verse: Psalm 5:12 *"Thou, O Lord, dost bless the righteous; as with a shield thou dost surround him with favor."*

OSWALD

Literal Meaning: DIVINE POWER
Suggested Character Quality: IN GOD'S STRENGTH
Suggested Lifetime Scripture Verse: Isaiah 40:31 *"But they that wait upon the Lord shall renew their strength; they shall mount up with wings of eagles; they shall run, and not be weary; and they shall walk, and not faint."**

OTIS

Literal Meaning: KEEN OF HEARING (GREEK)
Suggested Character Quality: ATTENTIVE SPIRIT
Suggested Lifetime Scripture Verse: Proverbs 8:34, 35 *"Blessed is the man that heareth me, watching daily at my gates, waiting at the posts of my doors. For whoso findeth me, findeth life, and shall obtain favor of the Lord."**

OTTO

Literal Meaning: PROSPEROUS; WEALTHY ONE (GERMAN)
Suggested Character Quality: PROSPEROUS ONE
Suggested Lifetime Scripture Verse: Psalm 37:3 *"Trust in the Lord, and do good; so shalt thou dwell in the land, and verily thou shalt be fed."**

OVETTA

Literal Meaning: ETTA — THE LITTLE
Suggested Character Quality: LIVELY
Suggested Lifetime Scripture Verse: Psalm 40:3 *"And He hath put a new song in my mouth, even praise unto our God: many shall see it, and fear, and shall trust in the Lord."**

OWEN

Literal Meaning: "YOUTH" — Welsh
Suggested Character Quality: YOUTHFUL HEART
Suggested Lifetime Scripture Verse: Psalm 103:2, 5 *"Bless the Lord, O my soul, and forget not all His benefits, . . . who satisfies you throughout life with good things, so that your youth is renewed like the eagle's."*

PAIGE

Literal Meaning: ATTENDANT
Suggested Character Quality: OBEDIENT SPIRIT
Suggested Lifetime Scripture Verse: Proverbs 15:33 *"Reverence of the Lord is the instruction of wisdom, for before honor must be humility."*

PALMER

Literal Meaning: PILGRIM (LATIN)
Suggested Character Quality: SEEKING HEART
Suggested Lifetime Scripture Verse: Matthew 6:33 *"But seek ye first the kingdom of God, and His righteousness; and all these things shall be added unto you."* *

PAM

Literal Meaning: LOVING; KIND; ALL HONEY
Suggested Character Quality: SWEET SPIRIT
Suggested Lifetime Scripture Verse: Proverbs 16:24 *"Pleasant words are as a honeycomb, sweet to the soul and healing to the bones."*

PAMELA

Literal Meaning: ALL HONEY
Suggested Character Quality: SWEET SPIRIT
Suggested Lifetime Scripture Verse: Proverbs 16:24 *"Pleasant words are as a honeycomb, sweet to the soul and healing to the bones."*

PARKE

Literal Meaning: DWELLER AT THE PARK
Suggested Character Quality: JOYOUS SPIRIT
Suggested Lifetime Scripture Verse: Psalm 16:11 *"Thou wilt show me the path of life: in Thy presence is fulness of joy; at Thy right hand there are pleasures for evermore."* *

PARKER

Literal Meaning: PARK KEEPER
Suggested Character Quality: GREAT PROTECTOR
Suggested Lifetime Scripture Verse: Psalm 121:5 *"The Lord is thy keeper: the Lord is thy shade upon thy right hand."* *

PAT (F)
Literal Meaning: NOBLE ONE
Suggested Character Quality: FULL OF HONOR
Suggested Lifetime Scripture Verse: Psalm 62:7 *"My salvation and my glory depend on God; the rock of my defense, my refuge is in God."*

PAT (M)
Literal Meaning: "OF NOBLE BIRTH" — Latin
Suggested Character Quality: FULL OF HONOR
Suggested Lifetime Scripture Verse: Psalm 26:3 *"For Thy lovingkindness is before my eyes, and I have walked in Thy truth."*

PATIENCE
Literal Meaning: PATIENCE
Suggested Character Quality: PATIENT
Suggested Lifetime Scripture Verse: James 1:4 *"But let patience have her perfect work, that ye may be perfect and entire, wanting nothing."* *

PATRICE
Literal Meaning: NOBLE ONE
Suggested Character Quality: FULL OF HONOR
Suggested Lifetime Scripture Verse: Psalm 62:7 *"My salvation and my glory depend on God; the rock of my defense, my refuge is in God."*

PATRICIA
Literal Meaning: NOBLE ONE
Suggested Character Quality: FULL OF HONOR
Suggested Lifetime Scripture Verse: Psalm 62:7 *"My salvation and my glory depend on God; the rock of my defense, my refuge is in God."*

PATRICK
Literal Meaning: NOBLE ONE
Suggested Character Quality: FULL OF HONOR
Suggested Lifetime Scripture Verse: Psalm 62:7 *"My salvation and my glory depend on God; the rock of my defense, my refuge is in God."*

PATSY
Literal Meaning: NOBLE ONE
Suggested Character Quality: FULL OF HONOR
Suggested Lifetime Scripture Verse: Psalm 62:7 *"My salvation and my glory depend on God; the rock of my defense, my refuge is in God."*

PATTI
Literal Meaning: NOBLE ONE
Suggested Character Quality: FULL OF HONOR
Suggested Lifetime Scripture Verse: Psalm 62:7 *"My salvation and my glory depend on God; the rock of my defense, my refuge is in God."*

PATTY

Literal Meaning: NOBLE ONE
Suggested Character Quality: FULL OF HONOR
Suggested Lifetime Scripture Verse: Psalm 62:7 *"My salvation and my glory depend on God; the rock of my defense, my refuge is in God."*

PAUL

Literal Meaning: LITTLE
Suggested Character Quality: DEPENDENT ON GOD
Suggested Lifetime Scripture Verse: Psalm 73:28 *"But as for me, drawing near to God is good for me; I have made the Lord my refuge, so that I may announce all Thy works."*

PAULA

Literal Meaning: LITTLE
Suggested Character Quality: DEPENDENT ON GOD
Suggested Lifetime Scripture Verse: Psalm 73:28 *"But as for me, drawing near to God is good for me; I have made the Lord my refuge, so that I may announce all Thy works."*

PAULETTE

Literal Meaning: LITTLE
Suggested Character Quality: DEPENDENT ON GOD
Suggested Lifetime Scripture Verse: Psalm 73:28 *"But as for me, drawing near to God is good for me; I have made the Lord my refuge, so that I may announce all Thy works."*

PAULINE

Literal Meaning: LITTLE
Suggested Character Quality: DEPENDENT ON GOD
Suggested Lifetime Scripture Verse: Psalm 73:28 *"But as for me, drawing near to God is good for me; I have made the Lord my refuge, so that I may announce all Thy works."*

PEARCE

Literal Meaning: ROCK OR STONE
Suggested Character Quality: STRONG IN SPIRIT
Suggested Lifetime Scripture Verse: Psalm 18:32 *"It is God that girdeth me with strength, and maketh my way perfect."* *

PEARL

Literal Meaning: "A JEWEL" — Latin
Suggested Character Quality: PURE HEART
Suggested Lifetime Scripture Verse: Psalm 33:1 *"Rejoice, ye righteous, in the Lord; praise becomes the upright!"*
Explanation: A pearl is the symbol of purity.

PEDER

Literal Meaning: ROCK; STONE
Suggested Character Quality: STRONG IN HEART
Suggested Lifetime Scripture Verse: Psalm 27:14 *"Wait for the Lord, take courage, and He will give strength to your heart; yes, wait for the Lord."*

PEGGY

Literal Meaning: A PEARL
Suggested Character Quality: PRECIOUS ONE
Suggested Lifetime Scripture Verse: Matthew 5:8 *"Blessed are the pure in heart: for they shall see God."* *

PENNY

Literal Meaning: "WEAVER" — Greek
Suggested Character Quality: CREATIVE SPIRIT
Suggested Lifetime Scripture Verse: Psalm 51:10 *"Create in me a clean heart, O God, and renew a steadfast spirit within me."*
Explanation: One who weaves creates.

PEPIN

Literal Meaning: PERSERVERANT; PETITIONER
Suggested Character Quality: PERSERVERANT
Suggested Lifetime Scripture Verse: Ephesians 6:18 *"Praying always with all prayer and supplication in the Spirit, and watching thereunto with all perserverance and supplication for all saints."* *

PERCY

Literal Meaning: THE PERCEPTIVE
Suggested Character Quality: SEEKER OF WISDOM
Suggested Lifetime Scripture Verse: Psalm 111:10 *"The fear of the Lord is the beginning of wisdom: a good understanding have all they that do His commandments: His praise endureth forever."* *

PERRIN

Literal Meaning: PEAR TREE
Suggested Character Quality: ABUNDANT PROVIDER
Suggested Lifetime Scripture Verse: Psalm 1:3 *"And he shall be like a tree planted by the rivers of water, that bringeth forth his fruit in his season; his leaf also shall not wither; and whatsoever he doeth shall prosper."* *

PERRY

Literal Meaning: PEAR TREE
Suggested Character Quality: ABUNDANT PROVIDER
Suggested Lifetime Scripture Verse: Psalm 1:3 *"And he shall be like a tree planted by the rivers of water, that bringeth forth his fruit in his season; his leaf also shall not wither; and whatsoever he doeth shall prosper."* *

PETE

Literal Meaning: ROCK
Suggested Character Quality: STRONG IN SPIRIT
Suggested Lifetime Scripture Verse: Psalm 27:14 *"Wait for the Lord; take courage, and He will give strength to your heart; yes, wait for the Lord."*

PETER

Literal Meaning: ROCK
Suggested Character Quality: STRONG IN SPIRIT
Suggested Lifetime Scripture Verse: Psalm 27:14 *"Wait for the Lord, take courage, and He will give strength to your heart; yes, wait for the Lord."*

PETRINA

Literal Meaning: A ROCK
Suggested Character Quality: STRONG IN SPIRIT
Suggested Lifetime Scripture Verse: Psalm 18:2 *"The Lord is my rock, and my fortress, and my deliverer; my God, my strength, in Whom I trust; my buckler, and the horn of my salvation, and my high tower."* *

PHIL

Literal Meaning: LOVER OF HORSES
Suggested Character Quality: STRONG IN SPIRIT
Suggested Lifetime Scripture Verse: Matthew 6:33 *"But you, seek first His kingdom and His righteousness and all these things will be added to you."*
Explanation: See Philip

PHILIP

Literal Meaning: LOVER OF HORSES
Suggested Character Quality: STRONG IN SPIRIT
Suggested Lifetime Scripture Verse: Matthew 6:33 *"But you, seek first His kingdom and His righteousness and all these things will be added to you."*
Explanation: Characteristically, a lover of horses has a strong, free spirit with an element of sensitivity.

PHILIPPA

Literal Meaning: LOVER OF HORSES
Suggested Character Quality: TENDERHEARTED
Suggested Lifetime Scripture Verse: Ephesians 4:32 *"And be ye kind one to another, tenderhearted, forgiving one another, even as God for Christ's sake hath forgiven you."* *
Explanation: See Philip

PHILLIP

Literal Meaning: LOVER OF HORSES
Suggested Character Quality: STRONG IN SPIRIT
Suggested Lifetime Scripture Verse: Matthew 6:33 *"But you, seek first His kingdom and His righteousness and all these things will be added to you."*
Explanation: See Philip

PHILOMENA
Literal Meaning: FRIENDLY; LOVING (GREEK)
Suggested Character Quality: LOVING FRIEND
Suggested Lifetime Scripture Verse: Proverbs 17:17 *"A friend loveth at all times . . ."* *

PHOEBE
Literal Meaning: RADIANT; BRIGHT
Suggested Character Quality: SHINING RADIANCE
Suggested Lifetime Scripture Verse: Proverbs 4:18 *"But the path of the just is as the shining light, that shineth more and more unto the perfect day."* *

PHYLLIS
Literal Meaning: LEAF
Suggested Character Quality: TENDERHEARTED
Suggested Lifetime Scripture Verse: Psalm 116:1 *"I love the Lord, for He hears my voice, my supplications."*

PIERCE
Literal Meaning: ROCK; STONE
Suggested Character Quality: STRONG IN SPIRIT
Suggested Lifetime Scripture Verse: Psalm 18:32 *"It is God that girdeth me with strenth, and maketh my way perfect."* *

PIPER
Literal Meaning: ONE WHO PIPES
Suggested Character Quality: CHEERFUL ONE
Suggested Lifetime Scripture Verse: Psalm 35:9 *"And my soul shall be joyful in the Lord: it shall rejoice in His salvation."* *

PIXIE
Literal Meaning: A MISCHIEVOUS ELF
Suggested Character Quality: FULL OF JOY
Suggested Lifetime Scripture Verse: Isaiah 61:10a *"I will greatly rejoice in the Lord, my soul shall be joyful in my God . . ."* *

PLACID
Literal Meaning: PEACEFUL; UNDISTURBED
Suggested Character Quality: PEACEFUL
Suggested Lifetime Scripture Verse: Psalm 119:165 *"Great peace have they which love Thy law: and nothing shall offend them."* *

POLLY
Literal Meaning: BITTER; MYRRH
Suggested Character Quality: LIVING FRAGRANCE
Suggested Lifetime Scripture Verse: II Corinthians 2:15 *"For we are unto God a sweet savor of Christ, in them that are saved, and in them that perish."* *

POLLYANNA

Literal Meaning: BITTER; MYRRH; GRACIOUS
Suggested Character Quality: GRACIOUS FRAGRANCE
Suggested Lifetime Scripture Verse: II Corinthians 9:8 *"And God is able to make all grace abound toward you; that ye, always having all sufficiency in all things, may abound to every good work."* *

PORTER

Literal Meaning: DOORKEEPER
Suggested Character Quality: WATCHFUL ONE
Suggested Lifetime Scripture Verse: Psalm 84:10 *"For a day in Thy courts is better than a thousand. I had rather be a doorkeeper in the house of my God, than to dwell in the tents of wickedness."* *

PRENTICE

Literal Meaning: LEARNER, APPRENTICE
Suggested Character Quality: INCREASING FAITHFULNESS
Suggested Lifetime Scripture Verse: Philippians 1:6 *"Being confident of this very thing, that He which hath begun a good work in you will perform it until the day of Jesus Christ."* *

PRESLEY

Literal Meaning: DWELLER AT THE PRIEST MEADOW
Suggested Character Quality: PEACEFUL SPIRIT
Suggested Lifetime Scripture Verse: Isaiah 26:3 *"Thou wilt keep him in perfect peace, whose mind is stayed on Thee; because he trusteth in Thee."* *

PRESTON

Literal Meaning: FROM THE PRIEST'S TOWN
Suggested Character Quality: NOBLE SERVANT
Suggested Lifetime Scripture Verse: I Kings 10:8 *"Happy are thy men, happy are these thy servants, which stand continually before thee, and that hear thy wisdom."* *

PRISCILLA

Literal Meaning: ANCIENT BIRTH
Suggested Character Quality: FULL OF HONOR
Suggested Lifetime Scripture Verse: Micah 7:7 *"I will wait on the Lord; I will hope in the God of my salvation; my God will hear me."*
Explanation: Ancient birth suggests an honorable family.

PRUDENCE

Literal Meaning: DISCRETION (LATIN)
Suggested Character Quality: WISE ONE
Suggested Lifetime Scripture Verse: James 3:17 *"But the wisdom that is from above is first pure, then peaceable, gentle, and easy to be entreated, full of mercy and good fruits, without partiality, and without hypocrisy."* *

QUENTIN

Literal Meaning: "FIFTH" — Latin
Suggested Character Quality: A MANLY HEART
Suggested Lifetime Scripture Verse: Psalm 50:23 *"He who offers a sacrifice of praise honors Me; to him who prepares his way I will show the salvation of God."*
Explanation: Five is used in Scripture as a symbol of man or humanity; therefore the number five in this case suggests manliness.

QUINN

Literal Meaning: WISE
Suggested Character Quality: FULL OF WISDOM
Suggested Lifetime Scripture Verse: Psalm: 111:10 *"For reverence of the Lord is the beginning of wisdom. There is insight in all who observe it. His praise is everlasting."*

RACHAEL

Literal Meaning: LITTLE LAMB
Suggested Character Quality: LITTLE LAMB
Suggested Lifetime Scripture Verse: Isaiah 40:11 *"He will feed His flock like a shepherd; He will gather the lambs in His arms, carrying them in His bosom and gently leading those that are with young."*

RACHEL

Literal Meaning: LITTLE LAMB
Suggested Character Quality: LITTLE LAMB
Suggested Lifetime Scripture Verse: Isaiah 40:11 *"He will feed His flock like a shepherd; He will gather the lambs in His arms, carrying them in His bosom and gently leading those that are with young."*

RACHELLE

Literal Meaning: LITTLE LAMB (FRENCH)
Suggested Character Quality: LITTLE LAMB
Suggested Lifetime Scripture Verse: Psalm 79:13 *"So we Thy people and the sheep of Thy pasture will give Thee thanks forever: we will show forth Thy praise to all generations."* *

RAE — FEMALE

Literal Meaning: LITTLE LAMB
Suggested Character Quality: LITTLE LAMB
Suggested Lifetime Scripture Verse: Isaiah 40:11 *"He will feed His flock like a shepherd; He will gather the lambs in His arms, carrying them in His bosom and gently leading those that are with young."*

RAE — MALE

Literal Meaning: THE KING
Suggested Character Quality: WISE PROTECTOR
Suggested Lifetime Scripture Verse: Proverbs 2:6 *"For the Lord giveth wisdom: out of His mouth cometh knowledge and understanding."* *

RAINIE

Literal Meaning: THE ROYAL; A QUEEN
Suggested Character Quality: CROWNED ONE
Suggested Lifetime Scripture Verse: Psalm 103:4 *"Who redeemeth thy life from destruction; who crowneth thee with lovingkindness and tender mercies."* *

RALEIGH

Literal Meaning: DWELLER AT THE ROE-DEER MEADOW
Suggested Character Quality: QUIET SPIRIT
Suggested Lifetime Scripture Verse: Isaiah 32:17 *"And the work of righteousness shall be peace; and the effect of righteousness quietness and assurance forever."* *

RALPH

Literal Meaning: WOLF-COUNSEL
Suggested Character Quality: BRAVE ADVISOR
Suggested Lifetime Scripture Verse: Proverbs 27:9 *"Oil and perfume make the heart rejoice, as does the pleasantness of a friend's suggestions from the heart."*

RAMONA

Literal Meaning: WISE PROTECTOR (SPANISH)
Suggested Character Quality: WISE GUARDIAN
Suggested Lifetime Scripture Verse: Daniel 12:3 *"And they that be wise shall shine as the brightness of the firmament; and they that turn many to righteousness as the stars forever and ever."* *

RAMSEY

Literal Meaning: WOODED; OR STRONG ISLAND
Suggested Character Quality: STEADFAST PROTECTION
Suggested Lifetime Scripture Verse: Ephesians 3:16 *"That He would grant you, according to the riches of His glory, to be strengthened with might by His Spirit in the inner man."* *

RANAE

Literal Meaning: BORN AGAIN
Suggested Character Quality: TRANSFORMED HEART
Suggested Lifetime Scripture Verse: Jeremiah 29:13 *"You will seek Me and find Me when you will seek Me with all your heart."*

RAND

Literal Meaning: SHIELD-WOLF
Suggested Character Quality: LOYAL ONE
Suggested Lifetime Scripture Verse: Psalm 116:2 *"Because He has inclined His ear to me, therefore I will call on Him as long as I live."*

RANDAL

Literal Meaning: SHIELD-WOLF
Suggested Character Quality: LOYAL ONE
Suggested Lifetime Scripture Verse: Psalm 116:2 *"Because He has inclined His ear to me, therefore, I will call on Him as long as I live."*

RANDALPH

Literal Meaning: "SHIELD-WOLF" — Anglo-saxon
Suggested Character Quality: LOYAL ONE
Suggested Lifetime Scripture Verse: Psalm 116:2 *"Because He has inclined His ear to me, therefore I will call on Him as long as I live."*

RANDOLPH

Literal Meaning: SHIELD-WOLF
Suggested Character Quality: LOYAL ONE
Suggested Lifetime Scripture Verse: Psalm 116:2 *"Because He has inclined His ear to me, therefore I will call on Him as long as I live."*

RANDY

Literal Meaning: SHIELD-WOLF
Suggested Character Quality: LOYAL ONE
Suggested Lifetime Scripture Verse: Psalm 116:2 *"Because He has inclined His ear to me, therefore I will call on Him as long as I live."*

RAPHAEL

Literal Meaning: GOD HEALS (HEBREW)
Suggested Character Quality: HEALED BY GOD
Suggested Lifetime Scripture Verse: Psalm 103:2, 3 *"Bless the Lord, O my soul, and forget not all His benefits: who forgiveth all thine iniquities; who healeth all thy diseases."* *

RAQUEL

Literal Meaning: INNOCENT; LIKE A LAMB
Suggested Character Quality: LITTLE LAMB
Suggested Lifetime Scripture Verse: Psalm 79:13 *"So we, Thy people and sheep of Thy pasture, will give Thee thanks forever: we will show forth Thy praise to all generations."* *

RAY

Literal Meaning: "MIGHTY OR WISE PROTECTOR" — Germanic
Suggested Character Quality: WISE PROTECTOR
Suggested Lifetime Scripture Verse: Psalm 28:7 *"The Lord is my defense and my shield; my heart trusted in Him, and I am helped. Therefore, my heart rejoices, and with my song I will praise Him."*

RAYFORD

Literal Meaning: MIGHTY PROTECTOR
Suggested Character Quality: MIGHTY PROTECTOR
Suggested Lifetime Scripture Verse: Ephesians 6:10 *"Finally, my brethren, be strong in the Lord, and in the power of His might."* *

RAYMOND

Literal Meaning: COUNSEL-PROTECTION
Suggested Character Quality: MIGHTY
Suggested Lifetime Scripture Verse: Psalm 28:7 *"The Lord is my strength and my shield; my heart trusted in Him, and I am helped. Therefore, my heart rejoices, and with my song I will praise Him."*

RAYNOLD

Literal Meaning: COUNSEL-PROTECTION
Suggested Character Quality: MIGHTY, POWERFUL
Suggested Lifetime Scripture Verse: Psalm 28:7 *"The Lord is my strength and my shield; my heart trusted in Him, and I am helped. Therefore, my heart rejoices, and with my song I will praise Him."*

REAGAN

Literal Meaning: REGAL
Suggested Character Quality: ESTEEMED ONE
Suggested Lifetime Scripture Verse: Isaiah 33:15, 116 *"He that walketh righteously, and speaketh uprightly; he that despiseth the gain of oppressions, that shaketh his hands from holding of bribes, that stoppeth his ears from hearing of blood, and shutteth his eyes from seeing evil; He shall dwell on high: his place of defense shall be the munitions of rocks: bread shall be given him; his waters shall be sure."* *

REBECCA

Literal Meaning: YOKE
Suggested Character Quality: EARNEST DEVOTEE
Suggested Lifetime Scripture Verse: Psalm 73:28 *"But as for me, drawing near to God is good for me; I have made the Lord my refuge, so that I may announce all Thy works."*

REBEKAH

Literal Meaning: YOKE
Suggested Character Quality: DEVOTED ONE
Suggested Lifetime Scripture Verse: Psalm 73:28 *"But as for me, drawing near to God is good for me; I have made the Lord my refuge, so that I may announce all Thy works."*

REDMOND

Literal Meaning: PROTECTIVE COUNSEL
Suggested Character Quality: COUNSELOR
Suggested Lifetime Scripture Verse: Proverbs 11:14 *"Where no counsel is, the people fall: but in the multitude of counselors there is safety."* *

REED

Literal Meaning: RED-HAIRED
Suggested Character Quality: COURAGEOUS
Suggested Lifetime Scripture Verse: Joshua 1:9 *"Have I not commanded thee? Be strong and of a good courage; be not afraid, neither be thou dismayed: for the Lord thy God is with thee withersoever thou goest."* *

REES

Literal Meaning: ARDENT ONE
Suggested Character Quality: RADIANT LIFE
Suggested Lifetime Scripture Verse: Matthew 5:16 *"Let your light so shine before men, that they may see your good works, and glorify your Father which is in heaven."* *

REESE

Literal Meaning: ARDENT ONE; A CHIEF
Suggested Character Quality: RADIANT LIFE
Suggested Lifetime Scripture Verse: Matthew 5:16 *"Let your light so shine before men, that they may see your good works, and glorify your Father which is in heaven."* *

REG

Literal Meaning: POWER-MIGHT
Suggested Character Quality: COURAGEOUS
Suggested Lifetime Scripture Verse: Isaiah 12:2 *"Behold, God is my salvation; I will trust and not be afraid, for Jehovah, the Lord, is my strength and my song; yes, He has become my salvation."*

REGGIE

Literal Meaning: POWER - MIGHT
Suggested Character Quality: COURAGEOUS
Suggested Lifetime Scripture Verse: Isaiah 12:2 *"Behold, God is my salvation; I will trust and not be afraid, for Jehovah, the Lord, is my strength and my song; yes, He has become my salvation."*

REGINA

Literal Meaning: A QUEEN (LATIN)
Suggested Character Quality: CROWNED WITH HONOR
Suggested Lifetime Scripture Verse: Proverbs 11:16a *"A gracious woman retaineth honor . . ."* *

REGINALD

Literal Meaning: "POWER-MIGHT" — Germanic
Suggested Character Quality: COURAGEOUS
Suggested Lifetime Scripture Verse: Isaiah 12:2 *"Behold, God is my salvation; I will trust and not be afraid, for Jehovah, the Lord, is my strength and my song; yes, He has become my salvation."*

REGIS

Literal Meaning: REGAL
Suggested Character Quality: MAN OF AUTHORITY
Suggested Lifetime Scripture Verse: Romans 13:1 *"Let every soul be subject unto the higher powers. For there is no power but of God: the powers that be are ordained of God."* *

REID

Literal Meaning: RED
Suggested Character Quality: COURAGEOUS
Suggested Lifetime Scripture Verse: I Corinthians 16:13 *"Be alert; stand firm in the faith; play the man; be strong."*
Explanation: The color red associated with a man's name gives the impression of boldness and courage.

REINHART

Literal Meaning: STRONG COUNSEL
Suggested Character Quality: COUNSELOR
Suggested Lifetime Scripture Verse: Proverbs 11:14 *"Where no counsel is, the people fall: but in the multitude of counselors there is safety."* *

REITA

Literal Meaning: A PEARL
Suggested Character Quality: A PEARL
Suggested Lifetime Scripture Verse: Matthew 5:8 *"Blessed are the pure in heart: for they shall see God."* *

RENEE

Literal Meaning: BORN AGAIN
Suggested Character Quality: BORN ANEW
Suggested Lifetime Scripture Verse: Psalm 119:174 *"I long for Thy salvation, O Lord; Thy law is my delight."*

RESA

Literal Meaning: REAPER
Suggested Character Quality: GOD'S LABORER
Suggested Lifetime Scripture Verse: I Corinthians 3:9 *"For we are laborers together with God: ye are God's husbandry, ye are God's building."* *

RETA

Literal Meaning: A PEARL
Suggested Character Quality: A PEARL
Suggested Lifetime Scripture Verse: Matthew 5:8 *"Blessed are the pure in heart: for they shall see God."* *

RETTA

Literal Meaning: THE TYPE OF PERFECT WOMAN
Suggested Character Quality: INDUSTRIOUS
Suggested Lifetime Scripture Verse: Proverbs 31:27 *"She looks well to the ways of her household and eats no bread of idleness."*

REUBEN

Literal Meaning: BEHOLD A SON (HEBREW)
Suggested Character Quality: GIFT OF GOD
Suggested Lifetime Scripture Verse: John 15:9 *"As the Father hath loved me, so have I loved you: continue ye in my love."*

REVA

Literal Meaning: TO GAIN STRENGTH
Suggested Character Quality: STRONG AND WOMANLY
Suggested Lifetime Scripture Verse: Proverbs 31:25 *"Strength and honor are her clothing; and she shall rejoice in time to come."* *

REX

Literal Meaning: KING
Suggested Character Quality: MAN OF AUTHORITY
Suggested Lifetime Scripture Verse: Job 17:9 *"Yet the righteous will maintain his way, and he who has clean hands will grow stronger."*

REYNOLD

Literal Meaning: MIGHTY AND POWERFUL
Suggested Character Quality: MIGHTY AND POWERFUL
Suggested Lifetime Scripture Verse: Colossians 4:2 *"Keep persevering in prayer; attend to it diligently with the offering of thanks."*

RHEA

Literal Meaning: MOTHERLY; A STREAM (GREEK)
Suggested Character Quality: GIVER OF LOVE
Suggested Lifetime Scripture Verse: I Corinthians 13:13 *"There remain then faith, hope, love, these three; but the greatest of these is love."*

RHODA

Literal Meaning: A ROSE
Suggested Character Quality: FRAGRANT SPIRIT
Suggested Lifetime Scripture Verse: Psalm 54:6 *"With a freewill offering I will sacrifice to Thee; I will praise Thy name O Lord, for it is good."*

RHONDA

Literal Meaning: GRAND
Suggested Character Quality: STRENGTH OF CHARACTER
Suggested Lifetime Scripture Verse: Proverbs 31:30-31 *"Charm is deceitful and beauty is passing, but a woman who reveres the Lord will be praised. Acknowledge the product of her hands; let her works praise her in the gates."*

RICH

Literal Meaning: POWERFUL RULER
Suggested Character Quality: BRAVE
Suggested Lifetime Scripture Verse: II Timothy 1:7 *"For God has not given us a spirit of cowardice, but of power and love and self-control."*

RICHARD

Literal Meaning: POWERFUL RULER
Suggested Character Quality: BRAVE
Suggested Lifetime Scripture Verse: II Timothy 1:7 *"For God has not given us a spirit of cowardice, but of power and love and self-control."*

RICK

Literal Meaning: POWERFUL RULER
Suggested Character Quality: BRAVE
Suggested Lifetime Scripture Verse: II Timothy 1:7 *"For God has not given us a spirit of cowardice, but of power and love and self-control."*

RICKY

Literal Meaning: POWERFUL RULER
Suggested Character Quality: BRAVE
Suggested Lifetime Scripture Verse: II Timothy 1:7 *"For God has not given us a spirit of cowardice, but of power and love and self-control."*

RITA

Literal Meaning: A PEARL
Suggested Character Quality: A PEARL
Suggested Lifetime Scripture Verse: Matthew 5:8 *"Blessed are the pure in heart: for they shall see God."* *

ROANNA

Literal Meaning: GRACIOUS ROSE
Suggested Character Quality: INNER BEAUTY
Suggested Lifetime Scripture Verse: Psalm 29:2 *"Ascribe to the Lord the glory of His name; worship the Lord in sacred adornment."*

ROB

Literal Meaning: SHINING WITH FAME
Suggested Character Quality: EXCELLENT WORTH
Suggested Lifetime Scripture Verse: Psalm 24:3, 4 *"Who shall go up into the mountain of the Lord; who shall stand in His holy place? He who has clean hands and a pure heart, who has not lifted up his soul to falsehood, who has not sworn deceptively."*

ROBERT

Literal Meaning: SHINING WITH FAME
Suggested Character Quality: EXCELLENT WORTH
Suggested Lifetime Scripture Verse: Psalm 24:3, 4 *"Who shall go up into the mountain of the Lord; who shall stand in His holy place? He who has clean hands and a pure heart, who has not lifted up his soul to falsehood, who has not sworn deceptively."*

ROBERTA

Literal Meaning: SHINING WITH FAME
Suggested Character Quality: EXCELLENT WORTH
Suggested Lifetime Scripture Verse: Philippians 4:13 *"I have strength for every situation through Him who empowers me."*

ROBIN — FEMALE

Literal Meaning: SHINING WITH FAME
Suggested Character Quality: STRENGTH OF CHARACTER
Suggested Lifetime Scripture Verse: Philippians 4:13 *"I have strength for every situation through Him who empowers me."*

ROBIN — MALE

Literal Meaning: OF BRIGHT SHINING FAME
Suggested Character Quality: EXCELLENT WORTH
Suggested Lifetime Scripture Verse: Psalm 24:3, 4 *"Who shall go up into the mountain of the Lord; who shall stand in His holy place? He who has clean hands and a pure heart, who has not lifted up his soul to falsehood, who has not sworn deceptively."*

ROBINSON

Literal Meaning: SHINING WITH FAME
Suggested Character Quality: EXCELLENT WORTH
Suggested Lifetime Scripture Verse: Psalm 24:3, 4 *"Who shall go up into the mountain of the Lord; who shall stand in His holy place? He who has clean hands and a pure heart, who has not lifted up his soul to falsehood, who has not sworn deceptively."*

ROBYN

Literal Meaning: SHINING WITH FAME
Suggested Character Quality: STRENGTH OF CHARACTER
Suggested Lifetime Scripture Verse: Philippians 4:13 *"I have strength for every situation through Him who empowers me."*

ROCCO

Literal Meaning: ROCK
Suggested Character Quality: STRONG IN SPIRIT
Suggested Lifetime Scripture Verse: Joshua 1:9 *"Have not I commanded thee? Be strong and of a good courage; be not afraid, neither be thou dismayed: for the Lord thy God is with these whithersoever thou goest."* *

ROCHELLE

Literal Meaning: THE LITTLE ROCK (FRENCH)
Suggested Character Quality: STRONG IN HEART
Suggested Lifetime Scripture Verse: Psalm 28:7 *"The Lord is my strength and my shield; my heart trusted in Him, and I am helped: therefore my heart greatly rejoiceth; and with my song will I praise Him."* *

ROD

Literal Meaning: "FAMOUS RULER" — Germanic
Suggested Character Quality: ESTEEMED ONE
Suggested Lifetime Scripture Verse: Psalm 112:6 *"Such a man will never be laid low, for the just shall be held in remembrance forever."*

RODDY

Literal Meaning: RICH IN FAME
Suggested Character Quality: EXCELLENT WORTH
Suggested Lifetime Scripture Verse: Psalm 1:1, 2 *"Blessed is the man that walketh not in the counsel of the ungodly, nor standeth in the way of sinners, nor sitteth in the seat of the scornful: But his delight is in the law of the Lord; and in His law doth he meditate day and night."* *

RODGER

Literal Meaning: FAMOUS SPEARMAN
Suggested Character Quality: GOD'S WARRIOR
Suggested Lifetime Scripture Verse: II Corinthians 10:4 *"For the weapons of our warfare are not physical, but they are powerful with God's help for the tearing down of fortresses."*

RODNEY

Literal Meaning: FAMOUS ONE'S ISLAND
Suggested Character Quality: ESTEEMED ONE
Suggested Lifetime Scripture Verse: Psalm 112:6 *"Such a man will never be laid low, for the just shall be held in remembrance forever."*

ROGER

Literal Meaning: FAMOUS SPEARMAN
Suggested Character Quality: GOD'S WARRIOR
Suggested Lifetime Scripture Verse: II Corinthians 10:4 *"For the weapons of our warfare are not physical, but they are powerful with God's help for the tearing down of fortresses."*

ROLAN

Literal Meaning: FAME OF THE LAND
Suggested Character Quality: STRONG; MANLY
Suggested Lifetime Scripture Verse: Philippians 4:13 *"I have strength for every situation through Him who empowers me."*

ROLAND

Literal Meaning: FAME OF THE LAND
Suggested Character Quality: STRONG; MANLY
Suggested Lifetime Scripture Verse: Philippians 4:13 *"I have strength for every situation through Him who empowers me."*

ROLF

Literal Meaning: FAME-WOLF
Suggested Character Quality: STRONG; MANLY
Suggested Lifetime Scripture Verse: Joshua 1:9 *"Have I not commanded you? Be resolute and strong! Be not afraid, and be not dismayed; for the Lord your God is with you everywhere you go."*

ROLLIE

Literal Meaning: FAME OF THE LAND
Suggested Character Quality: STRONG; MANLY
Suggested Lifetime Scripture Verse: Philippians 4:13 *"I have strength for every situation through Him who empowers me."*

ROLLIN

Literal Meaning: FROM THE FAMOUS LAND
Suggested Character Quality: STRONG; MANLY
Suggested Lifetime Scripture Verse: Philippians 4:13 *"I have strength for every situation through Him who empowers me."*

ROMAN

Literal Meaning: FROM ROME
Suggested Character Quality: NOBLE AND JUST
Suggested Lifetime Scripture Verse: Romans 1:16, 17 *"For I am not ashamed of the gospel of Christ: for it is the power of God unto salvation to everyone that believeth; to the Jew first, and also to the Greek. For therein is the righteousness of God revealed from faith to faith: as it is written, the just shall live by faith."* *

RON

Literal Meaning: MIGHTY POWER
Suggested Character Quality: STRONG ONE
Suggested Lifetime Scripture Verse: Ephesians 6:10 *"In conclusion, be strong in the Lord and in the strength of His might."*

RONALD

Literal Meaning: MIGHTY POWER
Suggested Character Quality: STRONG ONE
Suggested Lifetime Scripture Verse: Ephesians 6:10 *"In conclusion, be strong in the Lord and in the strength of His might."*

RONDA

Literal Meaning: GRAND
Suggested Character Quality: STRENGTH OF CHARACTER
Suggested Lifetime Scripture Verse: Proverbs 31:30-31 *"Charm is deceitful, and beauty is vain, but a woman who fears the Lord is to be praised. Give her the fruit of her hands, and let her works praise her in the gates."*

RONI

Literal Meaning: POWERFUL, OR QUEENLY
Suggested Character Quality: GOD'S PRINCESS
Suggested Lifetime Scripture Verse: Isaiah 62:3 *"Thou shalt also be a crown of glory in the hand of the Lord, and a royal diadem in the hand of thy God."* *

RONNA

Literal Meaning: OF MIGHTY POWER
Suggested Character Quality: STRENGTH OF CHARACTER
Suggested Lifetime Scripture Verse: Proverbs 31:30-31 *"Charm is deceitful, and beauty is vain, but a woman who fears the Lord is to be praised. Give her the fruit of her hands, and let her works praise her in the gates."*

RONNIE

Literal Meaning: MIGHTY POWER
Suggested Character Quality: STRONG ONE
Suggested Lifetime Scripture Verse: Ephesians 6:10 *"In conclusion, be strong in the Lord and in the strength of His might."*

ROONEY

Literal Meaning: RED HAIR
Suggested Character Quality: DISTINCTIVE GIFT
Suggested Lifetime Scripture Verse: I Thessalonians 5:18 *"In everything give thanks: for this is the will of God in Christ Jesus concerning you."* *

ROOSEVELT

Literal Meaning: FROM THE ROSE FIELD (GERMAN)
Suggested Character Quality: MAN OF DISTINCTION
Suggested Lifetime Scripture Verse: I Thessalonians 5:23, 24 *"And the very God of peace sanctify you wholly; and I pray God your whole spirit and soul and body be preserved blameless unto the coming of the Lord Jesus Christ. Faithful is He that calleth you, who also will do it."* *

RORY

Literal Meaning: THE RUDDY; RED KING
Suggested Character Quality: GOD'S WARRIOR
Suggested Lifetime Scripture Verse: II Timothy 2:4 *"No man that warreth entangleth himself with the affairs of this life; that he may please Him who hath chosen him to be a soldier."* *

ROSA

Literal Meaning: ROSE
Suggested Character Quality: GIVER OF LOVE
Suggested Lifetime Scripture Verse: I Corinthians 13:13 *"There remain then, faith, hope, love, these three; but the greatest of these is love."*

ROSALIE

Literal Meaning: A ROSE
Suggested Character Quality: GIVER OF LOVE
Suggested Lifetime Scripture Verse: I Corinthians 13:13 "There remain then, faith, hope, love, these three; but the greatest of these is love."

ROSALIND

Literal Meaning: FAIR ROSE
Suggested Character Quality: GIVER OF LOVE
Suggested Lifetime Scripture Verse: I Corinthians 13:13 *"There remain then, faith, love, these three; but the greatest of these is love."*

ROSAMOND

Literal Meaning: ROSE
Suggested Character Quality: GIVER OF LOVE
Suggested Lifetime Scripture Verse: I Corinthians 13:13 *"There remain then faith, hope, love, these three; but the greatest of these is love."*

ROSANNE

Literal Meaning: ROSE OF GRACE
Suggested Character Quality: GIVER OF LOVE
Suggested Lifetime Scripture Verse: I Corinthians 13:13 *"There remain then, faith, love, these three; but the greatest of these is love."*

ROSE

Literal Meaning: A ROSE
Suggested Character Quality: GIVER OF LOVE
Suggested Lifetime Scripture Verse: I Corinthians 13:13 *"There remain then, faith, love, these three; but the greatest of these is love."*

ROSEMARIE

Literal Meaning: THE ROSE OF ST. MARY
Suggested Character Quality: GIVER OF LOVE
Suggested Lifetime Scripture Verse: I Corinthians 13:13 *"There remain then, faith, love, these three; but the greatest of these is love."*

ROSEMARY

Literal Meaning: ROSE OF ST. MARY
Suggested Character Quality: GIVER OF LOVE
Suggested Lifetime Scripture Verse: I Corinthians 13:13 *"There remain then, faith, love, these three; but the greatest of these is love."*

ROSETTE

Literal Meaning: ROSE
Suggested Character Quality: COMPASSIONATE SPIRIT
Suggested Lifetime Scripture Verse: I Corinthians 13:13 *"There remain then, faith, hope, love, these three; but the greatest of these is love."*

ROSS

Literal Meaning: FROM THE PENINSULA
Suggested Character Quality: GALLANT
Suggested Lifetime Scripture Verse: Psalm 27:14 *"Wait for the Lord; take courage, and He will give strength to your heart; yes, wait for the Lord."*

ROWEN

Literal Meaning: THE FAMED
Suggested Character Quality: EXCELLENT WORTH
Suggested Lifetime Scripture Verse: Psalm 37:37 *"Mark the perfect man, and behold the upright: for the end of that man is peace."* *

ROXANNA

Literal Meaning: BRILLIANT ONE
Suggested Character Quality: COMING WITH LIGHT
Suggested Lifetime Scripture Verse: Psalm 27:1 *"The Lord is my light and my salvation; whom shall I fear? The Lord is the stronghold of my life; of whom shall I be afraid?"*

ROXANNE

Literal Meaning: BRILLIANT ONE
Suggested Character Quality: COMING WITH LIGHT
Suggested Lifetime Scripture Verse: Psalm 27:1 *"The Lord is my light and my salvation; whom shall I fear? The Lord is the stronghold of my life; of whom shall I be afraid?"*

ROXIE

Literal Meaning: BRILLIANT ONE
Suggested Character Quality: COMING WITH LIGHT
Suggested Lifetime Scripture Verse: Psalm 27:1 *"The Lord is my light and my salvation; whom shall I fear? The Lord is the stronghold of my life; of whom shall I be afraid?"*

ROY

Literal Meaning: KINGLY
Suggested Character Quality: GRACIOUS; MANLY
Suggested Lifetime Scripture Verse: Jeremiah 17:7 *"Blessed is the man who trusts in the Lord, whose trust is the Lord."*
Explanation: These qualities characterize a kingly man.

ROYAL

Literal Meaning: THE KINGLY
Suggested Character Quality: GRACIOUS AND JUST
Suggested Lifetime Scripture Verse: Micah 6:8 *"He hath shewed thee, O man, what is good; and what doth the Lord require of thee, but to do justly, and to love mercy, and to walk humbly with thy God?"* *

ROYCE

Literal Meaning: SON OF THE KING
Suggested Character Quality: GOD'S HEIR
Suggested Lifetime Scripture Verse: I John 3:2 *"Beloved, now are we the sons of God, and it doth not yet appear what we shall be: but we know that, when He shall appear, we shall be like Him; for we shall see Him as He is."* *

RUBY

Literal Meaning: RED JEWEL
Suggested Character Quality: EXCELLENT SPIRIT
Suggested Lifetime Scripture Verse: Psalm 7:8 *". . . May the Lord judge the people. Vindicate me, O Lord, according to my righteousness and according to the integrity that is upon me."*
Explanation: A jewel must have excellent qualities to be considered precious.

RUDOLPH

Literal Meaning: FAMOUS WOLF
Suggested Character Quality: LOYAL ONE
Suggested Lifetime Scripture Verse: Psalm 116:2 *"Because He has inclined His ear to me, therefore I will call on Him as long as I live."*

RUDY

Literal Meaning: FAMOUS WOLF
Suggested Character Quality: LOYAL ONE
Suggested Lifetime Scripture Verse: Psalm 116:2 *"Because he has inclined His ear to me, therefore I will call on Him as long as I live.'*

RUPERT

Literal Meaning: SHINING WITH FAME
Suggested Character Quality: EXCELLENT WORTH
Suggested Lifetime Scripture Verse: Psalm 24:3, 4 *"Who shall go into the mountain of the Lord; who shall stand in His holy place? He who has clean hands and a pure heart, who has not lifted up his soul to falsehood, who has not sworn deceptively."*

RUSH

Literal Meaning: RED HAIRED
Suggested Character Quality: DISTINCTIVE GIFT
Suggested Lifetime Scripture Verse: I Thessalonians 5:18 *"In everything give thanks: for this is the will of God in Christ Jesus concerning you."* *

RUSSELL

Literal Meaning: RED-HAIRED ONE
Suggested Character Quality: WISE DISCRETION
Suggested Lifetime Scripture Verse: Isaiah 28:26 *"His God correctly instructs and teaches him."*

RUSTY

Literal Meaning: RED-HAIRED ONE
Suggested Character Quality: DISTINCTIVE GIFT
Suggested Lifetime Scripture Verse: I Thessalonians 5:18 *"In everything give thanks: for this is the will of God in Christ Jesus concerning you."* *

RUTH

Literal Meaning: COMPASSIONATE, BEAUTIFUL
Suggested Character Quality: COMPASSIONATE
Suggested Lifetime Scripture Verse: Proverbs 31:20 *"She opens her palm to the poor and reaches out her hands to the needy."*

RYAN

Literal Meaning: LITTLE KING
Suggested Character Quality: MAN OF DISTINCTION
Suggested Lifetime Scripture Verse: Psalm 112:5 *"It is well with him who is generous and ready to lend, the man who conducts his business with fairness."*

RYDER

Literal Meaning: ONE WHO RIDES; A HORSEMAN
Suggested Character Quality: SKILLFUL
Suggested Lifetime Scripture Verse: Colossians 3:23 *"And whatsoever ye do, do it heartily, as to the Lord, and not unto men."* *

RYNAE

Literal Meaning: BORN AGAIN
Suggested Character Quality: BORN ANEW
Suggested Lifetime Scripture Verse: Psalm 119:174 *"I long for Thy salvation, O Lord; Thy law is my delight."*

SABLE

Literal Meaning: THIRD BORN CHILD
Suggested Character Quality: GOD'S HEIR
Suggested Lifetime Scripture Verse: Luke 6:35, 36 *"But love ye your enemies, and do good, and lend, hoping for nothing again; and your reward shall be great, and ye shall be the children of the Highest: for He is kind unto the unthankful and to the evil. Be ye therefore merciful, as your Father also is merciful."* *

SABRINA

Literal Meaning: TO REST; FROM THE BORDER
Suggested Character Quality: PEACEFUL WOMAN
Suggested Lifetime Scripture Verse: Isaiah 32:17 *"And the work of righteousness shall be peace; and the effect of righteousness quietness and assurance forever."* *

SACHA

Literal Meaning: HELPMATE
Suggested Character Quality: GOD'S HELPER
Suggested Lifetime Scripture Verse: Psalm 100:2 *"Serve the Lord with gladness: come before His presence with singing."* *

SADIE

Literal Meaning: PRINCESS
Suggested Character Quality: GOD'S PRINCESS
Suggested Lifetime Scripture Verse: I Peter 2:9 *"But you are a chosen race, a royal priethood, a holy nation, a people of His acquisition, so that you may proclaim the perfections of Him who called you out of darkness into His marvelous light."*

SAL

Literal Meaning: TO SAVE
Suggested Character Quality: MERCIFUL
Suggested Lifetime Scripture Verse: Proverbs 11:17 *"The merciful man doeth good to his own soul: but he that is cruel troubleth his own flesh."* *

SALLY

Literal Meaning: PRINCESS
Suggested Character Quality: GOD'S PRINCESS
Suggested Lifetime Scripture Verse: I Peter 2:9 *"But you are a chosen race, a royal priesthood, a holy nation, a people of His acquisition, so that you may proclaim the perfections of Him who called you out of darkness into His marvelous light.'*

SALOME

Literal Meaning: PEACE (HEBREW)
Suggested Character Quality: PEACEMAKER
Suggested Lifetime Scripture Verse: Matthew 5:9 *"Blessed are the peace-makers: for they shall be called the children of God."* *

SAMANTHA

Literal Meaning: THE LISTENER
Suggested Character Quality: TEACHABLE ONE
Suggested Lifetime Scripture Verse: Psalm 25:4, 5 *"Show me Thy ways, O Lord; teach me Thy paths. Lead me in Thy truth, and teach me: for Thou art the God of my salvation; on Thee do I wait all the day."* *

SAMPSON

Literal Meaning: SUN'S MAN; STRONG MAN
Suggested Character Quality: MAN OF STRENGTH
Suggested Lifetime Scripture Verse: Proverbs 24:5 *"A wise man is strong; yea, a man of knowledge increaseth strength."* *

SAMUEL

Literal Meaning: HIS NAME IS GOD — HEARD OR ASKED OF GOD
Suggested Character Quality: INTEGRITY
Suggested Lifetime Scripture Verse: Proverbs 21:3 *"To practice righteousness and justice is more acceptable to the Lord than sacrifice."*

SANDI

Literal Meaning: HELPER; DEFENDER OF MANKIND
Suggested Character Quality: COMPASSION WITH HUMILITY
Suggested Lifetime Scripture Verse: Proverbs 31:20 *"She opens her palm to the poor and reaches out her hands to the needy."*

SANDRA

Literal Meaning: HELPER; DEFENDER OF MANKIND
Suggested Character Quality: COMPASSION WITH HUMILITY
Suggested Lifetime Scripture Verse: Proverbs 31:20 *"She opens her palm to the poor and reaches out her hands to the needy."*

SANDY

Literal Meaning: HELPER; DEFENDER OF MANKIND
Suggested Character Quality: COMPASSION WITH HUMILITY
Suggested Lifetime Scripture Verse: Proverbs 31:20 *"She opens her palm to the poor and reaches out her hands to the needy."*

SANFORD

Literal Meaning: BY THE SANDY CROSSING
Suggested Character Quality: LOYAL
Suggested Lifetime Scripture Verse: Psalm 31:23 *"O love the Lord, all ye His saints: for the Lord preserveth the faithful, and plentifully rewardeth the proud doer."* *

SARA

Literal Meaning: PRINCESS
Suggested Character Quality: GOD'S PRINCESS
Suggested Lifetime Scripture Verse: I Peter 2:9 *"But you are a chosen race, a royal priesthood, a holy nation, a people of His acquisition, so that you may proclaim the perfection of Him who called you out of darkness into His marvelous light."*

SARAH

Literal Meaning: PRINCESS
Suggested Character Quality: GOD'S PRINCESS
Suggested Lifetime Scripture Verse: I Peter 2:9 *"But you are a chosen race, a royal priesthood, a holy nation, a people of His acquisition, so that you may proclaim the perfections of Him who called you out of darkness into His marvelous light."*

SCOTT

Literal Meaning: FROM SCOTLAND
Suggested Character Quality: LOYAL
Suggested Lifetime Scripture Verse: Romans 12:9-10 *"Let your love be sincere, clinging to the right with abhorrence of evil. Be joined together in a brotherhood of mutual love, trying to outdo one another in showing respect."*

SEAN

Literal Meaning: GOD IS GRACIOUS
Suggested Character Quality: GOD'S GIFT
Suggested Lifetime Scripture Verse: Isaiah 43:10 *"You are My witness, says the Lord, and My servant whom I have chosen, in order that you may know and believe Me, and understand that I am He. Before Me no God was formed, nor shall there be after Me."*

SEBASTIAN

Literal Meaning: RESPECTED; REVERENCED
Suggested Character Quality: IN HIGH ESTEEM
Suggested Lifetime Scripture Verse: Psalm 5:12 *"For Thou, Lord, wilt bless the righteous; with favor wilt Thou compass him as with a shield."* *

SELENA

Literal Meaning: THE MOON (GREEK)
Suggested Character Quality: REFLECTOR OF LIGHT
Suggested Lifetime Scripture Verse: Psalm 37:6 *"And He shall bring forth thy righteousness as the light, and thy judgment as the noonday."* *

SELINA

Literal Meaning: THE MOON (GREEK)
Suggested Character Quality: REFLECTOR OF LIGHT
Suggested Lifetime Scripture Verse: Psalm 37:6 *"And He shall bring forth thy righteousness as the light, and thy judgment as the noonday."* *

SELMA

Literal Meaning: PROTECTED BY GOD
Suggested Character Quality: DIVINELY PROTECTED
Suggested Lifetime Scripture Verse: Isaiah 41:10 *"Fear thou not; for I am with thee: be not dismayed; for I am thy God: I will strengthen thee; yea, I will help thee; yea, I will uphold thee with the right hand of my righteousness."* *

SELMER

Literal Meaning: NO LITERAL MEANING FOUND
Suggested Character Quality: STRONG IN FAITH
Suggested Lifetime Scripture Verse: Habakkuk 3:18 *"Yet I will rejoice in the Lord, I will joy in the God of my salvation."* *

SERENA

Literal Meaning: SERENE OR TRANQUIL (LATIN)
Suggested Character Quality: PEACEFUL
Suggested Lifetime Scripture Verse: John 14:27 *"Peace I leave with you, My peace I give unto you: not as the world giveth, give I unto you. Let not your heart be troubled, neither let it be afraid."* *

SETH

Literal Meaning: THE APPOINTED (HEBREW)
Suggested Character Quality: CHOSEN OF GOD
Suggested Lifetime Scripture Verse: Psalm 65:4 *"Blessed is the man whom Thou chooses, and causest to approach unto Thee, that he may dwell in Thy courts: we shall be satisfied with the goodness of Thy house, even of Thy holy temple."* *

SEWARD

Literal Meaning: DEFENDER OF THE COAST
Suggested Character Quality: WISE PROTECTOR
Suggested Lifetime Scripture Verse: Ephesians 6:13 *"Wherefore take unto you the whole armor of God, that ye may be able to withstand in the evil day, and having done all, to stand."* *

SHANE (F)

Literal Meaning: SLOW WATERS; GOD IS GRACIOUS
Suggested Character Quality: GOD'S GRACIOUS GIFT
Suggested Lifetime Scripture Verse: Isaiah 30:18 *"Nevertheless the Lord longs to be gracious to you! Therefore He shall rise up to bestow mercy on you; for the Lord is a God of justice. Blessed are they who wait for Him."*

SHANE (M)

Literal Meaning: GRACIOUS GIFT OF GOD (MODERN IRISH)
Suggested Character Quality: GOD'S GRACIOUS GIFT
Suggested Lifetime Scripture Verse: Numbers 6:25 *"The Lord make His face shine upon you and be gracious to you."*

SHANNA

Literal Meaning: GOD IS GRACIOUS
Suggested Character Quality: GOD'S GRACIOUS GIFT
Suggested Lifetime Scripture Verse: Isaiah 30:18 *"Nevertheless the Lord longs to be gracious to you! Therefore He shall rise up to bestow mercy on you; for the Lord is a God of justice. Blessed are they who wait for Him."*

SHANNON

Literal Meaning: LITTLE-WISE ONE
Suggested Character Quality: GRACIOUS SPIRIT
Suggested Lifetime Scripture Verse: Psalm 84:11 *"For the Lord God is a sun and shield, the Lord bestows mercy and honor. He holds back nothing good from those who walk uprightly."*

SHARI

Literal Meaning: A PRINCESS
Suggested Character Quality: A PRINCESS
Suggested Lifetime Scripture Verse: I Peter 2:9 *"But you are a chosen race, a royal priesthood, a holy nation, a people of His acquisition, so that you may proclaim the perfections of Him who called you out of darkness into His light."*

SHARON

Literal Meaning: A PRINCESS
Suggested Character Quality: A PRINCESS
Suggested Lifetime Scripture Verse: I Peter 2:9 *"But you are a chosen race, a royal priesthood, a holy nation, a people of His acquisition, so that you may proclaim the perfections of Him who called you out of darkness into His light."*

SHAWN

Literal Meaning: JEHOVAH HAS BEEN GRACIOUS
Suggested Character Quality: GOD'S GIFT
Suggested Lifetime Scripture Verse: Isaiah 43:10 *"You are My witnesses, says the Lord, and My servant whom I have chosen, in order that you may know and believe Me, and understand that I am He. Before Me no God was formed, nor shall there be after Me."*

SHAWNA
Literal Meaning: SLOW WATERS; GOD IS GRACIOUS
Suggested Character Quality: GOD'S GRACIOUS GIFT
Suggested Lifetime Scripture Verse: Isaiah 30:18 *"Nevertheless the Lord longs to be gracious to you! Therefore He shall rise up to bestow mercy on you; for the Lord is a God of justice. Blessed are they who wait for Him."*

SHEILA
Literal Meaning: IRISH HEAVENLY
Suggested Character Quality: CONTENTED HEART
Suggested Lifetime Scripture Verse: Psalm 18:28 *"For Thou causest my lamp to shine; the Lord my God, illumines my darkness."*

SHELBY
Literal Meaning: FROM THE LEDGE ESTATE
Suggested Character Quality: WHERE GOD DWELLS
Suggested Lifetime Scripture Verse: Jeremiah 7:7 *"Then I will let you dwell in this place, in the land that I gave to your fathers forever."*

SHELLEY
Literal Meaning: FROM THE MEADOW ON THE LEDGE
Suggested Character Quality: PROTECTOR OF LIFE
Suggested Lifetime Scripture Verse: Psalm 23:1-2 *"The Lord is my Shepherd, I shall not lack; He makes me to lie down in green pastures."*

SHELLY
Literal Meaning: SHELL ISLAND
Suggested Character Quality: PEACEFUL HEART
Suggested Lifetime Scripture Verse: Psalm 23:1-2 *"The Lord is my shepherd; I shall not lack; He makes me to lie down in green pastures."*

SHERI
Literal Meaning: LITTLE WOMANLY ONE
Suggested Character Quality: CHERISHED ONE
Suggested Lifetime Scripture Verse: Zephaniah 3:17 *"The Lord, your God, is in your midst, a Mighty One who will save. He will rejoice over you with delight; He will rest you in His love; He will be joyful over you with singing."*

SHERIDAN
Literal Meaning: WILD MAN (IRISH)
Suggested Character Quality: CHOSEN OF GOD
Suggested Lifetime Scripture Verse: John 15:16 *"Ye have not chosen me but I have chosen you, and ordained you, that ye should go and bring forth fruit, and that your fruit should remain: that whatsoever ye shall ask of the Father in my name, He may give it you."* *

SHERMAN

Literal Meaning: CLOTH-CUTTER
Suggested Character Quality: INDUSTRIOUS
Suggested Lifetime Scripture Verse: Matthew 5:16 *"Similarly let your light shine for everyone in the house."*

SHERRI

Literal Meaning: LITTLE WOMANLY ONE
Suggested Character Quality: CHERISHED ONE
Suggested Lifetime Scripture Verse: Zephaniah 3:17 *"The Lord, your God, is in your midst, a Mighty One who will save. He will rejoice over you with delight; He will rest you in His love; He will be joyful over you with singing."*

SHERRY

Literal Meaning: LITTLE WOMANLY ONE
Suggested Character Quality: CHERISHED ONE
Suggested Lifetime Scripture Verse: Zephaniah 3:17 *"The Lord, your God, is in your midst, a Mighty One who will save. He will rejoice over you with delight; He will rest you in His love; He will be joyful over you with singing."*

SHERRYL

Literal Meaning: SHINING MEADOW
Suggested Character Quality: RADIANT PEACE
Suggested Lifetime Scripture Verse: Romans 8:38, 39 *"For I am persuaded, that neither death, nor life, nor angels, nor principalities, nor powers, nor things present, nor things to come, nor height, nor depth, nor any other creature, shall be able to separate us from the love of God, which is in Christ Jesus our Lord."* *

SHIRLEY

Literal Meaning: FROM THE BRIGHT MEADOW
Suggested Character Quality: RESTFUL SPIRIT
Suggested Lifetime Scripture Verse: Isaiah 26:4 *"Trust in the Lord forever, for the Lord God is the Rock of Ages."*

SIDNEY

Literal Meaning: "SAINT DENIS" — Form of French
Suggested Character Quality: DISCERNER OF EXCELLENCE
Suggested Lifetime Scripture Verse: Matthew 6:33 *"But you, seek first His kingdom and His righteousness and all these things will be added to you."*
Explanation: Taken from the meaning for Dennis.

SIEG

Literal Meaning: VICTORIOUS; PEACEFUL
Suggested Character Quality: VICTORIOUS SPIRIT
Suggested Lifetime Scripture Verse: Romans 12:21 *"Be not overcome of evil, but overcome evil with good."* *

SIEGFRIED

Literal Meaning: VICTORIOUS, PEACEFUL
Suggested Character Quality: VICTORIOUS SPIRIT
Suggested Lifetime Scripture Verse: Romans 12:21 *"Be not overcome of evil, but overcome evil with good."* *

SILAS

Literal Meaning: OF THE FOREST
Suggested Character Quality: DEEP IN WISDOM
Suggested Lifetime Scripture Verse: Proverbs 11:30 *"The fruit of the righteous is a tree of life; and he that winneth souls is wise."* *

SILVIA

Literal Meaning: FROM THE FOREST
Suggested Character Quality: SECURE ONE
Suggested Lifetime Scripture Verse: Job 11:18 *"You will feel confident; because you have hoped, you will look around and lie down without fear."*

SIMON

Literal Meaning: HEARING
Suggested Character Quality: OBEDIENT SPIRIT
Suggested Lifetime Scripture Verse: Psalm 37:5 *"Commit your way to the Lord; trust in Him, too, and He will bring it about."*

SIMONE

Literal Meaning: HEARER; ONE WHO HEARS
Suggested Character Quality: OBEDIENT SPIRIT
Suggested Lifetime Scripture Verse: Psalm 37:5 *"Commit your way to the Lord; trust in Him, too, and He will bring it about."*

SLADE

Literal Meaning: DWELLER IN THE VALLEY
Suggested Character Quality: PROSPEROUS ONE
Suggested Lifetime Scripture Verse: III John 1:2 *"Beloved, I wish above all things that thou mayest prosper and be in health, even as thy soul prosperth."* *

SLOAN

Literal Meaning: WARRIOR — IN SERVICE OF HIS COUNTRY
Suggested Character Quality: LOYAL ONE
Suggested Scripture Verse: Psalm 31:23 *"O love the Lord, all ye His saints: for the Lord preserveth the faithful, and plnetifully rewardeth the proud doer."*

SONDRA

Literal Meaning: HELPER OF MANKIND
Suggested Character Quality: COMPASSIONATE CARING HEART
Suggested Lifetime Scripture Verse: Proverbs 31:20 *"She opens her palm to the poor and reaches out her hands to the needy."*

SONIA

Literal Meaning: WISDOM
Suggested Character Quality: WOMAN OF WISDOM
Suggested Lifetime Scripture Verse: Proverbs 2:6 *"For the Lord gives wisdom; from His mouth come knowledge and discernment."*

SONJA

Literal Meaning: WISDOM
Suggested Character Quality: WOMAN OF WISDOM
Suggested Lifetime Scripture Verse: Proverbs 2:6 *"For the Lord gives wisdom; from His mouth come knowledge and discernment."*

SONJIA

Literal Meaning: WISDOM
Suggested Character Quality: WOMAN OF WISDOM
Suggested Lifetime Scripture Verse: Proverbs 2:6 *"For the Lord gives wisdom; from His mouth come knowledge and discernment."*

SONYA

Literal Meaning: WISE
Suggested Character Quality: WOMAN OF WISDOM
Suggested Lifetime Scripture Verse: Proverbs 2:6 *"For the Lord gives wisdom; from His mouth come knowledge and discernment."*

SOPHIA

Literal Meaning: WISE
Suggested Character Quality: WOMAN OF WISDOM
Suggested Lifetime Scripture Verse: Proverbs 2:6 *"For the Lord gives wisdom; from His mouth come knowledge and discernment."*

SOPHIE

Literal Meaning: WISDOM
Suggested Character Quality: WOMAN OF WISDOM
Suggested Lifetime Scripture Verse: Proverbs 2:6 *"For the Lord gives wisdom; from His mouth come knowledge and discernment."*

SPENCER

Literal Meaning: DISPENSER OF PROVISIONS
Suggested Character Quality: FAITHFUL STEWARD
Suggested Lifetime Scripture Verse: Deuteronomy 11:1 *"Love the Lord your God, therefore, and always heed His charge, His laws, His ordinances, and His commandments. Of the Lord your God's discipline you must be ever mindful."*

STACIA

Literal Meaning: RESURRECTION
Suggested Character Quality: TRANSFORMED HEART
Suggested Lifetime Scripture Verse: Psalm 11:7 *"For the Lord is righteous; He loves acts of righteousness; His countenance beholds the upright."*

STACIE

Literal Meaning: OF THE RESURRECTION
Suggested Character Quality: TRANSFORMED HEART
Suggested Lifetime Scripture Verse: Psalm 11:7 *"For the Lord is righteous; He loves acts of righteousness; His countenance beholds the upright."*

STACEY

Literal Meaning: OF THE RESURRECTION
Suggested Character Quality: TRANSFORMED HEART
Suggested Lifetime Scripture Verse: Psalm 11:7 *"For the Lord is righteous; He loves acts of righteousness; His countenance beholds the upright."*

STACY

Literal Meaning: OF THE RESURRECTION
Suggested Character Quality: TRANSFORMED HEART
Suggested Lifetime Scripture Verse: Psalm 11:7 *"For the Lord is righteous; He loves acts of righteousness; His countenance beholds the upright."*

STAN

Literal Meaning: DWELLER AT THE ROCKY MEADOW
Suggested Character Quality: STURDY SPIRIT
Suggested Lifetime Scripture Verse: Micah 6:8 *"He has declared to you, O man, what is good, and what does the Lord require of you but to do justice, to love mercy, and to walk humbly with your God."*
Explanation: See Stanley

STANLEY

Literal Meaning: DWELLER AT THE ROCKY MEADOW
Suggested Character Quality: STURDY SPIRIT
Suggested Lifetime Scripture Verse: Micah 6:8 *"He has declared to you, O man, what is good, and what does the Lord require of you but to do justice, to love mercy, and to walk humbly with your God."*
Explanation: A rocky meadow suggests that one would need a sturdy, steadfast spirit in order to survive.

STEFFEN

Literal Meaning: CROWNED; GARLAND
Suggested Character Quality: CROWNED ONE
Suggested Lifetime Scripture Verse: Psalm 103:2, 4 *"Bless the Lord, O my soul and forget none of His benefits . . . Who redeems your life from the grave, who crowns you with lovingkindness and mercy."*

STELLA

Literal Meaning: "A STAR" — Latin
Suggested Character Quality: WOMAN OF ESTEEM
Suggested Lifetime Scripture Verse: Proverbs 2:6 *"For the Lord gives wisdom; from His mouth come knowledge and discernment."*

STEPHANIE

Literal Meaning: CROWNED ONE
Suggested Character Quality: CROWNED ONE
Suggested Lifetime Scripture Verse: Isaiah 58:14 *"Then you shall find your delight in the Lord, and I will make you ride on the highways of the earth; I will nourish you with the heritage of Jacob, your father, for the mouth of the Lord has spoken it."*

STEPHEN

Literal Meaning: CROWNED ONE
Suggested Character Quality: CROWNED ONE
Suggested Lifetime Scripture Verse: Psalm 103:2, 4 *"Bless the Lord, O my soul and forget none of His benefits . . . Who redeems your life from the grave, who crowns you with lovingkindness and mercy."*

STERLING

Literal Meaning: STANDARD OF EXCELLENT QUALITY
Suggested Character Quality: EXCELLENT CHARACTER
Suggested Lifetime Scripture Verse: Job 23:10 *"But He knows the way which I take, and when He has tested me I shall come forth as gold."*

STEVE

Literal Meaning: CROWNED ONE
Suggested Character Quality: CROWNED ONE
Suggested Lifetime Scripture Verse: Psalm 103:2, 4 *"Bless the Lord, O my soul and forget none of His benefits . . . Who redeems your life from the grave, who crowns you with lovingkindness and mercy."*

STEVEN

Literal Meaning: CROWNED ONE
Suggested Character Quality: CROWNED ONE
Suggested Lifetime Scripture Verse: Psalm 103:2, 4 *"Bless the Lord, O my soul and forget none of His benefits . . . Who redeems your life from the grave, who crowns you with lovingkindness and mercy."*

STEWART

Literal Meaning: CARETAKER
Suggested Character Quality: HELPFUL SPIRIT
Suggested Lifetime Scripture Verse: Romans 15:14 *"I myself am convinced about you, my brothers, that you are full of goodness, amply furnished with knowledge, and competent to advise one another."*

STUART

Literal Meaning: CARETAKER
Suggested Character Quality: HELPFUL SPIRIT
Suggested Lifetime Scripture Verse: Romans 15:14 *"I myself am convinced about you, my brothers, that you are full of goodness, amply furnished with knowledge, and competent to advise one another."*

SUE

Literal Meaning: LILY OR GRACEFUL LILY
Suggested Character Quality: FULL OF GRACE
Suggested Lifetime Scripture Verse: Psalm 84:11 *"For the Lord God is a sun and shield; the Lord bestows mercy and honor. He holds back nothing good from those who walk uprightly."*

SUMMER

Literal Meaning: A SEASON
Suggested Character Quality: REFRESHING ONE
Suggested Lifetime Scripture Verse: Isaiah 40:31 *"But they that wait upon the Lord will renew their strength; they shall mount up with wings as eagles; they shall run, and not be weary; and they shall walk, and not faint."* *

SUSAN

Literal Meaning: LILY OR GRACEFUL LILY
Suggested Character Quality: FULL OF GRACE
Suggested Lifetime Scripture Verse: Psalm 84:11 *"For the Lord God is a sun and shield; the Lord bestows mercy and honor. He holds back nothing good from those who walk uprightly."*

SUSANNAH

Literal Meaning: LILY; GRACEFUL LILY
Suggested Character Quality: PURE IN GRACE
Suggested Lifetime Scripture Verse: Psalm 84:11 *"For the Lord God is a sun and shield; the Lord bestows mercy and honor. He holds back nothing good from those who walk uprightly."*

SUSANNE

Literal Meaning: LILY; GRACEFUL LILY
Suggested Character Quality: PURE IN GRACE
Suggested Lifetime Scripture Verse: Psalm 84:11 *"For the Lord God is a sun and shield; the Lord bestows mercy and honor. He holds back nothing good from those who walk uprightly."*

SUZANNE

Literal Meaning: LILY; GRACEFUL LILY
Suggested Character Quality: PURE IN GRACE
Suggested Lifetime Scripture Verse: Psalm 84:11 *"For the Lord God is a sun and shield; the Lord bestows mercy and honor. He holds back nothing good from those who walk uprightly."*

SVEN

Literal Meaning: YOUTHFUL
Suggested Character Quality: YOUTHFUL ONE
Suggested Lifetime Scripture Verse: Colossians 3:10 *"And have put on the new man, which is renewed in knowledge after the image of Him that created him."* *

SYLVESTER

Literal Meaning: OF THE FOREST
Suggested Character Quality: SECURE ONE
Suggested Lifetime Scripture Verse: Proverbs 18:10 *"The name of the Lord is a strong tower: the righteous runneth into it, and is safe."* *

SYLVIA

Literal Meaning: FROM THE FOREST
Suggested Character Quality: SECURE ONE
Suggested Lifetime Scripture Verse: Job 11:18 *"You will feel confident, because you have hoped; you will look around and lie down without fear."*

TABATHA

Literal Meaning: A GAZELLE
Suggested Character Quality: STRONG OR GRACEFUL
Suggested Lifetime Scripture Verse: Psalm 27:14 *"Wait on the Lord: be of good courage, and He shall strengthen thine heart; wait, I say, on the Lord."* *

TABITHA

Literal Meaning: A GAZELLE
Suggested Character Quality: STRONG AND GRACEFUL
Suggested Lifetime Scripture Verse: Psalm 27:14 *"Wait on the Lord: be of good courage, and He shall strengthen thine heart: wait, I say, on the Lord."* *

TAD

Literal Meaning: GIFT OF GOD
Suggested Character Quality: GIFT OF GOD
Suggested Lifetime Scripture Verse: Isaiah 43:10 *"You are My witnesses, says the Lord, and My servant whom I have chosen, in order that you may know and believe Me, and understand that I am He. Before Me no God was formed, nor shall there be after Me."*

TAGGART

Literal Meaning: SON OF THE PRELATE (CHURCH DIGNITARY)
Suggested Character Quality: ONE WHO REVERENCES GOD
Suggested Lifetime Scripture Verse: Psalm 89:7 *"God is greatly to be feared in the assembly of the saints, and to be had in reverence of all them that are about Him."* *

TALITHA

Literal Meaning: MAIDEN
Suggested Character Quality: PURE ONE
Suggested Lifetime Scripture Verse: Psalm 29:2 *"Give unto the Lord the glory due unto His name; worship the Lord in the beauty of holiness."* *

TAMMY

Literal Meaning: A TWIN
Suggested Character Quality: SEEKER OF TRUTH
Suggested Lifetime Scripture Verse: Psalm 63:1 *"O God, Thou art my God, I seek Thee earnestly; my soul thirsts for Thee, my flesh longs for Thee in a dry and wornout land, where there is no water."*

TANIA

Literal Meaning: A FAIRY QUEEN
Suggested Character Quality: NOBLE SPIRIT
Suggested Lifetime Scripture Verse: Proverbs 31:31 *"Acknowledge the product of her hands; let her works praise her in the gates."*

TATE

Literal Meaning: CHEERFUL
Suggested Character Quality: CHEERFUL ONE
Suggested Lifetime Scripture Verse: Proverbs 16:20 *"He that handleth a matter wisely shall find good: and whoso trusteth in the Lord, happy is he."* *

TAYLOR

Literal Meaning: A TAILOR
Suggested Character Quality: INDUSTRIOUS ONE
Suggested Lifetime Scripture Verse: I Thessalonians 4:11, 12 *"And that ye study to be quiet, and to do your own business, and to work with your own hands, as we commanded you; That ye may walk honestly toward them that are without, and that ye may have lack of nothing."* *

TED

Literal Meaning: GIFT OF GOD
Suggested Character Quality: GIFT OF GOD
Suggested Lifetime Scripture Verse: Isaiah 43:10 *"You are My witnesses, says the Lord, and My servant whom I have chosen, in order that you may know and believe Me, and understand that I am He. Before Me no God was formed, nor shall there be after Me."*

TERESA

Literal Meaning: REAPER
Suggested Character Quality: INDUSTRIOUS
Suggested Lifetime Scripture Verse: Psalm 18:32 *"It is God that girdeth me with strength, and maketh my way perfect."* *

TERRENCE

Literal Meaning: SMOOTH-POLISHED ONE
Suggested Character Quality: SMOOTH-POLISHED ONE
Suggested Lifetime Scripture Verse: Philippians 1:6 *"Of this I am convinced, that He who has begun a good work in you will bring it to completion in the day of Christ Jesus."*

TERRI (F)

Literal Meaning: REAPER
Suggested Character Quality: CARING ONE
Suggested Lifetime Scripture Verse: Jude 1:21 *"Keep yourselves in the Love of God, all the while awaiting the mercy of our Lord Jesus Christ for eternal life."*

TERRI (M)

Literal Meaning: SMOOTH-POLISHED ONE
Suggested Character Quality: SMOOTH-POLISHED ONE
Suggested Lifetime Scripture Verse: Philippians 1:6 *"Of this I am convinced, that He who has begun a good work in you will bring it to completion in the day of Christ Jesus."*

TERRY

Literal Meaning: SMOOTH-POLISHED ONE
Suggested Character Quality: SMOOTH-POLISHED ONE
Suggested Lifetime Scripture Verse: Philippians 1:6 *"Of this I am convinced, that He who has begun a good work in you will bring it to completion in the day of Christ Jesus."*

THEA

Literal Meaning: GODDESS (GREEK)
Suggested Character Quality: GIFT OF GOD
Suggested Lifetime Scripture Verse: Ephesians 5:1, 2 *"Be ye therefore followers of God as dear children: and walk in love, as Christ also hath loved us, and hath given Himself for us an offering and a sacrifice to God for a sweetsmelling savor."* *

THELMA

Literal Meaning: NURSING
Suggested Character Quality: TRUSTFUL HEART
Suggested Lifetime Scripture Verse: Isaiah 30:15 *"For thus said the Lord God, the Holy One of Israel. In returning and resting you shall be saved; in quietness and in trust shall be your strength."*

THEODORE

Literal Meaning: GIFT OF GOD
Suggested Character Quality: GIFT OF GOD
Suggested Lifetime Scripture Verse: Isaiah 43:10 *"You are My witnesses, says the Lord, and My servant whom I have chosen, in order that you may know and believe Me, and understand that I am He. Before me no God was formed, nor shall there be after Me."*

THERESA

Literal Meaning: REAPER
Suggested Character Quality: INDUSTRIOUS
Suggested Lifetime Scripture Verse: Psalm 18:32 *"It is God who girds me with strength, and makes my way perfect."*

THOMAS

Literal Meaning: A TWIN
Suggested Character Quality: SEEKER OF TRUTH
Suggested Lifetime Scripture Verse: Psalm 63:1 *"O God Thou art my God, I seek Thee earnestly; my soul thirsts for Thee in a dry and worn-out land, where there is no water."*

THURSTON

Literal Meaning: THOR'S JEWEL
Suggested Character Quality: OF GREAT WORTH
Suggested Lifetime Scripture Verse: Psalm 1:3 *"And he shall be like a tree planted by the rivers of water, that bringeth forth his fruit in his season; his leaf also shall not wither; and whatsoever he doeth shall prosper."* *

TIFFANY

Literal Meaning: APPEARANCE OF GOD
Suggested Character Quality: IN GOD'S IMAGE
Suggested Lifetime Scripture Verse: Psalm 37:6 *"He will bring forth your righteousness like the light, and your life as the noonday brightness."*

TILLIE

Literal Meaning: BRAVE IN BATTLE
Suggested Character Quality: MIGHTY IN SPIRIT
Suggested Lifetime Scripture Verse: Colossians 1:11 *"Strengthened with all might, according to His glorious power, unto all patience and longsuffering with joyfulness."* *

TILLMAN

Literal Meaning: FROM A FERTILE VALLEY
Suggested Character Quality: ABUNDANT PROVIDER
Suggested Lifetime Scripture Verse: Matthew 6:33 *"But seek ye first the kingdom of God, and His righteousness; and all these things shall be added unto you."* *

TIM

Literal Meaning: HONORING GOD
Suggested Character Quality: HONORING GOD
Suggested Lifetime Scripture Verse: Psalm 104:1 *"Bless the Lord, O my soul! O Lord my God, Thou art very great; Thou art clothed with honor and majesty."* *

TIMOTHY

Literal Meaning: HONORING GOD
Suggested Character Quality: HONORING GOD
Suggested Lifetime Scripture Verse: Psalm 104:1 *"Bless the Lord, O my soul! O Lord my God, Thou art very great; Thou art clothed with honor and majesty."* *

TINA

Literal Meaning: No Literal Meaning Found
Suggested Character Quality: OBEDIENT HEART
Suggested Lifetime Scripture Verse: Psalm 18:22 *"For all His ordinance.*
were before me, and His statutes I did not put away from me."
Explanation: Since this name has no real meaning of its own a combination
of meanings from Christina and Ernestina was used.

TOBY

Literal Meaning: GOD IS GOOD
Suggested Character Quality: GOD'S GOODNESS
Suggested Lifetime Scripture Verse: Psalm 34:8 *"O taste and see that the*
Lord is good: blessed is the man that trusteth in Him." *

TODD

Literal Meaning: A FOX
Suggested Character Quality: WISE CHOOSER
Suggested Lifetime Scripture Verse: Proverbs 3:5, 6 *"Trust in the Lord*
with all your heart and lean not on your own understanding; in all your
ways acknowledge Him, and He will direct your paths."

TOM

Literal Meaning: A TWIN
Suggested Character Quality: SEEKER OF TRUTH
Suggested Lifetime Scripture Verse: Psalm 63:1 *"O God, Thou art my*
God, I seek Thee earnestly; my soul thirsts for Thee; my flesh longs for
Thee in a dry and worn-out land, where there is no water."
Explanation: See Thomas

TONI

Literal Meaning: PRICELESS
Suggested Character Quality: PRICELESS ONE
Suggested Lifetime Scripture Verse: Proverbs 31:10, 31 *"Who can find a*
virtuous woman? for her price is far above rubies. Give her of the fruit of
her hands; and let her own works praise her in the gates." *

TONY

Literal Meaning: INESTIMABLE
Suggested Character Quality: PRICELESS ONE
Suggested Lifetime Scripture Verse: Psalm 21:6 *"Yes, forever Thou dost*
make him most blessed; Thou dost delight him with joy by Thy presence."

TRACEY

Literal Meaning: TO REAP
Suggested Character Quality: INDUSTRIOUS
Suggested Lifetime Scripture Verse: Proverbs 31:27 *"She looks well to the*
ways of her household and eats no bread of idleness."

TRACY (F)
Literal Meaning: TO REAP
Suggested Character Quality: INDUSTRIOUS
Suggested Lifetime Scripture Verse: Proverbs 31:27 *"She looks well to the ways of her household and eats no bread of idleness."*

TRACY (M)
Literal Meaning: ГО REAP
Suggested Character Quality: INDUSTRIOUS
Suggested Lifetime Scripture Verse: Ephesians 6:10 *"In conclusion, be strong in the Lord and in the strength of His might."*

TRAVIS
Literal Meaning: FROM THE CROSSROADS
Suggested Character Quality: DILIGENT SPIRIT
Suggested Lifetime Scripture Verse: Proverbs 24:5 *"A wise man is strong, and a man of knowledge adds to his strength."*

TRENT
Literal Meaning: TORRENT; RAPID STREAM
Suggested Character Quality: PERSERVERING
Suggested Lifetime Scripture Verse: Proverbs 28:20a *"A faithful man shall abound with blessings . . . "* *

TREVOR
Literal Meaning: PRUDENT; CAREFUL JUDGMENT
Suggested Character Quality: WATCHFUL ONE
Suggested Lifetime Scripture Verse: Ephesians 5:15, 16 *"See then that ye walk circumspectly, not as fools, but as wise, Redeeming the time, because the days are evil."* *

TRICIA
Literal Meaning: NOBLE ONE
Suggested Character Quality: FULL OF HONOR
Suggested Lifetime Scripture Verse: Psalm 62:7 *"My salvation and my glory depend on God; the rock of my defense, my refuge in God."*

TRINA
Literal Meaning: PURE
Suggested Character Quality: PURE HEART
Suggested Lifetime Scripture Verse: Matthew 5:8 *"Blessed are the pure in heart: for they shall see God."* *

TRISHA
Literal Meaning: NOBLE ONE
Suggested Character Quality: FULL OF HONOR
Suggested Lifetime Scripture Verse: Psalm 62:7 *"My salvation and my glory depend on God; the rock of my defense my refuge is in God."*

TROY

Literal Meaning: AT THE PLACE OF THE CURLY-HAIRED PEOPLE
Suggested Character Quality: RELIABLE
Suggested Lifetime Scripture Verse: Micah 6:8 *"He has declared to you, O man, what is good, and what does the Lord require of you but to do justice, to love mercy and to walk humbly with your God."*

TRUDY

Literal Meaning: LOVED ONE
Suggested Character Quality: BELOVED ONE
Suggested Lifetime Scripture Verse: I John 4:10, 11 *"Herein is love, not that we loved God, but that He loved us, and sent His Son to be the propitiation for our sins. Beloved, if God so loved us, we ought also to love one another."**

TRUMAN

Literal Meaning: FAITHFUL
Suggested Character Quality: FAITHFUL MAN
Suggested Lifetime Scripture Verse: II Timothy 4:7 *"I have fought a good fight, I have finished my course, I have kept the faith."* *

TUCKER

Literal Meaning: A TUCKER OF CLOTH; A DRUM BEATER
Suggested Character Quality: HUMBLE HEART
Suggested Lifetime Scripture Verse: James 4:10 *"Humble yourselves in the sight of the Lord, and He shall lift you up."* *

TWYLA

Literal Meaning: UNKNOWN
Suggested Character Quality: GOD'S GRACIOUS GIFT
Suggested Lifetime Scripture Verse: Proverbs 11:16a *"A gracious woman retaineth honor . . ."* *

TYLER

Literal Meaning: Occupational Name
Suggested Character Quality: INDUSTRIOUS ONE
Suggested Lifetime Scripture Verse: Hebrews 13:16 *"Do not forget to do good and be generous, for with such sacrifices God is well pleased."*

TYRONE

Literal Meaning: SOVEREIGN (GREEK)
Suggested Character Quality: ESTEEMED ONE
Suggested Lifetime Scripture Verse: I Peter 5:6 *"Humble yourselves therefore under the mighty hand of God, that He may exalt you in due time."* *

URBAN
Literal Meaning: FROM THE CITY; SOPHISTICATED (LATIN)
Suggested Character Quality: EXALTED ONE
Suggested Lifetime Scripture Verse: Philippians 1:6 *"Being confident of this very thing, that He which hath begun a good work in you will perform it until the day of Jesus Christ."* *

URIAH
Literal Meaning: MY LIGHT IS JEHOVAH
Suggested Character Quality: REFLECTOR OF LIGHT
Suggested Lifetime Scripture Verse: Matthew 5:16 *"Let your light so shine before men, that they may see your good works, and glorify your Father which is in heaven."* *

URSELLA
Literal Meaning: LITTLE SHE-BEAR
Suggested Character Quality: STRONG AND WOMANLY
Suggested Lifetime Scripture Verse: Psalm 138:3 *"In the day when I cried Thou answeredst me, and strengthenedst me with strength in my soul."* *

URSULA
Literal Meaning: LITTLE SHE-BEAR
Suggested Character Quality: STRONG AND WOMANLY
Suggested Lifetime Scripture Verse: Psalm 138:3 *"In the day when I cried Thou answeredst me, and strengthenedst me with strength in my soul."* *

VALERIE

Literal Meaning: "STRONG" — Latin
Suggested Character Quality: DETERMINED PURPOSE
Suggested Lifetime Scripture Verse: Psalm 27:14 *"Wait for the Lord; take courage, and He will give strength to your heart; yes, wait for the Lord."*

VALORIE

Literal Meaning: STRONG
Suggested Character Quality: DETERMINED PURPOSE
Suggested Lifetime Scripture Verse: Psalm 27:14 *"Wait for the Lord; take courage, and He will give strength to your heart; yes, wait for the Lord."*

VAN

Literal Meaning: THRESHER
Suggested Character Quality: INDUSTRIOUS SPIRIT
Suggested Lifetime Scripture Verse: Psalm 37:3 *"Trust in the Lord and do good; inhabit the land and practice faithfulness."*

VANCE

Literal Meaning: RESIDENT AT THE GRAIN-WINNOWING FANS
Suggested Character Quality: INDUSTRIOUS
Suggested Lifetime Scripture Verse: Psalm 128:1, 2 *"Blessed is everyone that feareth the Lord; that walketh in His ways. For thou shalt eat the labor of thine hands: happy shalt thou be, and it shall be well with thee."* *

VANESSA

Literal Meaning: No Literal Meaning Found
Suggested Character Quality: WALKS WITH GOD
Suggested Lifetime Scripture Verse: Psalm 37:5 *"Commit your way to the Lord; trust in Him, too, and He will bring it about."*

VAUGHN

Literal Meaning: THE SMALL
Suggested Character Quality: DEPENDENT ON GOD
Suggested Lifetime Scripture Verse: Psalm 23:1, 2 *"The Lord is my shepherd; I shall not want. He maketh me to lie down in green pastures: He leadeth me beside the still waters."* *

VELMA

Literal Meaning: RESOLUTE GUARDIAN
Suggested Character Quality: RESOLUTE PROTECTOR
Suggested Lifetime Scripture Verse: Psalm 121:2, 3 *"My help cometh from the Lord, which made heaven and earth. He will not suffer thy foot to be moved: He that keepeth thee will not slumber."* *

VERA

Literal Meaning: FAITH; TRUE
Suggested Character Quality: FAITHFUL SPIRIT
Suggested Lifetime Scripture Verse: Psalm 119:124 *"Deal with Thy servant according to Thy lovingkindness, and teach me Thy statutes."*

VERDA

Literal Meaning: YOUNG AND FRESH
Suggested Character Quality: REFRESHING ONE
Suggested Lifetime Scripture Verse: Psalm 104:33, 34 *"I will sing unto the Lord as long as I live: I will sing praise to my God while I have my being. My meditation of Him shall be sweet: I will be glad in the Lord."* *

VERDENE

Literal Meaning: YOUNG AND FRESH
Suggested Character Quality: REFRESHING ONE
Suggested Lifetime Scripture Verse: Psalm 104:33, 34 *"I will sing unto the Lord as long as I live: I will sing praise to my God while I have my being. My meditation of Him shall be sweet: I will be glad in the Lord."* *

VERDINE

Literal Meaning: YOUNG AND FRESH
Suggested Character Quality: REFRESHING ONE
Suggested Lifetime Scripture Verse: Psalm 104:33, 34 *"I will sing unto the Lord as long as I live: I will sing praise to my God while I have my being. My meditation of Him shall be sweet: I will be glad in the Lord."* *

VERLA

Literal Meaning: TRUE
Suggested Character Quality: TRUTHFUL
Suggested Lifetime Scripture Verse: I John 1:7 *"But if we walk in the light, as He is in the light, we have fellowship one with another, and the blood of Jesus Christ His Son cleanseth us from all sin."* *

VERLYN

Literal Meaning: TRUE
Suggested Character Quality: TRUTHFUL
Suggested Lifetime Scripture Verse: I John 1:7 *"But if we walk in the light, as He is in the light, we have fellowship one with another, and the blood of Jesus Christ His Son cleanseth us from all sin."* *

VERNA

Literal Meaning: SPRING-LIKE
Suggested Character Quality: ABUNDANT LIFE
Suggested Lifetime Scripture Verse: Psalm 52:8 *"But I am like a green olive tree in the house of God; I trust in God's lovingkindness forever and ever."*
Explanation: Spring is a time of new and abundant life.

VERNON

Literal Meaning: SPRING-LIKE
Suggested Character Quality: ABUNDANT LIFE
Suggested Lifetime Scripture Verse: Psalm 52:8 *"But I am like a green olive tree in the house of God; I trust in God's lovingkindness forever and ever."*
Explanation: See Verna

VERONICA

Literal Meaning: TRUE IMAGE
Suggested Character Quality: TRUE-HEARTED
Suggested Lifetime Scripture Verse: Psalm 119:132 *"Turn Thou to me and have mercy on me, as is Thy way with those who love Thy name."*

VICKI

Literal Meaning: VICTORY
Suggested Character Quality: VICTORIOUS SPIRIT
Suggested Lifetime Scripture Verse: Psalm 89:1 *"I will sing of the mercies of the Lord forever; I will make known Thy faithfulness with my mouth from generation to generation."*

VICTOR

Literal Meaning: CONQUEROR
Suggested Character Quality: VICTORIOUS LIFE
Suggested Lifetime Scripture Verse: I Corinthians 15:57 *"But thanks be to God, who gives us the victory through our Lord Jesus Christ!"*

VICTORIA

Literal Meaning: VICTORY
Suggested Character Quality: VICTORIOUS SPIRIT
Suggested Lifetime Scripture Verse: Psalm 89:1 *"I will sing of the mercies of the Lord forever; I will make known Thy faithfulness with my mouth from generation to generation."*

VINCE

Literal Meaning: CONQUERING ONE
Suggested Character Quality: STRONG IN VICTORY
Suggested Lifetime Scripture Verse: Psalm 118:14 *"The Lord is my strength and my song; He has become my salvation."*

VINCENT

Literal Meaning: CONQUERING ONE
Suggested Character Quality: STRONG IN VICTORY
Suggested Lifetime Scripture Verse: Psalm 118:14 *"The Lord is my strength and my song; He has become my salvation."*

VIOLA

Literal Meaning: A VIOLET FLOWER
Suggested Character Quality: HUMBLE
Suggested Lifetime Scripture Verse: Isaiah 30:15 *"For thus says the Lord God, the Holy One of Israel; in conversion and rest you shall be saved; in quietness and confidence shall be your strength."*
Explanation: See Violet

VIOLET

Literal Meaning: A VIOLET FLOWER
Suggested Character Quality: HUMBLE
Suggested Lifetime Scripture Verse: Isaiah 30:15 *"For thus says the Lord God, the Holy One of Israel; in conversion and rest you shall be saved; in quietness and confidence shall be your strength."*
Explanation: A violet is considered a humble flower.

VIRGIL

Literal Meaning: THE STAFF BEARER
Suggested Character Quality: THE STAFF OF AUTHORITY
Suggested Lifetime Scripture Verse: Matthew 18:4 *"Whosoever therefore shall humble himself as this little child, the same is the greatest in the kingdom of heaven."* *

VIRGINIA

Literal Meaning: MAIDENLY
Suggested Character Quality: PURE ONE
Suggested Lifetime Scripture Verse: Psalm 119:1 *"Blessed are those whose way is upright, who walk in the law of the Lord."*

VITA

Literal Meaning: LIFE
Suggested Character Quality: FULL OF LIFE
Suggested Lifetime Scripture Verse: John 10:7, 10 *"Then said Jesus unto them again . . . I am come that they might have life, and that they might have it more abundantly."* *

VIVA

Literal Meaning: LIVING; FULL OF LIFE
Suggested Character Quality: FULL OF LIFE
Suggested Lifetime Scripture Verse: Psalm 52:8 *"But I am like a green olive tree in the house of God; I trust in God's lovingkindness forever and ever."*

VIVIAN

Literal Meaning: ALIVE
Suggested Character Quality: FULL OF LIFE
Suggested Lifetime Scripture Verse: Psalm 52:8 *"But I am like a green olive tree in the house of God; I trust in God's lovingkindness forever and ever."*

VIVIENNE

Literal Meaning: LIVING; FULL OF LIFE
Suggested Character Quality: FULL OF LIFE
Suggested Lifetime Scripture Verse: Psalm 52:8 *"But I am like a green olive tree in the house of God; I trust in God's lovingkindness forever and ever."*

WADE

Literal Meaning: THE ADVANCER
Suggested Character Quality: CHAMPION
Suggested Lifetime Scripture Verse: Philippians 3:14 *"I push on to the goal for the prize of God's heavenly call in Christ Jesus."*

WALLACE

Literal Meaning: MAN FROM WALES
Suggested Character Quality: INDUSTRIOUS
Suggested Lifetime Scripture Verse: Matthew 5:16 *"Similarly let your light shine among the people, so that they observe your good works and give glory to your heavenly Father."*

WALTER

Literal Meaning: POWERFUL WARRIOR; ARMY RULER
Suggested Character Quality: POWERFUL
Suggested Lifetime Scripture Verse: Philippians 4:13 *"I have strength for every situation through Him who empowers me."*

WANDA

Literal Meaning: WANDERER
Suggested Character Quality: WALKS WITH GOD
Suggested Lifetime Scripture Verse: Psalm 37:5 *"Commit your way to the Lord; trust in Him, too, and He will bring it about."*

WARD

Literal Meaning: GUARD
Suggested Character Quality: SECURE SPIRIT
Suggested Lifetime Scripture Verse: Nahum 1:7 *"The Lord is good, a stronghold in the day of trouble; He knows those who commit themselves to Him."*
Explanation: A guard provides security.

WARNER

Literal Meaning: PROTECTING WARRIOR
Suggested Character Quality: PROTECTOR
Suggested Lifetime Scripture Verse: Psalm 125:1 *"They that trust in the Lord shall be as Mount Zion which cannot be removed, but abideth forever."* *

WARREN

Literal Meaning: PROTECTING FRIEND
Suggested Character Quality: ONE WHO PROTECTS
Suggested Lifetime Scripture Verse: Psalm 11:7 *"For the Lord is righteous; He loves acts of righteousness; His countenance beholds the upright."*

WAYLAND

Literal Meaning: FROM THE PATHWAY LAND
Suggested Character Quality: LED OF GOD
Suggested Lifetime Scripture Verse: Psalm 31:3 *"For Thou art my rock and my fortress; therefore for Thy name's sake lead me, and guide me."* *

WAYNE

Literal Meaning: WAGONER OR WAGONMAKER
Suggested Character Quality: LIFTER OF CARES
Suggested Lifetime Scripture Verse: Galatians 6:2 *"Carry one another's burden and thus fulfill the law of Christ."*

WEBSTER

Literal Meaning: WEAVER
Suggested Character Quality: INDUSTRIOUS SPIRIT
Suggested Lifetime Scripture Verse: I Corinthians 15:58 *"Therefore, my beloved brethren, be ye steadfast, unmovable, always abounding in the work of the Lord, forasmuch as ye know that your labor is not in vain in the Lord."* *

WENDELL

Literal Meaning: WANDERER
Suggested Character Quality: TRUSTS IN GOD
Suggested Lifetime Scripture Verse: Isaiah 26:3 *"Thou wilt keep him in perfect peace, whose mind is stayed on Thee: because he trusteth in Thee."* *

WENDY

Literal Meaning: WANDERER
Suggested Character Quality: WALKS WITH GOD
Suggested Lifetime Scripture Verse: Psalm 37:5 *"Commit your way to the Lord; trust in Him, too, and He will bring it about."*

WERNER

Literal Meaning: PROTECTING WARRIOR
Suggested Character Quality: STRONG LEADER
Suggested Lifetime Scripture Verse: II Timothy 2:1 *"Thou therefore, my son, be strong in the grace that is in Christ Jesus."* *

WESLEY

Literal Meaning: WEST FIELD
Suggested Character Quality: PROSPEROUS SPIRIT
Suggested Lifetime Scripture Verse: Psalm 13:6 *"Let me sing to the Lord because He has dealt generously with me."*
Explanation: Those names which have to do with fields, meadows, or land suggest prosperity.

WHITMAN

Literal Meaning: WHITEHEADED MAN
Suggested Character Quality: MAN OF REASON
Suggested Lifetime Scripture Verse: Psalm 111:10 *"The fear of the Lord is the beginning of wisdom: a good understanding have all they that do His commandments: His praise endureth forever."* *

WHITNEY

Literal Meaning: FROM THE WHITE-HAIRED ONE'S ISLAND
Suggested Character Quality: SEEKER OF WISDOM
Suggested Lifetime Scripture Verse: Psalm 111:10 *"For reverence of the Lord is the beginning of wisdom. There is insight in all who observe it. His praise is everlasting."*

WILBUR

Literal Meaning: BRIGHT PLEDGE
Suggested Character Quality: NOBLE IN HONOR
Suggested Lifetime Scripture Verse: Psalm 29:1 *"Give to the Lord, O you sons of the mighty, give to the Lord glory and strength."*

WILEY

Literal Meaning: THE WILY OR BEGUILING
Suggested Character Quality: HONEST
Suggested Lifetime Scripture Verese: Zechariah 8:16 *"These are things that ye shall do; Speak ye every man the truth to his neighbor; execute the judgment of truth and peace in your gates."* *

WILFRED

Literal Meaning: FIRM PEACEMAKER
Suggested Character Quality: PEACEMAKER
Suggested Lifetime Scripture Verse: Matthew 5:9 *"Blessed are the peacemakers: for they shall be called the children of God."* *

WILL

Literal Meaning: OF RESOLUTE WILL
Suggested Character Quality: OR RESOLUTE SPIRIT
Suggested Lifetime Scripture Verse: Psalm 1:2 *"But his delight is in the law of the Lord and His law he ponders day and night."*

WILLARD

Literal Meaning: RESOLUTE AND BRAVE
Suggested Character Quality: OF RESOLUTE SPIRIT
Suggested Lifetime Scripture Verse: Psalm 1:2 *"But his delight is in the law of the Lord and His law he ponders day and night."*

WILLIAM

Literal Meaning: RESOLUTE PROTECTOR
Suggested Character Quality: GREAT PROTECTOR
Suggested Lifetime Scripture Verse: Micah 6:8 *"And what does the Lord require of you but to do justice, to love mercy and to walk humbly with your God."*

WILLIS

Literal Meaning: RESOLUTE PROTECTOR
Suggested Character Quality: DEFENDER
Suggested Lifetime Scripture Verse: Psalm 62:1, 2 *"Truly my soul waiteth upon God: from Him cometh my salvation. He only is my rock and my salvation; He is my defense; I shall not be greatly moved."* *

WILMA

Literal Meaning: WILL HELMET
Suggested Character Quality: GIVER OF SECURITY
Suggested Lifetime Scripture Verse: Romans 15:13 *"So may God, the fountain of hope, fill you with all joy and peace in your believing, so that you may enjoy overflowing hope by the power of the Holy Spirit."*
Explanation: One who guards gives security.

WILSON

Literal Meaning: SON OF WILLIAM; RESOLUTE PROTECTOR
Suggested Character Quality: GREAT PROTECTOR
Suggested Lifetime Scripture Verse: Micah 6:8 *"And what does the Lord require of you but to do justice, to lover mercy and to walk humbly with your God."*

WINIFRED

Literal Meaning: WHITE WAVE
Suggested Character Quality: PURE OF HEART
Suggested Lifetime Scripture Verse: Psalm 119:1 *"Blessed are those whose way is upright, who walk in the law of the Lord!"*

WINSLOW

Literal Meaning: FROM THE FRIENDLY HILL
Suggested Character Quality: FRIENDLY
Suggested Lifetime Scripture Verse: Ephesians 4:32 *"And be ye kind one to another, tenderhearted, forgiving one another, even as God for Christ's sake hath forgiven you."* *

WINSTON

Literal Meaning: "FRIEND" — Anglo-Saxon
Suggested Character Quality: FRIENDLY SPIRIT
Suggested Lifetime Scripture Verse: Proverbs 18:24 *"A man has many friends for companionship, but there is a friend who sticks closer than a brother."*

WOODROW

Literal Meaning: FROM THE WOODS
Suggested Character Quality: WALKS WITH GOD
Suggested Lifetime Scripture Verse: Colossians 1:10 *"That ye might walk worthy of the Lord unto all pleasing, being fruitful in every good work, and increasing in the knowledge of God."* *

WYATT

Literal Meaning: A GUIDE; LITTLE WARRIOR
Suggested Character Quality: GOD'S SOLDIER
Suggested Lifetime Scripture Verse: I Timothy 6:11b, 12a *"... follow after righteousness, godliness, faith, love, patience, meekness. Fight the good fight of faith ..."* *

YALE
Literal Meaning: ONE WHO PAYS OR YIELDS
Suggested Character Quality: OBEDIENT SPIRIT
Suggested Lifetime Scripture Verse: James 1:22a *"But be ye doers of the word, and not hearers only . . . "* *

YOLANDA
Literal Meaning: A VIOLET
Suggested Character Quality: FULL OF HUMILITY
Suggested Lifetime Scripture Verse: Isaiah 30:15 *"For thus says the Lord God, the Holy One of Israel, in conversion and rest you shall be saved; in quietness and confidence shall be your strength."*

YVETTE
Literal Meaning: BOWMAN; HERO; YOUTH
Suggested Character Quality: JOYFUL LIFE
Suggested Lifetime Scripture Verse: Psalm 100:2 *"Serve the Lord with gladness: come before His presence with singing."* *

YVONNE
Literal Meaning: "HERO" — Anglo-Saxon
Suggested Character Quality: COURAGEOUS HEART
Suggested Lifetime Scripture Verse: Psalm 7:10 *"My shield depends upon God, who saves the upright in heart."*

ZACHARY

Literal Meaning: "JEHOVAH HAS REMEMBERED" — Hebrew
Suggested Character Quality: THE LORD REMEMBERS
Suggested Lifetime Scripture Verse: Psalm 17:7 *"In a marvelous way show Thine unfailing love, O Thou, who savest those who look for refuge from their adversaries at Thy right hand."*

ZELDA

Literal Meaning: THE HEROINE
Suggested Character Quality: MIGHTY IN SPIRIT
Suggested Lifetime Scripture Verse: Philippians 4:13 *"I can do all things through Christ which strengtheneth me."* *

ZOE

Literal Meaning: LIFE; COME (GREEK)
Suggested Character Quality: FULL OF LIFE
Suggested Lifetime Scripture Verse: Acts 17:27, 28a *"That they should seek the Lord, if haply they might feel after Him, and find Him, though He be not far away from every one of us: For in Him we live, and move, and have our being . . ."* *